It's *your* country. Learn it. Love it. Explore it.

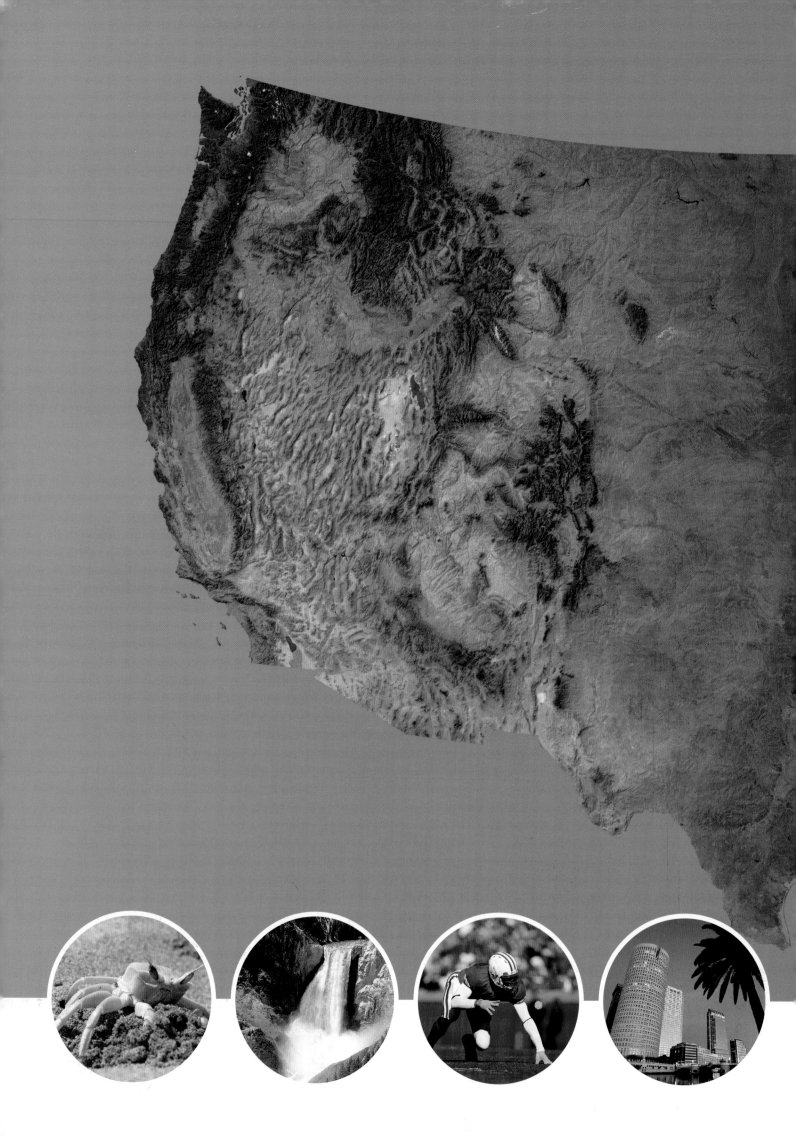

NATIONAL GEOGRAPHIC KiDS

United States
Atlas

Fifth Edition

NATIONAL GEOGRAPHIC

WASHINGTON, D.C.

Table
of Contents

Northeast: Maine lighthouse, pp. 34–35

Southeast: Manatee in Florida waters, p. 62

Title page: Atlantic sand crab; Lower Falls of the Yellowstone, Wyoming; football player; skyline, Tampa, Florida; sage grouse; skyline, Seattle, Washington State; American girl; Organ Pipe Cactus National Monument, Arizona

Territories: Festival dancers, American Samoa, pp. 156–157

Southwest: Albuquerque balloon festival, p. 120

Midwest: Illinois hay field with tractor, pp. 88–89

West: Wyoming ranch, p. 152

How to Use This Atlas

This atlas is much more than just another book of maps about the United States. Of course you will find plenty of maps—country, regional, and state—that will help you learn about the people and places that make up our country. But there's much more. This atlas includes essays filled with history and current facts about each state, and photos that provide an up close view of natural and cultural features. In addition, you will discover state flags and nicknames, state flowers and birds, facts and statistics, and even graphs and charts. Follow the captions below and to the right to discover all the special features that are waiting for you in this atlas.

COLOR BARS

Each section of the atlas has its own color to make it easy to move from one to another. Look for the color in the Table of Contents and across the top of the pages in the atlas. The name of the section and the title for each topic or map is in the color bar.

THE NORTHEAST
THE SOUTHEAST
THE MIDWEST
THE SOUTHWEST
THE WEST
THE TERRITORIES

STATE FACT BOX

The fact box is full of key information you need at a glance about a state: its nickname and flag, statehood, statistics about land and population*, racial and ethnic makeup** and other population characteristics, plus some fascinating Geo Whiz facts and the state bird and flower.

Population figures are for 2015 unless otherwise noted; city populations are for city proper unless metropolitan area is specified.

*** Racial percentages total less than 100 percent because very small racial groups are not included. Hispanics are an ethnic group and can be included in any racial group.*

WHERE ARE THE PICTURES?

If you want to know where a picture in any of the regional sections in the atlas was taken, check the map in the regional photo essay. Find the label that describes the photograph you are curious about, and follow the line to its location.

CHARTS AND GRAPHS

The photo essay for each state includes a chart or graph that highlights economic, physical, cultural, or some other type of information related to the state.

BAR SCALE

Each map has a bar scale in miles and kilometers to help you find out how far on Earth's surface it is from one place to another on the map.

YOU ARE HERE

Locator maps show you where each region and state within the region is in relation to the rest of the United States. Regions are shown in the regional color; featured states are in yellow.

MAP SYMBOLS

Maps use symbols to represent many physical, political, and economic features. Below is a complete list of the map symbols used in this atlas. In addition, each state map has its own key featuring symbols for major economic activities. Other abbreviations are listed on page 160.

• **Aspen** .... town of under 25,000 residents
• **Frankfort** .... town of 25,000 to 99,999
• **San Jose** .... city of 100,000 to 999,999
• **New York** ..... city of 1,000,000 and over

⊛ National capital
★ State capital
■ Point of interest
+ Mountain peak with elevation above sea level
• Low point with elevation below sea level
—— River
–– Intermittent river
⊥⊥⊥ Canal
—— Interstate or selected other highway
– – – Trail
•••••• State or national boundary
•••••• Continental divide
Lake and dam
Intermittent lake
Dry lake
Swamp
Glacier
National Wild & Scenic River, N.W.&S.R.

Sand
Lava
Area below sea level
Indian Reservation, I.R.
State Park, S.P.
State Historical Park, S.H.P.
State Historic Site, S.H.S.
National Battlefield, N.B.
National Battlefield Park, N.B.P.
National Battlefield Site, N.B.S.
National Historic Site, N.H.S.
National Historical Area, N.H.A.
National Historical Park, N.H.P.
National Lakeshore
National Military Park, N.M.P.
National Memorial, NAT. MEM.
National Monument, NAT. MON.
National Park, N.P.
National Parkway
National Preserve
National Recreation Area, N.R.A.
National River
National Riverway
National Scenic Area
National Seashore
National Volcanic Monument
National Forest, N.F.
National Grassland, N.G.
National Wildlife Refuge, N.W.R.

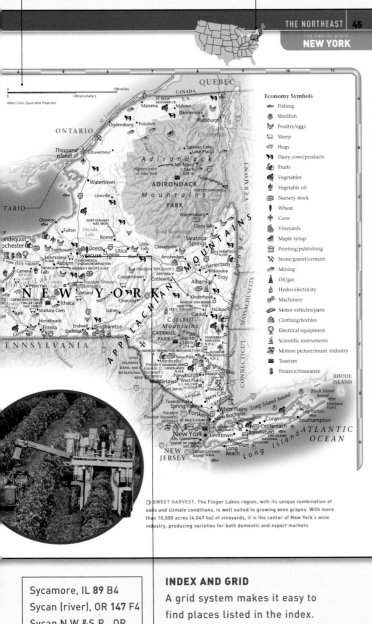

THE NORTHEAST   45
THE EMPIRE STATE
NEW YORK

SWEET HARVEST. The Finger Lakes region, with its unique combination of soils and climate conditions, is well suited to growing wine grapes. With more than 10,000 acres (4,047 ha) of vineyards, it is the center of New York's wine industry, producing varieties for both domestic and export markets.

INDEX AND GRID

A grid system makes it easy to find places listed in the index. For example, the listing for Syracuse, New York, is followed by **45 D5**. The bold type is the page number; D5 tells you the city is near the point where imaginary lines drawn from D and 5 on the grid bars meet.

Economy Symbols

Fishing
Lobster fishing
Shellfish
Poultry/eggs
Sheep
Hogs
Dairy cows/products
Beef cattle
Fruits
Vegetables
Vegetable oil
Peanuts
Nursery stock
Wheat
Corn
Rice
Soybeans
Sugarcane
Cotton
Tobacco
Coffee
Vineyards
Maple syrup
Timber/forest products
Furniture
Printing/publishing

Stone/gravel/cement
Mining
Coal
Oil/gas
Hydro-electricity
Machinery
Metal manufacturing
Metal products
Shipbuilding
Railroad equipment
Motor vehicles/parts
Rubber/plastics
Chemistry
Food processing
Clothing/textiles
Leather products
Glass/clay products
Jewelry
Electrical equipment
Computers/electronics
Scientific instruments
Aircraft/parts
Aerospace
Motion picture/music industry
Tourism
Finance/insurance

The Physical United States

Stretching from the Atlantic Ocean in the east to the Pacific in the west, the United States is the third largest country in area in the world. Its physical diversity ranges from mountains to fertile plains and from tropical forests to dry deserts. Shading on the map indicates changes in elevation, and colors suggest different vegetation patterns.

ALASKA AND HAWAI'I.
In addition to the states located on the main landmass, the United States has two states—Alaska and Hawai'i—that are not directly connected to the other 48 states. If Alaska and Hawai'i were shown in their correct relative sizes and locations, the map would not fit on the page. The locator globe shows the correct relative size and location of each.

San Francisco

Coast Ranges   Sierra Nevada   Great Basin   Rocky Mountains

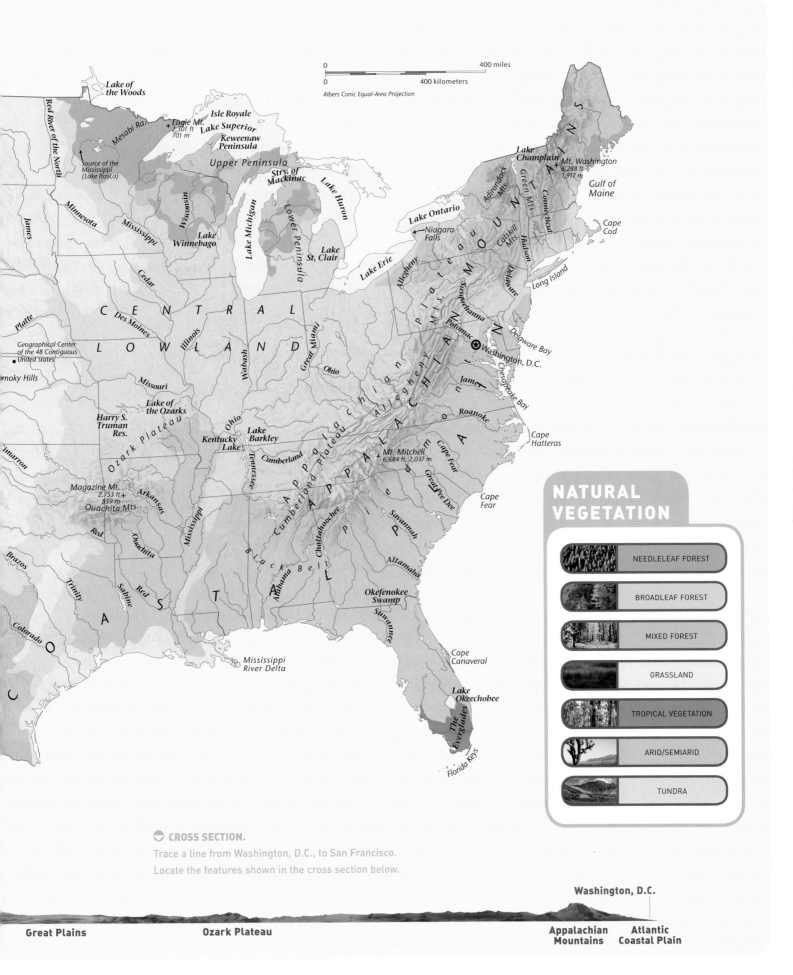

0 — 400 miles
0 — 400 kilometers
Albers Conic Equal-Area Projection

Lake of the Woods
Red River of the North
Source of the Mississippi (Lake Itasca)
Mesabi Ra.
Eagle Mt. 2,301 ft 701 m
Isle Royale
Lake Superior
Keweenaw Peninsula
Upper Peninsula
Strs. of Mackinac
Lake Huron
Lake Champlain
Mt. Washington 6,288 ft 1,917 m
Gulf of Maine
Minnesota
Wisconsin
Mississippi
James
Cedar
Lake Winnebago
Lake Michigan
Lower Peninsula
Lake St. Clair
Lake Ontario
Niagara Falls
Lake Erie
Adirondack Mts.
Green Mts.
Connecticut
Catskill Mts.
Hudson
Delaware
Cape Cod
Long Island
Platte
Des Moines
Illinois
Great Miami
Allegheny Plateau
Delaware Bay
Geographical Center of the 48 Contiguous United States
C E N T R A L   L O W L A N D
Wabash
Ohio
Susquehanna
Potomac
Washington, D.C.
Chesapeake Bay
moky Hills
Missouri
Lake of the Ozarks
Harry S. Truman Res.
Ozark Plateau
Ohio
Kentucky Lake
Lake Barkley
Cumberland
Tennessee
Appalachian Plateau
Cumberland Plateau
Allegheny Mts.
James
Roanoke
Cape Hatteras
cimarron
Magazine Mt. 2,753 ft 839 m
Ouachita Mts.
Arkansas
Mt. Mitchell 6,684 ft, 2,037 m
A P P A L A C H I A N   M O U N T A I N S
Cape Fear
Great Pee Dee
Cape Fear
Red
Ouachita
Mississippi
Black Belt
Chattahoochee
Alabama
Savannah
Altamaha
Cape Canaveral
Brazos
Trinity
Sabine
Red
A T L A N T I C   C O A S T A L   P L A I N
Okefenokee Swamp
Suwannee
Colorado
Mississippi River Delta
Lake Okeechobee
The Everglades
Florida Keys

NATURAL VEGETATION

	NEEDLELEAF FOREST
	BROADLEAF FOREST
	MIXED FOREST
	GRASSLAND
	TROPICAL VEGETATION
	ARID/SEMIARID
	TUNDRA

◔ **CROSS SECTION.**

Trace a line from Washington, D.C., to San Francisco.
Locate the features shown in the cross section below.

Washington, D.C.

Great Plains   **Ozark Plateau**   **Appalachian Mountains**   **Atlantic Coastal Plain**

Natural Environment

A big part of the natural environment of the United States is the climate. With humid areas near the coasts, dry interior regions far from any major water body, and land areas that extend from northern Alaska to southern Florida and Hawai'i, the country experiences great variation in climate. Location is the key. Distance from the Equator, nearness to water, wind patterns, temperature of nearby water bodies, and elevation are things that influence temperature and precipitation. Climate affects the types of vegetation that grow in a particular place and plays a part in soil formation.

CHANGING CLIMATE

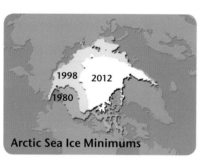

Arctic Sea Ice Minimums

1980 1998 2012

Scientists believe that a warming trend that has occurred in recent decades may be more than a natural cycle and that human activity is a contributing factor. An increase in average temperatures could result in more severe storms, changes in precipitation patterns, and the spread of deserts. Rising temperatures may also play a part in the melting of glaciers, which could lead to a rise in ocean levels and the shrinking of the Arctic ice cover. NASA satellite images indicate that Arctic ice is shrinking as much as 9 percent each decade. Many believe that this puts polar bears at risk, because they normally hunt and raise their young on ice floes.

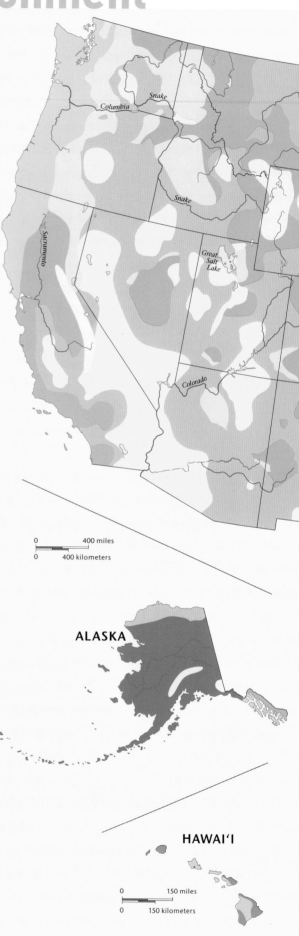

0 — 400 miles
0 — 400 kilometers

ALASKA

HAWAI'I

0 — 150 miles
0 — 150 kilometers

0 ____ 400 miles
0 ____ 400 kilometers
Albers Conic Equal-Area Projection

Climate Zones

Tropical
- Tropical wet
- Tropical wet and dry

Dry
- Semiarid
- Arid

Mild
- Marine west coast
- Mediterranean
- Humid subtropical

Continental
- Hot summer
- Warm summer
- Subarctic

Polar
- Tundra and ice

High Elevations
- Highlands

🌀 **CLIMATE MOSAIC.**
The United States includes every major climate
type, shown in different colors on the map above.

WARMING UP

Evidence indicates that Earth is experiencing a warming pattern unlike any
in recorded history. In 2015 every state
reported above average temperatures, and
four states saw record-setting averages.
Overall the average temperature in the
lower 48 states was 2.4°F (1.3°C) warmer
than the 20th-century average.

Average Temperature Ranks in 2015 (by State)
No data | Above average | Much above average | Record warmest

Natural Hazards

The natural environment of the United States provides much diversity, but it also poses many dangers, especially when people locate homes and businesses in places at risk of natural disasters. Tornadoes bring destructive winds, and hurricanes bring strong winds, rain, and more; shifting of Earth's crust along fault lines rattles buildings; flood waters and wildfires threaten lives and property. More than one-third of the U.S. population lives in hazard-prone areas. Compare this natural hazards map to the population map on pages 16–17.

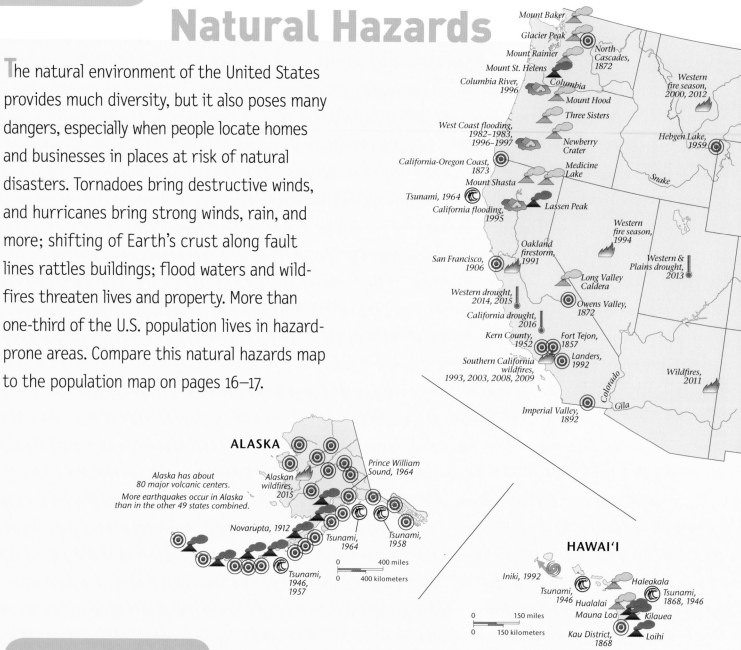

Mount Baker
Glacier Peak
Mount Rainier
North Cascades, 1872
Mount St. Helens
Columbia River, 1996
Columbia
Western fire season, 2000, 2012
West Coast flooding, 1982–1983, 1996–1997
Mount Hood
Three Sisters
Newberry Crater
Hebgen Lake, 1959
California-Oregon Coast, 1873
Medicine Lake
Snake
Mount Shasta
Tsunami, 1964
Lassen Peak
California flooding, 1995
Western fire season, 1994
San Francisco, 1906
Oakland firestorm, 1991
Western & Plains drought, 2013
Western drought, 2014, 2015
Long Valley Caldera
California drought, 2016
Owens Valley, 1872
Kern County, 1952
Fort Tejon, 1857
Southern California wildfires, 1993, 2003, 2008, 2009
Landers, 1992
Wildfires, 2011
Imperial Valley, 1892
Colorado
Gila

ALASKA

Alaska has about 80 major volcanic centers.
More earthquakes occur in Alaska than in the other 49 states combined.

Alaskan wildfires, 2015
Prince William Sound, 1964
Novarupta, 1912
Tsunami, 1964
Tsunami, 1958
Tsunami, 1946, 1957

0   400 miles
0   400 kilometers

HAWAI'I

Iniki, 1992
Tsunami, 1946
Haleakala
Hualalai
Tsunami, 1868, 1946
Mauna Loa
Kilauea
Kau District, 1868
Loihi

0   150 miles
0   150 kilometers

NATURAL HAZARDS

BLIZZARD. Severe storm with bitter cold temperatures and wind-whipped snow and ice particles that reduce visibility to less than 650 feet (198 m), paralyzing transportation systems

FLOOD. Inundation of buildings or roadways caused by overflow of a river or stream swollen by heavy rainfall or rapid snowmelt; may involve displacement of people

DROUGHT. Long and con-tinuous period of abnormally low precipitation, resulting in water shortages that negatively affect people, animals, and plant life; may result in crop loss

HURRICANE. Tropical storm in the Atlantic, Caribbean, Gulf of Mexico, or eastern Pacific with a minimum sustained wind speed of 74 miles an hour (119 km/h)

ICE STORM. Damaging accumulations of ice associated with freezing rain; may pull down trees or utility lines, causing extensive damage and creating dangerous travel conditions

NATURAL HAZARDS

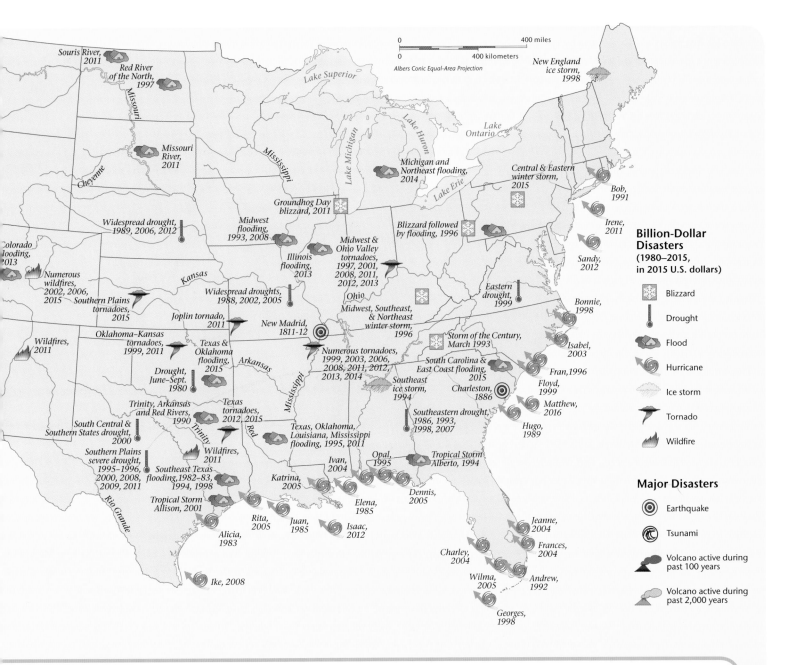

Souris River, 2011
Red River of the North, 1997
Missouri
Cheyenne
Missouri River, 2011
New England ice storm, 1998
Lake Superior
Lake Huron
Lake Michigan
Lake Ontario
Lake Erie
Lake
Michigan and Northeast flooding, 2014
Central & Eastern winter storm, 2015
Bob, 1991
Widespread drought, 1989, 2006, 2012
Groundhog Day blizzard, 2011
Midwest flooding, 1993, 2008
Blizzard followed by flooding, 1996
Irene, 2011
Colorado flooding, 2013
Mississippi
Midwest & Ohio Valley tornadoes, 1997, 2001, 2008, 2011, 2012, 2013
Sandy, 2012
Numerous wildfires, 2002, 2006, 2015
Kansas
Illinois flooding, 2013
Ohio
Eastern drought, 1999
Bonnie, 1998
Southern Plains tornadoes, 2015
Widespread droughts, 1988, 2002, 2005
Midwest, Southeast, & Northeast winter storm, 1996
Wildfires, 2011
Joplin tornado, 2011
New Madrid, 1811-12
Storm of the Century, March 1993
Isabel, 2003
Oklahoma–Kansas tornadoes, 1999, 2011
Texas & Oklahoma flooding, 2015
Arkansas
Numerous tornadoes, 1999, 2003, 2006, 2008, 2011, 2012, 2013, 2014
South Carolina & East Coast flooding, 2015
Fran, 1996
Drought, June–Sept. 1980
Southeast ice storm, 1994
Charleston, 1886
Floyd, 1999
Matthew, 2016
Trinity, Arkansas and Red Rivers, 1990
Texas tornadoes, 2012, 2015
Mississippi
Southeastern drought, 1986, 1993, 1998, 2007
Hugo, 1989
South Central & Southern States drought, 2000
Texas, Oklahoma, Louisiana, Mississippi flooding, 1995, 2011
Ivan, 2004
Opal, 1995
Tropical Storm Alberto, 1994
Southern Plains severe drought, 1995–1996, 2000, 2008, 2009, 2011
Wildfires, 2011
Southeast Texas flooding, 1982–83, 1994, 1998
Katrina, 2005
Dennis, 2005
Tropical Storm Allison, 2001
Rita, 2005
Juan, 1985
Elena, 1985
Jeanne, 2004
Rio Grande
Isaac, 2012
Frances, 2004
Alicia, 1983
Charley, 2004
Wilma, 2005
Andrew, 1992
Ike, 2008
Georges, 1998
Red
Trinity

Scale:
0 — 400 miles
0 — 400 kilometers
Albers Conic Equal-Area Projection

Billion-Dollar Disasters
(1980–2015, in 2015 U.S. dollars)

- ❄ Blizzard
- 🌡 Drought
- ☁ Flood
- 🌀 Hurricane
- ☁ Ice storm
- 🌪 Tornado
- 🔥 Wildfire

Major Disasters

- ◎ Earthquake
- ◉ Tsunami
- 🌋 Volcano active during past 100 years
- 🌋 Volcano active during past 2,000 years

TORNADO. Violently rotating column of air that, when it reaches the ground, is the most damaging of all atmospheric phenomena; most common in the central region of the country

WILDFIRE. Free-burning, uncontained fire in a forest or grassland; may result from lightning strikes or accidental or deliberate human activity in areas where conditions are dry

EARTHQUAKE. Shaking or vibration created by energy released by movement of Earth's crust along tectonic plate boundaries; can cause structural damage and loss of life

TSUNAMI. Series of unusually large ocean waves caused by an underwater earthquake, landslide, or volcanic eruption; very destructive in coastal areas

VOLCANO. Vent or opening in Earth's surface through which molten rock called lava, ash, and gases are released; often associated with tectonic plate boundaries

The Political United States

Like a giant patchwork quilt, the United States is made up of 50 states, each uniquely different but together making a national fabric held together by a Constitution and a federal government. State boundaries, outlined in various colors on the map, set apart internal political units within the country. The national capital—Washington, D.C.—is marked by a star in a double circle on the map. The capital of each state is marked by a star in a single circle.

9:00 AM

10:00 AM

7:00 AM
HAWAI'I-ALEUTIAN TIME

8:00 AM
ALASKA TIME

7:00 AM
HAWAI'I-ALEUTIAN TIME

TIME ZONES. Earth is divided into 24 time zones, each about 15 degrees of longitude wide, reflecting the distance Earth turns from west to east each hour. The U.S. is divided into six time zones, indicated by red dotted lines on these maps. When it is noon in Boston, what is the time in Seattle?

WESTWARD EXPANSION. The United States had its origins in 13 British colonies established along the Atlantic coast. After gaining independence in 1783, the young country began adding new territories—some by treaty, others by purchase or by war. The map traces the country's expansion and shows the date each territory was acquired.

Population

More than 324 million* and growing! The population of the United States topped the 300 million mark in 2006, and it continues to grow by more than 2 million people each year. Before the arrival of European settlers, the population consisted of Native Americans living in tribal groups scattered across the country. In the 16th and 17th centuries, Europeans, some with slaves from Africa, settled first along the eastern seaboard and later moved westward. In 1790 the U.S. population was not quite 4 million people. Today, New York City alone has a population more than double that number. The country's population is unevenly distributed. The map shows the number of people per square mile for each county in every state. The greatest densities are in the East and along the West Coast, especially around major cities. The most rapid growth is occurring in the South and the West—an area referred to as the Sunbelt—as well as in suburban areas around cities.

*August 2016 figure

Seattle
Portland
Ogden-Layton
Salt Lake City
Provo-Orem
Sacramento
San Francisco-Oakland
San Jose
Fresno
Bakersfield
Las Vegas
Los Angeles-Long Beach-Santa Ana
Riverside-San Bernardino
Mission Viejo
Temecula-Murrieta
Phoenix-Mesa
San Diego
Tucson

ALASKA

0   400 miles
0   400 kilometers

Anchorage

HAWAI'I
Honolulu

0   150 miles
0   150 kilometers

◉ **COMMUTER RUSH HOUR.** Crowds of people press toward trains in New York City's Grand Central Station. With more than three-quarters of the population living in urban areas, commuter transportation poses a major challenge to cities in the United States.

◗ **WHERE WE LIVE.** The first U.S. census in 1790 revealed that only 5 percent of people lived in towns. As industry has grown and agriculture has become increasingly mechanized, people have left farms (green), moving to urban places (blue) and their surrounding suburbs (orange).

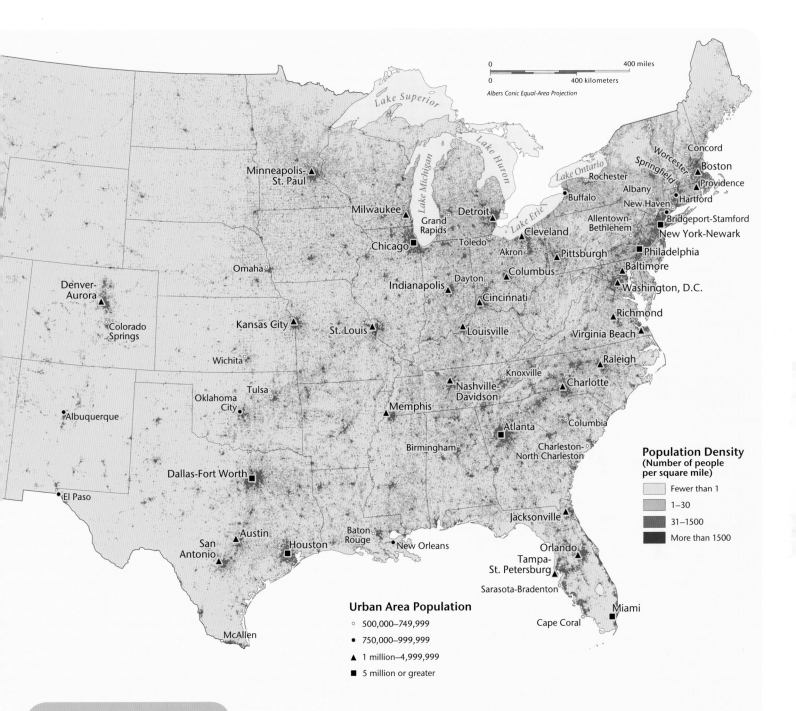

0   400 miles
0   400 kilometers
Albers Conic Equal-Area Projection

Lake Superior
Lake Michigan
Lake Huron
Lake Erie
Lake Ontario

Minneapolis-St. Paul
Milwaukee
Grand Rapids
Detroit
Cleveland
Chicago
Toledo
Akron
Pittsburgh
Columbus
Dayton
Indianapolis
Cincinnati
Louisville
St. Louis
Kansas City
Omaha
Denver-Aurora
Colorado Springs
Wichita
Tulsa
Oklahoma City
Albuquerque
El Paso
Dallas-Fort Worth
San Antonio
Austin
Houston
Baton Rouge
New Orleans
McAllen
Memphis
Nashville-Davidson
Birmingham
Atlanta
Knoxville
Charlotte
Raleigh
Columbia
Charleston-North Charleston
Jacksonville
Orlando
Tampa-St. Petersburg
Sarasota-Bradenton
Cape Coral
Miami
Concord
Worcester
Boston
Springfield
Providence
Rochester
Albany
Buffalo
New Haven
Hartford
Allentown-Bethlehem
Bridgeport-Stamford
New York-Newark
Philadelphia
Baltimore
Washington, D.C.
Richmond
Virginia Beach

Population Density
(Number of people per square mile)

Fewer than 1
1–30
31–1500
More than 1500

Urban Area Population

○ 500,000–749,999
● 750,000–999,999
▲ 1 million–4,999,999
■ 5 million or greater

HOW OLD ARE WE?

Population pyramids show the distribution of population by sex and age groups, called cohorts. In 1960 the largest cohorts, born after World War II and known as Baby Boomers, were under 15 years of age. By 2000 Baby Boomers had reached middle age. By 2040 they will reach the top of the pyramid.

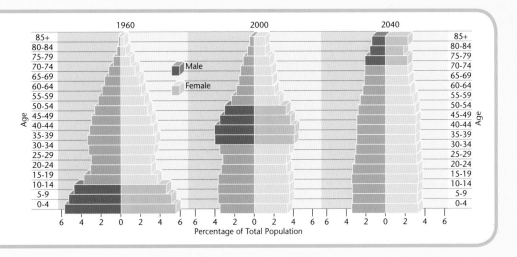

Male
Female

1960   2000   2040

85+
80-84
75-79
70-74
65-69
60-64
55-59
50-54
45-49
40-44
35-39
30-34
25-29
20-24
15-19
10-14
5-9
0-4

Age

6 4 2 0 2 4 6   6 4 2 0 2 4 6   6 4 2 0 2 4 6
Percentage of Total Population

People on the Move

From earliest human history, the land of the United States has been a focus of migration. Native peoples arrived thousands of years ago. The first European settlers came in the 16th and 17th centuries, and slave ships brought people from Africa. Today, people are still on the move. Since the mid-20th century, most international migrants have come from Latin America—especially Mexico and countries of Central America and the Caribbean—and Asia, particularly China, the Philippines, and India. Although most of the population is still of European descent, certain regions have large minority concentrations, as shown on the map, that influence local cultural landscapes.

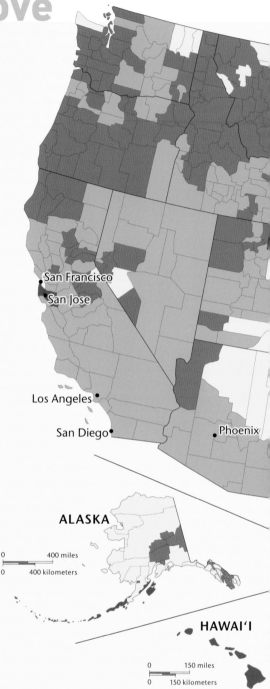

San Francisco
San Jose

Los Angeles
San Diego
Phoenix

ALASKA

0   400 miles
0   400 kilometers

HAWAI'I

0   150 miles
0   150 kilometers

⊖ **BRIDGE OF HOPE.** Many Mexicans enter the U.S. (foreground) by bridges across the Rio Grande, such as this one between Nuevo Laredo, Mexico, and Laredo, Texas.

⊖ **IMMIGRANT INFLUENCE.** With Hispanics making up more than 17 percent of the population, signs in Spanish are popping up everywhere—even at voting areas.

⊖ **SUNBELT SPRAWL.** Spreading suburbs are becoming a common feature of the desert Southwest as people flock to the Sunbelt.

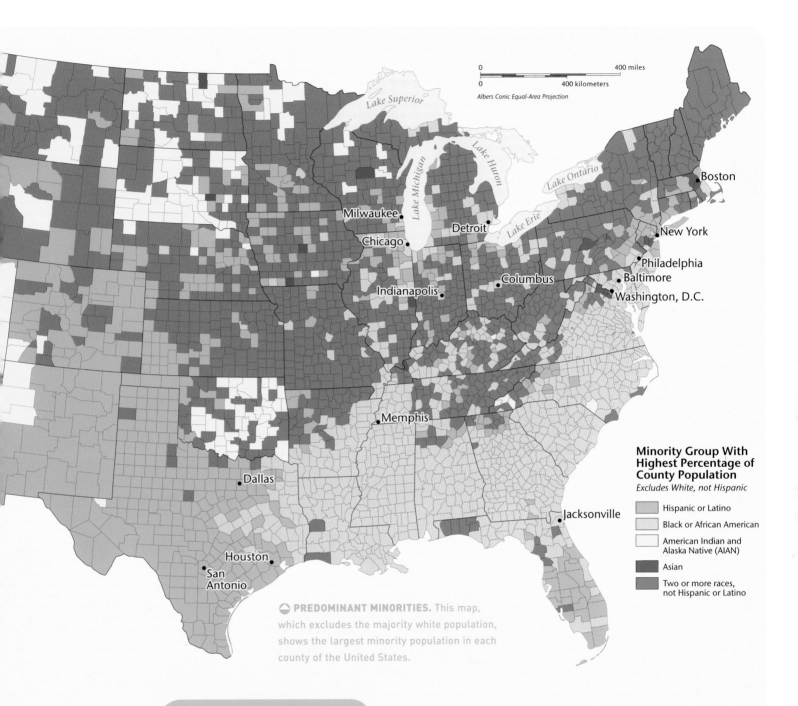

0   400 miles

0   400 kilometers

Albers Conic Equal-Area Projection

Lake Superior

Lake Michigan

Lake Huron

Lake Ontario

Lake Erie

Boston

Milwaukee

Detroit

New York

Chicago

Philadelphia

Columbus

Baltimore

Indianapolis

Washington, D.C.

Memphis

Dallas

Jacksonville

Houston

San
Antonio

**Minority Group With
Highest Percentage of
County Population**
Excludes White, not Hispanic

Hispanic or Latino

Black or African American

American Indian and
Alaska Native (AIAN)

Asian

Two or more races,
not Hispanic or Latino

⬭ **PREDOMINANT MINORITIES.** This map,
which excludes the majority white population,
shows the largest minority population in each
county of the United States.

POPULATION SHIFT

In the past half century, people have
begun moving from the historical
industrial and agricultural regions of
the Northeast and Midwest toward
the South and West, attracted by the
promise of jobs, generally lower
living costs, and a more relaxed way
of life. This continuing trend can be
seen in the population growth patterns shown in the map at right.

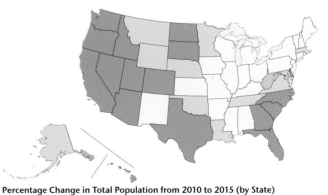

Percentage Change in Total Population from 2010 to 2015 (by State)

More than 5   2.6–5   0–2.5   Loss

Energy

People use energy every day in almost everything they do—from turning on a lamp, to using a computer, to riding a bus to school or work. Almost 40 percent of all energy consumption is used to create electricity, but another 27 percent goes to transportation. Energy sources fall into two main categories: nonrenewable and renewable. Nonrenewable energy resources include fossil fuels (petroleum, natural gas, and coal) and uranium (nuclear power). They have a limited supply that is not quickly replenished. Renewable energy includes wind, water, solar, geothermal, and biomass materials (wood, plant material, and garbage). These sources have an abundant supply that is constantly replenished. About 90 percent of all energy used in the United States comes from nonrenewable energy sources.

EARTHQUAKES & OIL PRODUCTION

Earthquake activity in the central U.S. has increased dramatically since 2009. Geophysicists—scientists who study forces at work within Earth, including earthquakes—have concluded that this increased earthquake activity results from drilling companies pumping wastewater—toxic water that occurs naturally in oil and natural gas deposits—back into the ground.

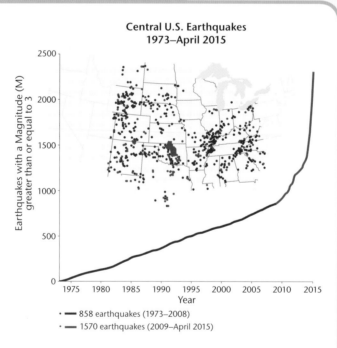

Central U.S. Earthquakes 1973–April 2015

- 858 earthquakes (1973–2008)
- 1570 earthquakes (2009–April 2015)

From 1973–2008 there were 858 earthquakes of magnitude 3 or greater (blue dots on the map, above) in the central U.S. But from 2009 to early 2016 there were 2,310 earthquakes of magnitude 3 or greater (red dots), with most concentrated in central Oklahoma. During this time the amount of toxic wastewater pumped back into the ground doubled. Scientists believe that this injection of wastewater increases pressure on deep underground faults, triggering earthquakes. The state of Oklahoma has now imposed strict limits on underground wastewater disposal.

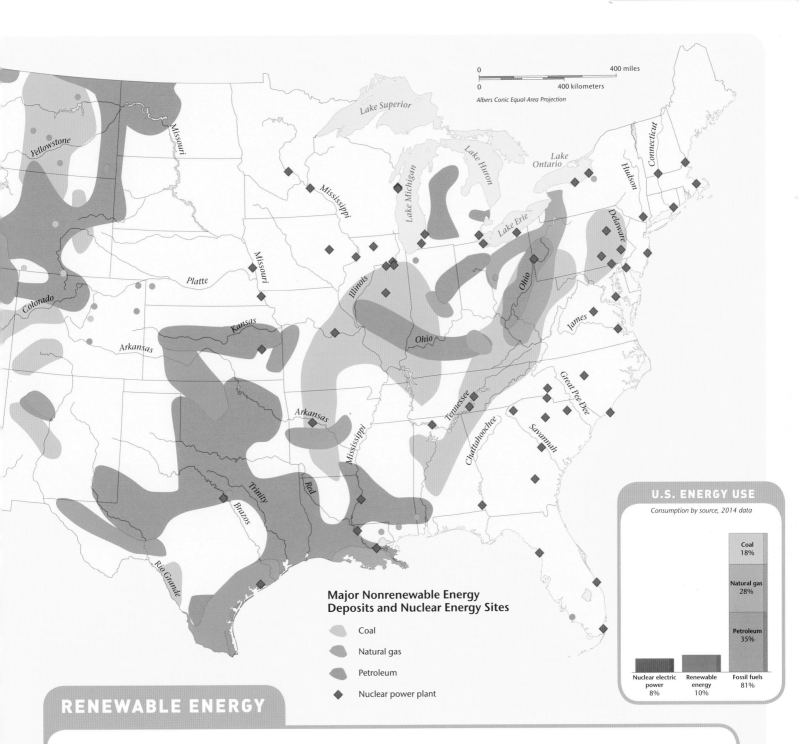

400 miles

400 kilometers

Albers Conic Equal-Area Projection

Major Nonrenewable Energy Deposits and Nuclear Energy Sites

- Coal
- Natural gas
- Petroleum
- ◆ Nuclear power plant

U.S. ENERGY USE

Consumption by source, 2014 data

| Coal 18% |
| Natural gas 28% |
| Petroleum 35% |

| Nuclear electric power 8% | Renewable energy 10% | Fossil fuels 81% |

RENEWABLE ENERGY

Renewable energy comes from sources that are readily available and naturally replenished. In the United States about 10 percent of all energy consumed comes from renewable sources, including hydroelectric energy from moving water; geothermal energy from heat within Earth's core; solar energy from the sun; wind energy (left) from moving air; and biomass energy from burning organic matter such as wood, plant material, and garbage.

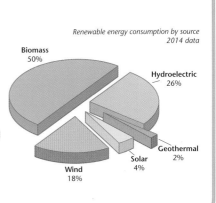

Renewable energy consumption by source 2014 data

- Biomass 50%
- Hydroelectric 26%
- Geothermal 2%
- Solar 4%
- Wind 18%

THE NATIONAL CAPITAL

The National Capital

Chosen as a compromise location between Northern and Southern interests and built on land ceded by Virginia and Maryland in the late 1700s, Washington, D.C., sits on a bank of the Potomac River. It is the seat of U.S. government and symbol of the country's history. Pierre L'Enfant, a French architect, was appointed by President George Washington to design the city, which is distinguished by a grid pattern cut by diagonal avenues. At the city's core is the National Mall, a broad park lined by monuments, museums, and stately government buildings.

THE BASICS

Founding
July 16, 1790

Total area (land and water)
68 sq mi (177 sq km)

Land area
61 sq mi (158 sq km)

Population
672,228

Racial/ethnic groups
44.1% white; 48.3% African American; 4.2% Asian; 0.7% Native American; 10.6% Hispanic (any race)

Foreign born
14.0%

Urban population
100.0% (2010)

Population density
11,020.1 per sq mi
(4,254.6 per sq km)

GEO WHIZ

License plates in the District of Columbia bear the slogan "Taxation Without Representation," reflecting the fact that residents have no voting representative in either house of the U.S. Congress.

The flag of the District of Columbia, with its three red stars and two red stripes, is based on the shield in George Washington's family coat of arms.

In 1790 Benjamin Banneker, a free black, helped survey the land that would become the capital city.

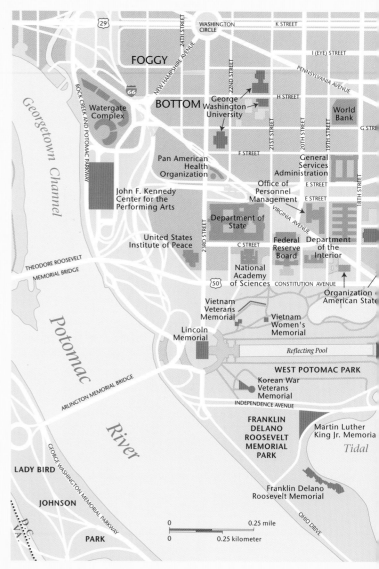

AMERICAN BEAUTY ROSE

WOOD THRUSH

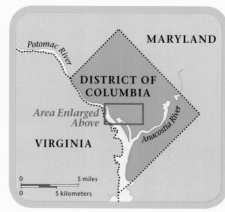

DISTRICT OF COLUMBIA. Originally on both sides of the Potomac River, the city returned land to Virginia in 1846.

GREAT LEADER. Abraham Lincoln, who was president during the Civil War and a strong opponent of slavery, is remembered in a monument that houses this seated statue at the west end of the National Mall.

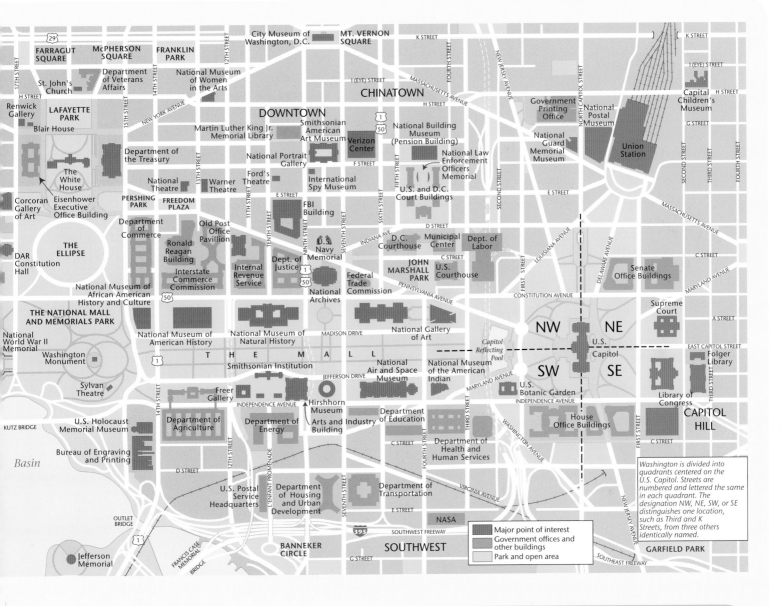

29

FARRAGUT SQUARE

McPHERSON SQUARE

FRANKLIN PARK

City Museum of Washington, D.C.

MT. VERNON SQUARE

K STREET

K STREET

I (EYE) STREET

Capital Children's Museum

H STREET

St. John's Church

Department of Veterans Affairs

National Museum of Women in the Arts

CHINATOWN

MASSACHUSETTS AVENUE

NEW JERSEY AVENUE

NORTH CAPITOL STREET

Government Printing Office

National Postal Museum

H STREET

Renwick Gallery

H STREET

LAFAYETTE PARK

DOWNTOWN

H STREET

National Guard Memorial Museum

G STREET

NEW YORK AVENUE

Blair House

Martin Luther King Jr. Memorial Library

Smithsonian American Art Museum

Verizon Center

National Building Museum (Pension Building)

Union Station

SECOND STREET

THIRD STREET

FOURTH STREET

Department of the Treasury

National Portrait Gallery

F STREET

National Law Enforcement Officers Memorial

The White House

National Theatre

Warner Theatre

Ford's Theatre

International Spy Museum

U.S. and D.C. Court Buildings

Corcoran Gallery of Art

Eisenhower Executive Office Building

PERSHING PARK

FREEDOM PLAZA

E STREET

FBI Building

D STREET

MASSACHUSETTS AVENUE

PENNSYLVANIA AVENUE

Senate Office Buildings

MARYLAND AVENUE

C STREET

Department of Commerce

Old Post Office Pavillion

D.C. Courthouse

Municipal Center

Dept. of Labor

LOUISIANA AVENUE

DELAWARE AVENUE

DAR Constitution Hall

THE ELLIPSE

Ronald Reagan Building

Interstate Commerce Commission

Internal Revenue Service

Dept. of Justice

U.S. Navy Memorial

JOHN MARSHALL PARK

U.S. Courthouse

FIRST STREET

National Museum of African American History and Culture

Federal Trade Commission

C STREET

CONSTITUTION AVENUE

Supreme Court

THE NATIONAL MALL AND MEMORIALS PARK

National Archives

PENNSYLVANIA AVENUE

NW

NE

A STREET

National World War II Memorial

National Museum of American History

MADISON DRIVE

National Gallery of Art

Capitol Reflecting Pool

U.S. Capitol

EAST CAPITOL STREET

Folger Library

Washington Monument

National Museum of Natural History

SW

SE

Sylvan Theatre

THE MALL

Smithsonian Institution

JEFFERSON DRIVE

National Air and Space Museum

National Museum of the American Indian

U.S. Botanic Garden

MARYLAND AVENUE

Library of Congress

THIRD STREET

CAPITOL HILL

Freer Gallery

Hirshhorn Museum

INDEPENDENCE AVENUE

U.S. Holocaust Memorial Museum

INDEPENDENCE AVENUE

KUTZ BRIDGE

Department of Agriculture

Department of Energy

Arts and Industry Building

Department of Education

WASHINGTON AVENUE

House Office Buildings

FIRST STREET

Bureau of Engraving and Printing

Department of Health and Human Services

C STREET

Basin

D STREET

C STREET

12TH STREET

14TH STREET

U.S. Postal Service Headquarters

Department of Housing and Urban Development

L'ENFANT PROMENADE

SEVENTH STREET

Department of Transportation

E STREET

FOURTH STREET

THIRD STREET

VIRGINIA AVENUE

NEW JERSEY AVENUE

OUTLET BRIDGE

NASA

GARFIELD PARK

SOUTHWEST FREEWAY

395

Washington is divided into quadrants centered on the U.S. Capitol. Streets are numbered and lettered the same in each quadrant. The designation NW, NE, SW, or SE distinguishes one location, such as Third and K Streets, from three others identically named.

BANNEKER CIRCLE

SOUTHWEST

G STREET

SOUTHEAST FREEWAY

Major point of interest

Government offices and other buildings

Park and open area

Jefferson Memorial

FRANCIS CASE MEMORIAL BRIDGE

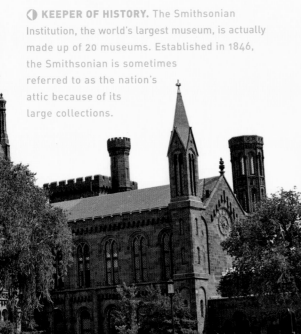

KEEPER OF HISTORY. The Smithsonian Institution, the world's largest museum, is actually made up of 20 museums. Established in 1846, the Smithsonian is sometimes referred to as the nation's attic because of its large collections.

NATIONAL ICON. The gleaming dome of the U.S. Capitol, home to the Senate and House of Representatives, is a familiar symbol of Washington's main business—the running of the country's government.

THE REGION

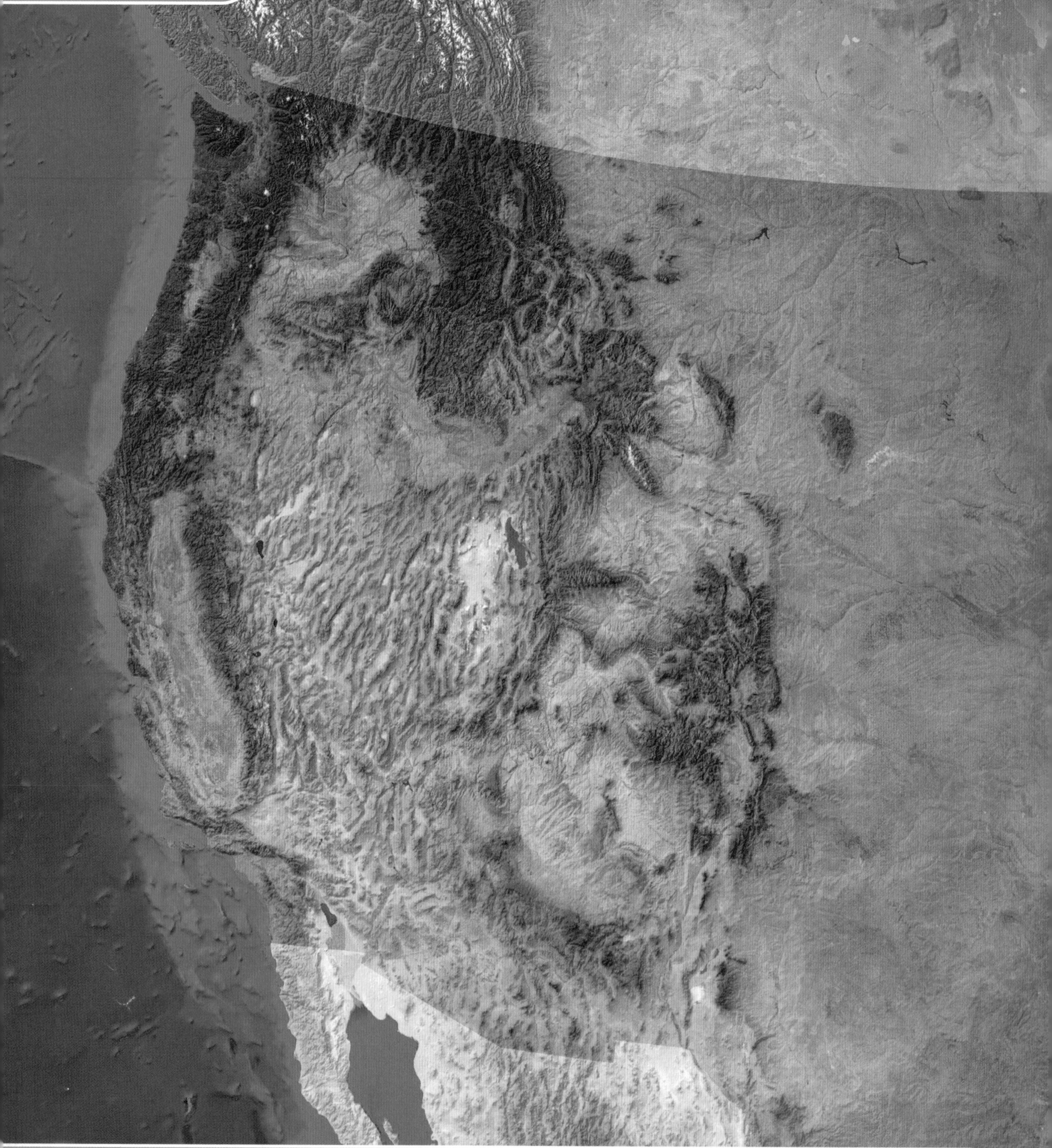

PHYSICAL

Total area
(land and water)
196,214 sq mi
(508,192 sq km)

Highest point
Mount Washington, NH
6,288 ft (1,917 m)

Lowest point
Sea level, shores of the
Atlantic Ocean

Longest rivers
St. Lawrence, Susquehanna,
Connecticut, Hudson

Largest lakes
Erie, Ontario, Champlain

Vegetation
Needleleaf, broadleaf, and
mixed forest

Climate
Continental to mild, with cool
to warm summers, cold winters,
and moderate precipitation
throughout the year

POLITICAL

Total population
59,645,340

States (11):
Connecticut, Delaware, Maine, Maryland,
Massachusetts, New Hampshire, New
Jersey, New York, Pennsylvania, Rhode
Island, Vermont

Largest state
New York: 54,555 sq mi (141,297 sq km)

Smallest state
Rhode Island: 1,545 sq mi (4,001 sq km)

Most populous state
New York: 19,795,791

Least populous state
Vermont: 626,042

Largest city proper
New York, NY: 8,550,405

The Northeast

A   B   C   D   E   F   G   H

NEW BRUNSWICK

NOVA SCOTIA

Bay of Fundy

St. John

St. Croix

CANADA
U.S.

Allagash

St. John

Mt. Katahdin
5,268 ft
1,606 m

Mt. Desert Island

Penobscot

M A I N E

Gulf of Maine

Kennebec

Saco

Mt. Washington
6,288 ft
1,917 m

White Mts.

N.H.

Merrimack

Cape Ann

Massachusetts Bay

Cape Cod

Nantucket Island

Martha's Vineyard

Mt. Mansfield
4,393 ft
1,339 m

Green Mts.

VT.

Connecticut

MASSACHUSETTS

Mt. Greylock
3,491 ft
1,064 m

CONN.

R.I.

Mt. Frissell
2,380 ft
725 m

Long Island Sound

Long Island

QUEBEC

CANADA
U.S.

Lake Champlain

Mt. Marcy
5,344 ft
1,629 m

Adirondack Mts.

Hudson

N E W   Y O R K

Catskill Mts.

High Point
1,803 ft
550 m

NEW JERSEY

C A N A D A

St. Lawrence

Raquette

Black

Oneida Lake

Mohawk

Erie Canal

Finger Lakes

Plateau

Genesee

A P P A L A C H I A N

Delaware

Fall Line

Pine Barrens

Cape May

Delaware Bay

DEL.

Delmarva Peninsula

COASTAL PLAIN

O N T A R I O

Lake Ontario

Niagara Falls

Allegheny

P E N N S Y L V A N I A

Allegheny Mountains

Blue Ridge

Piedmont

Susquehanna

448 ft
137 m

MARYLAND

D.C.

Chesapeake Bay

Potomac

Mt. Davis
3,213 ft
979 m

Backbone Mt.
3,360 ft
1,024 m

Monongahela

Ohio

WEST VIRGINIA

VIRGINIA

OHIO

Lake Erie

Lake Huron

ATLANTIC OCEAN

100 miles

100 kilometers

0

0

Albers Conic Equal-Area Projection

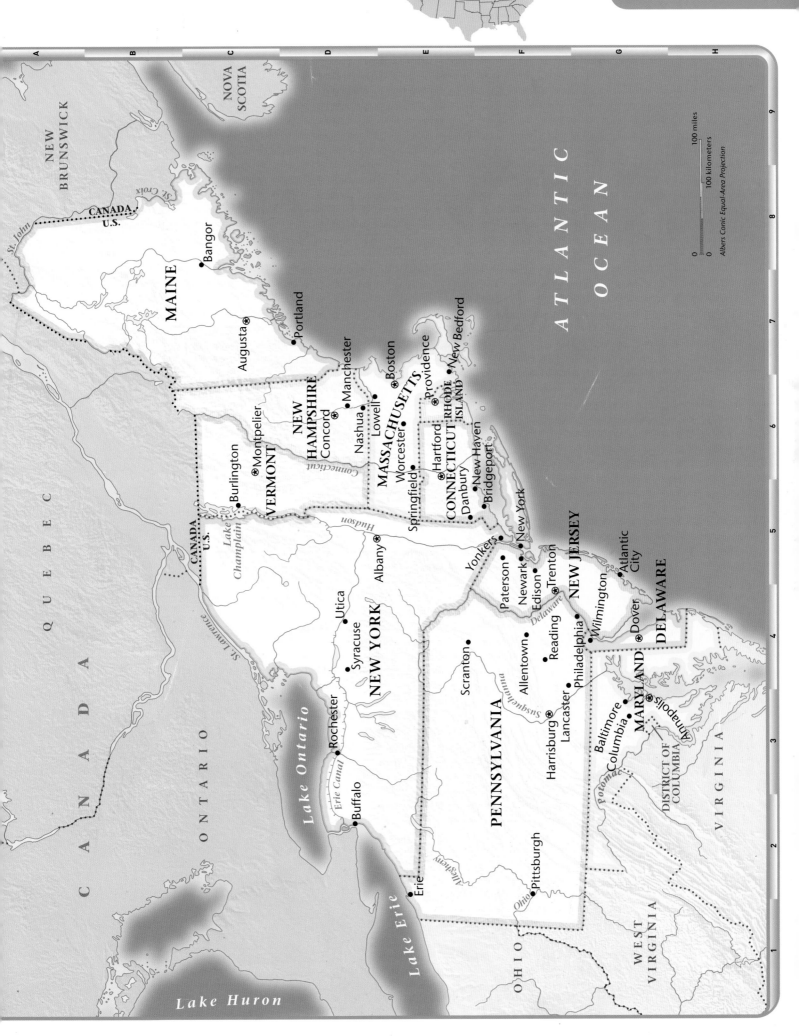

A B C D E F G H

9

8

7

6

5

4

3

2

1

NEW BRUNSWICK

NOVA SCOTIA

QUEBEC

CANADA

ONTARIO

OHIO

WEST VIRGINIA

VIRGINIA

ATLANTIC OCEAN

MAINE

Bangor

Portland

Augusta

NEW HAMPSHIRE

Manchester

Concord

Nashua

Lowell

Boston

Providence

New Bedford

VERMONT

Montpelier

Burlington

MASSACHUSETTS

Worcester

Springfield

Hartford

RHODE ISLAND

CONNECTICUT

New Haven

Danbury

Bridgeport

New York

Yonkers

NEW YORK

Albany

Utica

Syracuse

Rochester

Buffalo

Erie

Scranton

NEW JERSEY

Paterson

Newark

Edison

Trenton

Atlantic City

Wilmington

Dover

DELAWARE

PENNSYLVANIA

Allentown

Reading

Philadelphia

Harrisburg

Lancaster

Pittsburgh

Baltimore

Columbia

MARYLAND

Annapolis

DISTRICT OF COLUMBIA

St. Croix

St. John

CANADA U.S.

CANADA U.S.

Lake Champlain

St. Lawrence

Connecticut

Hudson

Lake Ontario

Lake Erie

Erie Canal

Susquehanna

Delaware

Allegheny

Ohio

Potomac

Lake Huron

100 miles

100 kilometers

Albers Conic Equal-Area Projection

The Northeast

BIRTHPLACE OF A NATION

The United States had its beginnings in the Northeast region. Early European traders and settlers were quickly followed by immigrants from around the globe, making the region's population the most diverse in the country. The region includes the country's financial center, New York City, and its political capital, Washington, D.C. Although the region boasts tranquil mountains, lakes, and rivers, its teeming cities have always been the heart of the Northeast.

DINNER DELICACY. Lobsters, a favorite food for many people, turn bright red when cooked. These crustaceans live in the cold waters of the Atlantic Ocean and are caught using baited traps.

MELTING POT. From colonial times, the Northeast has been a gateway for immigration. These young girls, dressed in traditional saris and performing in an India Cultural Festival in New Jersey, reflect the rich diversity of the region.

DEFENDER OF FREEDOM. Rising 548 feet (167 m) above Penn Square, Philadelphia's City Hall, with its statue of William Penn, is the country's largest municipal building. Penn was the founder of the Pennsylvania colony and a defender of equal rights for men and women.

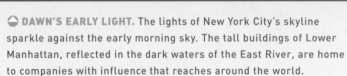

⬤ **DAWN'S EARLY LIGHT.** The lights of New York City's skyline sparkle against the early morning sky. The tall buildings of Lower Manhattan, reflected in the dark waters of the East River, are home to companies with influence that reaches around the world.

⬤ **STILL WATERS.** A father and son enjoy a quiet day of fishing on the smooth-as-glass waters of Lake Chocurua in New Hampshire's White Mountains. Deciduous trees turning red and gold will soon shed their leaves, and the hillsides will turn white with winter's snow, attracting skiers to the valley.

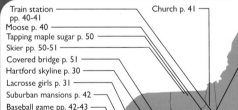

WHERE THE PICTURES ARE

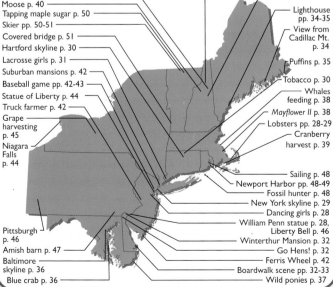

Train station pp. 40-41
Moose p. 40
Tapping maple sugar p. 50
Skier pp. 50-51
Covered bridge p. 51
Hartford skyline p. 30
Lacrosse girls p. 31
Suburban mansions p. 42
Baseball game pp. 42-43
Statue of Liberty p. 44
Truck farmer p. 42
Grape harvesting p. 45
Niagara Falls p. 44

Church p. 41

Canoers on lake pp. 28-29
Lighthouse pp. 34-35
View from Cadillac Mt. p. 34
Puffins p. 35
Tobacco p. 30
Whales feeding p. 38
Mayflower II p. 38
Lobsters pp. 28-29
Cranberry harvest p. 39
Sailing p. 48
Newport Harbor pp. 48-49
Fossil hunter p. 48
New York skyline p. 29
Dancing girls p. 28
William Penn statue p. 28, Liberty Bell p. 46
Winterthur Mansion p. 32
Go Hens! p. 32
Ferris Wheel p. 42
Boardwalk scene pp. 32-33
Wild ponies p. 37

Pittsburgh p. 46
Amish barn p. 47
Baltimore skyline p. 36
Blue crab p. 36

THE BASICS

Statehood
January 9, 1788; 5th state

Total area (land and water)
5,543 sq mi (14,357 sq km)

Land area
4,842 sq mi (12,542 sq km)

Population
3,590,886

Capital
Hartford
Population 124,006

Largest city
Bridgeport
Population 147,629

Racial/ethnic groups
80.8% white; 11.6% African American; 4.6% Asian; 0.5% Native American; 15.4% Hispanic origin (any race)

Foreign born
13.6%

Urban population
88.0% (2010)

Population density
741.6 per sq mi (286.3 per sq km)

GEO WHIZ

The sperm whale, Connecticut's state animal, has a brain larger than that of any other creature known to have lived on Earth.

The first hamburgers in U.S. history were served by Louis Lassen at his New Haven lunch wagon in 1895.

The nuclear-powered U.S.S. *Virginia*, the first of a class of technologically advanced submarines, was built at Groton, home of the U.S. Naval Submarine Base.

Connecticut

As early as 1614 Dutch explorers founded trading posts along the coast of Connecticut, but the first permanent European settlements were established in 1635 by English Puritans from nearby Massachusetts. The Connecticut Fundamental Orders, which in 1639 established a democratic system of government in the colony, were an important model for the writing of the U.S. Constitution in 1787. This earned the state its nickname—the Constitution State. Even in colonial times Connecticut was an important industrial center, producing goods that competed with factories in England. During the Revolutionary War, Connecticut produced military goods for the colonial army. Today, Connecticut industries produce jet aircraft engines, helicopters, and nuclear submarines. Connecticut is home to many international corporations, but it is best known as the "insurance state." Following independence, businessmen offered to insure ship cargoes in exchange for a share of the profits. Soon after, other types of insurance were offered. Now, Connecticut is home to more than 100 insurance companies.

**MOUNTAIN LAUREL
ROBIN**

⏚ **LEAFY HARVEST.** Tents protect shade tobacco, the state's leading agricultural export by value. Leaves from the plants, which are grown in the Connecticut River Valley, are used for premium cigar wrappers.

◖ **BRIGHT CITY LIGHTS.** Established as a fort in the early 1600s, Hartford was one of the earliest cities of colonial America. Today, this modern state capital is a center of economic growth and cultural diversity.

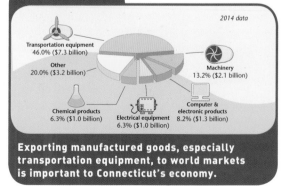

GLOBAL ECONOMY

2014 data

Transportation equipment
46.0% ($7.3 billion)

Other
20.0% ($3.2 billion)

Machinery
13.2% ($2.1 billion)

Chemical products
6.3% ($1.0 billion)

Electrical equipment
6.3% ($1.0 billion)

Computer & electronic products
8.2% ($1.3 billion)

Exporting manufactured goods, especially transportation equipment, to world markets is important to Connecticut's economy.

MASSACHUSETTS

Mt. Frissell
2,380 ft 725 m
Highest point
in Connecticut

Twin
Lakes

Canaan

Lakeville

Norfolk

East
Hartland

Congamond
Lakes

Hazardville

Staffordville
Reservoir

North Grosvenor
Dale

Quaddick
Res.

Thompson

Winsted

Granby

Enfield

Stafford

Putnam

APPALACHIAN
NATIONAL
SCENIC
TRAIL

Sharon

Windsor Locks

Broad Brook

Barkhamsted
Reservoir

Ellington

Dayville

FARMINGTON
NATIONAL WILD
& SCENIC RIVER

New
Hartford

Compensating
Reservoir

Simsbury

Windsor

Shenipsit
Lake

Storrs

Danielson

Torrington

Bloomfield

Vernon

Brooklyn

MACEDONIA BROOK
STATE PARK

Harwinton

Collinsville

Unionville

Hartford

Manchester

Mansfield
Hollow
Lake

Moosup

Litchfield

West
Hartford

East
Hartford

Coventry

Kent

Wethersfield

Glastonbury

Willimantic
Reservoir

Plainfield

Nepaug
Reservoir

Newington

Willimantic

Bantam
Lake

Plainville

Terryville

CONNECTICUT

Jewett City

Bethlehem

Bristol

New
Britain

Rocky Hill

DINOSAUR S.P.

Marlborough

Baltic

New
Milford

Watertown

Oakville

Waterbury

Southington

Middletown

Portland

East
Hampton

Colchester

Norwich

MASHANTUCKET
PEQUOT I.R.

Pocotopaug L.

Lake
Candlewood

Meriden

Prospect

Cheshire

SILVIO O. CONTE
NATIONAL FISH &
WILDLIFE REFUGE

Durham

Moodus

Gardner
Lake

Southbury

Naugatuck

MOHEGAN I.R.

Chesterfield

Quaker Hill

Lake
Lillinonah

Haddam

New Fairfield

Wallingford

Lake Zoar

Seymour

Hamden

President
George
W. Bush's
birthplace

North
Haven

Deep River

Essex

New
London

Groton

MYSTIC
SEAPORT

Pawcatuck

Danbury

Newtown

Lake
Gaillard

Mystic

Bethel

Ansonia

North
Branford

Poquonock
Bridge

Niantic

Ridgefield

Shelton

New Haven

Branford

Old
Saybrook

BLOCK ISLAND
SOUND

Saugatuck
Reservoir

Orange

Westbrook

WEIR FARM
N.H.S.

Trumbull

East
Haven

Guilford

East River

Madison

Clinton

STEWART B.
McKINNEY N.W.R.

NEW
YORK

Wilton

Stratford

West
Haven

Milford

Stratford
Point

New
Canaan

Westport

Bridgeport

STEWART B.
McKINNEY N.W.R.

Fairfield

Norwalk

Darien

LONG ISLAND SOUND

Stamford

Greenwich

0   20 miles
0   20 kilometers

Albers Conic Equal-Area Projection

NEW
YORK

Taconic Range

Housatonic

Shepaug

Housatonic

Naugatuck

Quinnipiac

Hammonasset

Connecticut

Salmon

Connecticut

Thames

Yantic

Shetucket

Quinebaug

Natchaug

Willimantic

Hockanum

Scantic

Farmington

West Branch Farmington

East Branch

RHODE ISLAND

Pachaug
Pond

Pawcatuck

Economy Symbols

Fishing		Printing/publishing	
Lobster fishing		Stone/gravel/cement	
Shellfish		Machinery	
Poultry/eggs		Metal manufacturing	
Sheep		Metal products	
Hogs		Shipbuilding	
Dairy cows		Chemistry	
Beef cattle		Electrical equipment	
Fruits		Computers/electronics	
Vegetables		Scientific instruments	
Nursery stock		Aircraft/parts	
Corn		Tourism	
Tobacco		Finance/insurance	

TEAM PLAY. Lacrosse can be traced back to games played by Native Americans of the Northeast. Adapted for women in the 1890s, the game has gained popularity. In 1982 the first national women's lacrosse championship was held in New Jersey.

DECEMBER 7, 1787

THE BASICS

Statehood
December 7, 1787; 1st state

Total area (land and water)
2,489 sq mi (6,446 sq km)

Land area
1,949 sq mi (5,047 sq km)

Population
945,934

Capital
Dover
Population 37,355 (2014)

Largest city
Wilmington
Population 71,948

Racial/ethnic groups
70.4% white; 22.4% African
American; 3.9% Asian; 0.7%
Native American; 9.0% Hispanic
origin (any race)

Foreign born
8.4%

Urban population
83.3% (2010)

Population density
485.3 per sq mi (187.4 per sq km)

GEO WHIZ

Each year contestants bring
their pumpkins and launch-
ing machines to the Punkin
Chunkin World Championship in
Bridgeville to see who can
catapult their big, orange
squash the farthest.

The Delaware Estuary is
one of the most important
shorebird migration sites in
the Western Hemisphere.

The first steam railroad to
provide regular service began
operations in New Castle in 1831.

Delaware

Second smallest among the states in the area, Delaware has played a big role in the history of the United States. The Delaware River Valley was explored at various times by the Spanish, Portuguese, and Dutch, but the Swedes established the first permanent European settlement in 1638. In 1655 the colony fell under Dutch authority, but in 1682 the land was annexed by William Penn and the Pennsylvania colony. In 1787 Delaware was the first state to ratify the new U.S. Constitution. Delaware's Atlantic coast beaches are popular with tourists. Its fertile farmland, mainly in the south, produces soybeans, corn, dairy products, and poultry. But the state's real economic power is located in the north, around Wilmington, where factories employ thousands of workers to process food products and produce machinery and chemicals. Industry has been a source of wealth, but it also poses a danger to the environment. Protecting the environment is a high priority for Delaware.

PEACH BLOSSOM
BLUE HEN CHICKEN

TEAM SPIRIT. Enthusiastic fans and the University of Delaware band support the "Fightin' Blue Hens." Located in Newark, the university traces its roots to 1743.

PAST GRANDEUR. Built in 1837 in the fashion of a British country house, Winterthur was expanded from 12 to 196 rooms by the du Ponts, chemical industry tycoons. In 1951 the house was opened to the public as a museum for the family's extensive collection of antiques and Americana.

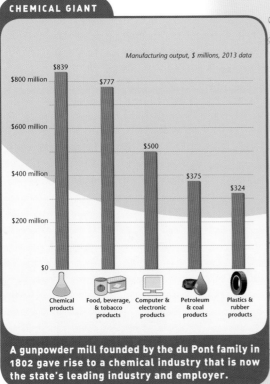

🐬 **SEASIDE RETREAT.** Originally established in 1873 as a church campground, Rehoboth Beach is still a popular getaway destination on Delaware's Atlantic coastline. A concrete dolphin overlooks the town's boardwalk, a popular promenade that separates shops and restaurants from the beach. The boardwalk has been destroyed on several occasions by storms.

CHEMICAL GIANT

Manufacturing output, $ millions, 2013 data

$839	Chemical products
$777	Food, beverage, & tobacco products
$500	Computer & electronic products
$375	Petroleum & coal products
$324	Plastics & rubber products

$800 million
$600 million
$400 million
$200 million
$0

A gunpowder mill founded by the du Pont family in 1802 gave rise to a chemical industry that is now the state's leading industry and employer.

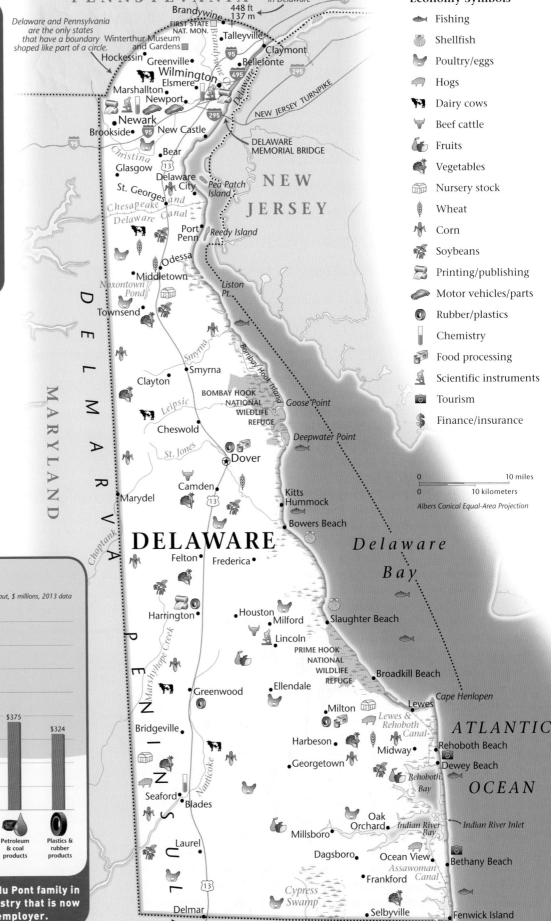

PENNSYLVANIA

Delaware and Pennsylvania are the only states that have a boundary shaped like part of a circle.

Highest point in Delaware
448 ft
137 m

Brandywine
FIRST STATE NAT. MON.
Winterthur Museum and Gardens
Talleyville
Claymont
Hockessin
Bellefonte
Greenville
Wilmington
Elsmere
Marshallton
Newport
Newark
Brookside
New Castle
Bear
Glasgow
Delaware City
St. Georges
Port Penn
Odessa
Middletown
Townsend
Noxontown Pond
Smyrna
Clayton
Cheswold
Dover
Camden
Marydel
Felton
Frederica
Harrington
Houston
Milford
Lincoln
Greenwood
Ellendale
Bridgeville
Milton
Harbeson
Midway
Georgetown
Seaford
Blades
Laurel
Oak Orchard
Millsboro
Dagsboro
Ocean View
Frankford
Delmar
Selbyville

Christina
Chesapeake and Delaware Canal
Pea Patch Island
Reedy Island
Liston Pt.
Bombay Hook Island
Goose Point
Deepwater Point
Kitts Hummock
Bowers Beach
Slaughter Beach
Broadkill Beach
Cape Henlopen
Lewes
Lewes & Rehoboth Canal
Rehoboth Beach
Dewey Beach
Rehoboth Bay
Indian River Inlet
Bethany Beach
Assawoman Canal
Cypress Swamp
Fenwick Island

NEW JERSEY
NEW JERSEY TURNPIKE
DELAWARE MEMORIAL BRIDGE

MARYLAND

DELMARVA PENINSULA

DELAWARE

Delaware Bay

ATLANTIC OCEAN

BOMBAY HOOK NATIONAL WILDLIFE REFUGE
PRIME HOOK NATIONAL WILDLIFE REFUGE

Leipsic
St. Jones
Smyrna
Choptank
Nanticoke
Marshyhope Creek
Indian River Bay

Economy Symbols

- 🐟 Fishing
- 🐚 Shellfish
- 🐔 Poultry/eggs
- 🐖 Hogs
- 🐄 Dairy cows
- 🐂 Beef cattle
- Fruits
- Vegetables
- Nursery stock
- Wheat
- Corn
- Soybeans
- Printing/publishing
- Motor vehicles/parts
- Rubber/plastics
- Chemistry
- Food processing
- Scientific instruments
- 📷 Tourism
- $ Finance/insurance

0   10 miles
0   10 kilometers
Albers Conical Equal-Area Projection

THE BASICS

Statehood
March 15, 1820; 23rd state

Total area (land and water)
35,380 sq mi (91,633 sq km)

Land area
30,843 sq mi (79,883 sq km)

Population
1,329,328

Capital
Augusta
Population 18,705 (2014)

Largest city
Portland
Population 66,881

Racial/ethnic groups
94.9% white; 1.4% African American; 1.2% Asian; 0.7% Native American; 1.6% Hispanic origin (any race)

Foreign born
3.4%

Urban population
38.7% (2010)

Population density
43.1 per sq mi (16.6 per sq km)

GEO WHIZ

With world shark populations declining, some conservation-minded deep-sea fishermen in Maine have turned the idea of a shark tournament upside down. They still compete to see who can catch the biggest fish, but they tag and release the sharks.

Forests cover more than 85 percent of Maine. No wonder it is called the Pine Tree State.

Glaciers formed during the last ice age carved hundreds of inlets out of Maine's shoreline and created some 2,000 islands off the coast.

Maine

Maine's story begins long before the arrival of European settlers in the 1600s. Evidence of native people dates to at least 3000 B.C., and Leif Erikson and his Viking sailors may have explored Maine's coastline 500 years before Columbus crossed the Atlantic. English settlements were established along the southern coast in the 1620s, and in 1677 the territory of Maine came under control of Massachusetts. Following the Revolutionary War, the people of Maine pressed for separation from Massachusetts, and in 1820 Maine entered the Union as a nonslave state under the terms of the Missouri Compromise. Most of Maine's population is concentrated in towns along the coast. Famous for its rugged beauty, the coast is the focus of the tourist industry. Cold offshore waters contribute to a lively fishing industry, and timber from the state's mountainous interior supports wood product and paper businesses. Maine, a leader in environmental awareness, seeks a balance between economic growth and environmental protection.

WHITE PINE CONE AND TASSEL

CHICKADEE

ACADIA NATIONAL PARK, established in 1929, attracts thousands of tourists each year. The park includes Cadillac Mountain, the highest point along the North Atlantic coast and the site from which the earliest sunrises in the United States can be viewed from October 7 through March 6.

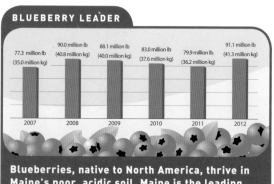

BLUEBERRY LEADER

2007	2008	2009	2010	2011	2012
77.3 million lb (35.0 million kg)	90.0 million lb (40.8 million kg)	88.1 million lb (40.0 million kg)	83.0 million lb (37.6 million kg)	79.9 million lb (36.2 million kg)	91.1 million lb (41.3 million kg)

Blueberries, native to North America, thrive in Maine's poor, acidic soil. Maine is the leading harvester of wild blueberries in the U.S.

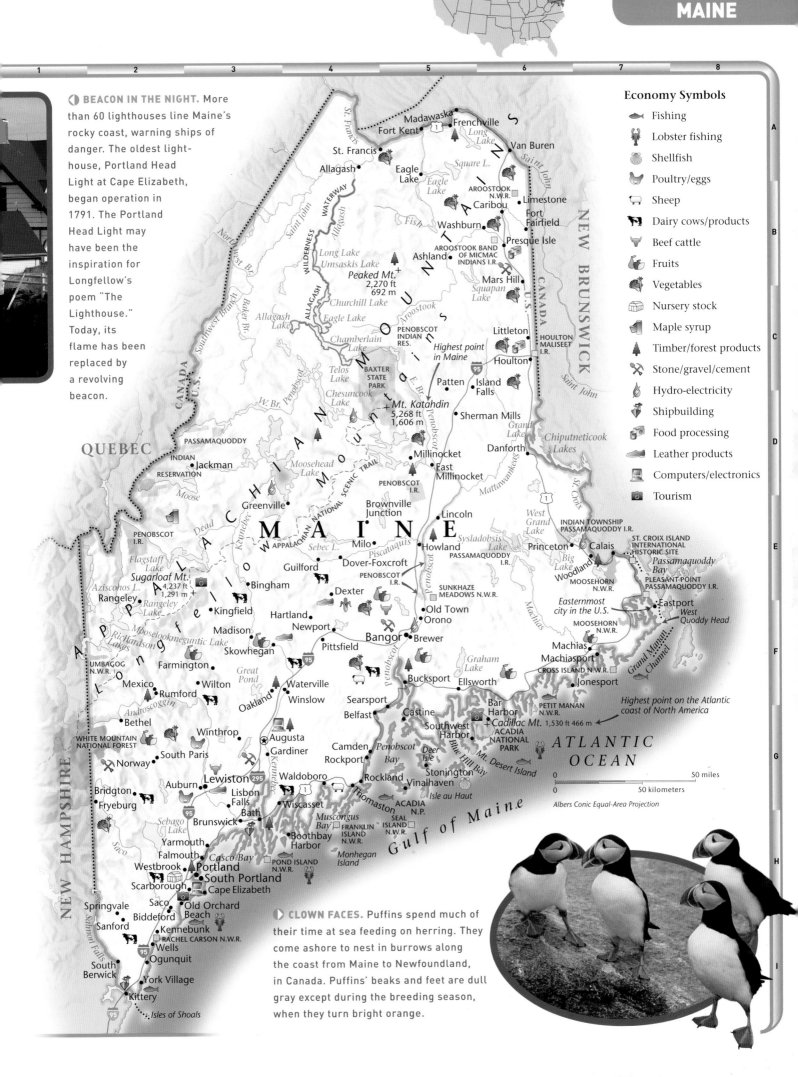

◖ **BEACON IN THE NIGHT.** More than 60 lighthouses line Maine's rocky coast, warning ships of danger. The oldest lighthouse, Portland Head Light at Cape Elizabeth, began operation in 1791. The Portland Head Light may have been the inspiration for Longfellow's poem "The Lighthouse." Today, its flame has been replaced by a revolving beacon.

Economy Symbols

- Fishing
- Lobster fishing
- Shellfish
- Poultry/eggs
- Sheep
- Dairy cows/products
- Beef cattle
- Fruits
- Vegetables
- Nursery stock
- Maple syrup
- Timber/forest products
- Stone/gravel/cement
- Hydro-electricity
- Shipbuilding
- Food processing
- Leather products
- Computers/electronics
- Tourism

QUEBEC

NEW BRUNSWICK

CANADA
U.S.

St. Francis
Madawaska
Fort Kent
Frenchville
Van Buren
St. Francis
Allagash
Eagle Lake
Long Lake
Square L.
Limestone
Caribou
Washburn
Fort Fairfield
AROOSTOOK N.W.R.
Ashland
Presque Isle
AROOSTOOK BAND OF MICMAC INDIANS I.R.
Mars Hill
Squapan Lake
Long Lake
Umsaskis Lake
Peaked Mt.
2,270 ft
692 m
Churchill Lake
Eagle Lake
Allagash Lake
PENOBSCOT INDIAN RES.
Littleton
Houlton
HOULTON MALISEET I.R.
Highest point in Maine
Telos Lake
BAXTER STATE PARK
Chesuncook Lake
Patten
Island Falls
Mt. Katahdin
5,268 ft
1,606 m
Sherman Mills
Danforth
Chiputneticook Lakes
Millinocket
East Millinocket
PENOBSCOT I.R.
Jackman
PASSAMAQUODDY INDIAN RESERVATION
Moosehead Lake
Moose
Greenville
Brownville Junction
Lincoln
West Grand Lake
INDIAN TOWNSHIP PASSAMAQUODDY I.R.
Princeton
Calais
ST. CROIX ISLAND INTERNATIONAL HISTORIC SITE
Woodland
MOOSEHORN N.W.R.
Passamaquoddy Bay
PLEASANT POINT PASSAMAQUODDY I.R.
Easternmost city in the U.S.
Eastport
West Quoddy Head
MOOSEHORN N.W.R.
PENOBSCOT I.R.
Flagstaff Lake
Sugarloaf Mt.
4,237 ft
1,291 m
Aziscohos L.
Rangeley
Rangeley Lake
Kingfield
Guilford
Dover-Foxcroft
Bingham
PENOBSCOT I.R.
Dexter
Sebec L.
Milo
Howland
Sysladobsis Lake
Big Lake
SUNKHAZE MEADOWS N.W.R.
Old Town
Orono
UMBAGOG N.W.R.
Madison
Skowhegan
Hartland
Newport
Pittsfield
Bangor
Brewer
Bucksport
Machias
Machiasport
Jonesport
CROSS ISLAND N.W.R.
Graham Lake
Moselookmeguntic Lake
Richardson Lakes
Farmington
Wilton
Great Pond
Waterville
Winslow
Oakland
Searsport
Ellsworth
Mexico
Rumford
Androscoggin
Bethel
Winthrop
Augusta
Gardiner
Camden
Rockport
Belfast
Castine
Southwest Harbor
Bar Harbor
PETIT MANAN N.W.R.
Highest point on the Atlantic coast of North America
Cadillac Mt. 1,530 ft 466 m
ACADIA NATIONAL PARK
ATLANTIC OCEAN
WHITE MOUNTAIN NATIONAL FOREST
South Paris
Norway
Auburn
Lewiston
Waldoboro
Rockland
Vinalhaven
Thomaston
Penobscot Bay
Deer Isle
Stonington
Mt. Desert Island
Blue Hill Bay
Bridgton
Fryeburg
Lisbon Falls
Wiscasset
Brunswick
Bath
ACADIA N.P.
Isle au Haut
Sebago Lake
Yarmouth
Falmouth
Casco Bay
Boothbay Harbor
Muscongus Bay
FRANKLIN ISLAND N.W.R.
SEAL ISLAND N.W.R.
Monhegan Island
Gulf of Maine
Westbrook
Portland
South Portland
Scarborough
Cape Elizabeth
POND ISLAND N.W.R.
Springvale
Saco
Old Orchard Beach
Biddeford
Sanford
Kennebunk
RACHEL CARSON N.W.R.
Wells
South Berwick
Ogunquit
York Village
Kittery
Isles of Shoals
NEW HAMPSHIRE
Salmon Falls

50 miles
50 kilometers
Albers Conic Equal-Area Projection

◗ **CLOWN FACES.** Puffins spend much of their time at sea feeding on herring. They come ashore to nest in burrows along the coast from Maine to Newfoundland, in Canada. Puffins' beaks and feet are dull gray except during the breeding season, when they turn bright orange.

THE BASICS

Statehood
April 28, 1788; 7th state

Total area (land and water)
12,406 sq mi (32,131 sq km)

Land area
9,707 sq mi (25,142 sq km)

Population
6,006,401

Capital
Annapolis
Population 38,856

Largest city
Baltimore
Population 621,849

Racial/ethnic groups
59.6% white; 30.5% African American; 6.5% Asian; 0.6% Native American; 9.5% Hispanic origin (any race)

Foreign born
14.0 %

Urban population
87.2% (2010)

Population density
618.8 per sq mi (238.9 per sq km)

GEO WHIZ

The Naval Support Facility Thurmont, better known as Camp David, is the mountain retreat of American presidents. It is part of Catoctin Mountain Park in north-central Maryland.

Residents on Smith Island, in the lower Chesapeake Bay, are being robbed of their land by rising sea levels and of their traditional livelihood by dwindling blue crab harvests. They fear a major Atlantic hurricane could wipe out their island home.

The name of Baltimore's professional football team— the Ravens—may have been inspired by the title of a poem by Edgar Allan Poe, who lived in Baltimore in the mid-1800s and whose grave is in that city.

Maryland

Native Americans, who raised crops and harvested oysters from the nearby waters of Chesapeake Bay, lived on the land that would become Maryland long before early European settlers arrived. In 1608 Captain John Smith explored the waters of the bay, and in 1634 English settlers established the colony of Maryland. In 1788 Maryland became the seventh state to ratify the new U.S. Constitution. Chesapeake Bay, the largest estuary in the United States, almost splits Maryland into two parts. East of the bay lies the flat coastal plain, and to the west the land rises through the hilly piedmont and mountainous panhandle. Chesapeake Bay, the state's economic and environmental focal point, supports a busy seafood industry. It is also a major transportation artery, linking Baltimore and other Maryland ports to the Atlantic Ocean. Most of the people of Maryland live in an urban corridor between Baltimore and Washington, D.C., where jobs in government, research, and high-tech businesses provide employment.

🌐 **GATEWAY CITY.** Since the early 1700s, Baltimore, near the upper Chesapeake Bay, has been a major seaport and focus of trade, industry, and immigration. Today, the Inner Harbor is not only a modern working port but also the city's vibrant cultural center.

BLACK-EYED SUSAN

NORTHERN (BALTIMORE) ORIOLE

◀ **COLORFUL CRUSTACEAN.** Blue crabs, found in Maryland's Chesapeake Bay waters, were a staple in the diet of Native Americans. They have been harvested commercially since the mid-1800s, and the tasty meat is a popular menu item—especially in crab cakes—in seafood restaurants throughout the area.

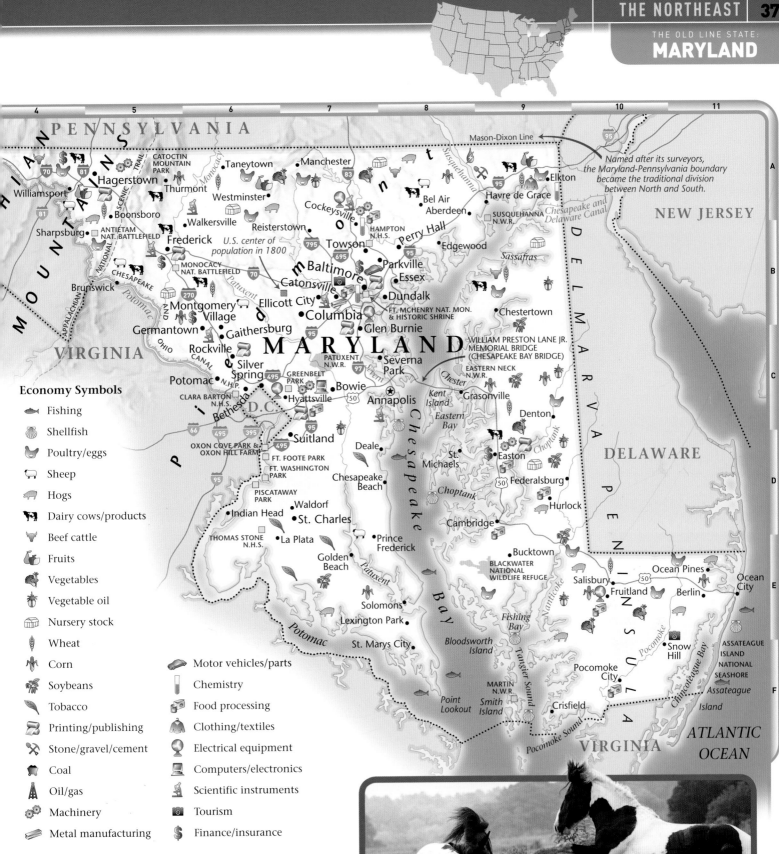

PENNSYLVANIA

Mason-Dixon Line

Named after its surveyors,
the Maryland-Pennsylvania boundary
became the traditional division
between North and South.

NEW JERSEY

VIRGINIA

DELAWARE

M A R Y L A N D

Williamsport
Hagerstown
Thurmont
Taneytown
Manchester
Elkton
Havre de Grace
Sharpsburg
Boonsboro
Westminster
Bel Air
Aberdeen
Walkersville
Reisterstown
Frederick
Cockeysville
Edgewood
Brunswick
Baltimore
Parkville
Essex
Catonsville
Dundalk
Chestertown
Ellicott City
Montgomery Village
Columbia
Glen Burnie
Germantown
Gaithersburg
Severna Park
Rockville
Silver Spring
Grasonville
Denton
Potomac
Bowie
Annapolis
Kent Island
Bethesda
Hyattsville
D.C.
Suitland
Deale
Easton
St. Michaels
Federalsburg
Chesapeake Beach
Hurlock
Waldorf
Indian Head
St. Charles
Cambridge
La Plata
Prince Frederick
Golden Beach
Bucktown
Ocean Pines
Salisbury
Ocean City
Solomons
Fruitland
Berlin
Lexington Park
Snow Hill
St. Marys City
Pocomoke City
Crisfield

ATLANTIC OCEAN

VIRGINIA

Chesapeake Bay

Assateague Island National Seashore

Economy Symbols

🪶 HORSEPLAY. Wild ponies have lived on Assateague Island since the 1600s. Some believe the original ponies were survivors from a Spanish galleon that sank offshore. Today, more than 300 ponies live on this Atlantic barrier island shared by Maryland and Virginia.

🐟 Fishing
🐚 Shellfish
🐔 Poultry/eggs
🐑 Sheep
🐗 Hogs
🐄 Dairy cows/products
🐂 Beef cattle
🍒 Fruits
🥬 Vegetables
🫒 Vegetable oil
🏠 Nursery stock
🌾 Wheat
🌽 Corn
🌱 Soybeans
🌿 Tobacco
🖨 Printing/publishing
⛏ Stone/gravel/cement
⬛ Coal
🛢 Oil/gas
⚙ Machinery
▬ Metal manufacturing

🚗 Motor vehicles/parts
🧪 Chemistry
📦 Food processing
👕 Clothing/textiles
🔦 Electrical equipment
💻 Computers/electronics
🔬 Scientific instruments
📷 Tourism
💲 Finance/insurance

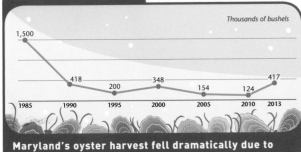

CHESAPEAKE HARVEST

Thousands of bushels

1,500
418
200
348
154
124
417

1985 1990 1995 2000 2005 2010 2013

Maryland's oyster harvest fell dramatically due to overharvesting, pollution, and disease, but it is now making a comeback.

THE BASICS

Statehood
February 6, 1788; 6th state

Total area (land and water)
10,554 sq mi (27,336 sq km)

Land area
7,800 sq mi (20,202 sq km)

Population
6,794,422

Capital
Boston
Population 667,137

Largest city
Boston
Population 667,137

Racial/ethnic groups
82.1% white; 8.4% African American; 6.6% Asian; 0.5% Native American; 11.2% Hispanic origin (any race)

Foreign born
15.0%

Urban population
92.0% (2010)

Population density
871.1 per sq mi
(336.3 per sq km)

GEO WHIZ

In 1717 the pirate ship *Whydah*, under the command of Captain Samuel Bellamy (also known as Black Sam), went down in a storm off Cape Cod. Treasure and artifacts recovered from the ship are on display at the Whydah Museum, in Provincetown.

Massachusetts is the birthplace of several famous inventors, including Eli Whitney, Samuel Morse, and Benjamin Franklin.

The country's first lighthouse was built on Little Brewster Island in Boston Harbor in 1716. It was automated in 1998 and opened to the public in 1999.

Stellwagen Bank National Marine Sanctuary helps make Cape Cod one of the world's best spots for whale-watching.

Massachusetts

The earliest human inhabitants of Massachusetts were Native Americans who arrived more than 10,000 years ago. The first Europeans to visit Massachusetts may have been Norsemen around A.D. 1000, and later fishermen came from France and Spain. But the first permanent European settlement was established in 1620, when people aboard the sailing ship *Mayflower* landed near Plymouth on the coast of Massachusetts. The Puritans arrived soon after, and by 1630 they had established settlements at Salem and Boston. By 1640 more than 16,000 people, most seeking religious freedom, had settled in Massachusetts. The early economy of Massachusetts was based on shipping, fishing, and whaling. By the 19th century, industry, taking advantage of abundant water power, had a firm foothold. Factory jobs attracted thousands of immigrants, mainly from Europe. In the late 20th century, Massachusetts experienced a boom in high-tech jobs, drawing on the state's skilled labor force and its 114 colleges and universities.

⬇ **REMINDER OF TIMES PAST.** Shrouded in morning mist, this replica of the *Mayflower* docked in Plymouth Harbor is a reminder of Massachusetts's early history.

CHICKADEE
MAYFLOWER

◗ **LEVIATHANS OF THE DEEP.** In the 19th century, Massachusetts was an important center for the whaling industry, with more than 300 registered whaling ships. Today, humpback whales swim in the protected waters of a marine sanctuary in Massachusetts Bay.

Map

NEW HAMPSHIRE

Amesbury
Newburyport
Haverhill
PARKER RIVER N.W.R.
Methuen
Lawrence
Ipswich
Winchendon
Lowell N.H.P.
Lowell
Dracut
Orange
Turners Falls
Athol
Fitchburg
Gardner
Chelmsford
Wilmington
Gloucester
Cape Ann
Greenfield
Deerfield
Leominster
OXBOW N.W.R.
SUDBURY, ASSABET & CONCORD NATIONAL WILD & SCENIC RIVER
Peabody
Danvers
Beverly
Salem Maritime N.H.S.
SILVIO O. CONTE N.W.R.
Quabbin Reservoir
Wachusett Res.
MINUTE MAN N.H.P.
Lexington
Concord
Boston N.H.P.
Woburn
SAUGUS IRON WORKS N.H.S.
Salem
Marblehead
ASSABET N.W.R.
Medford
Malden
Lynn
Amherst
Northampton
GREAT MEADOWS N.W.R.
Cambridge
Boston
Massachusetts
STELLWAGEN BANK NATIONAL MARINE SANCTUARY
Shrewsbury
Marlborough
Sudbury Res.
Wellesley
Brookline
BOSTON HARBOR ISLANDS N.R.A.
Bay
South Hadley
Easthampton
Ware
Worcester
Framingham
Milton
Quincy
Lake Quinsigamond
President Kennedy's birthplace
President George H.W. Bush's birthplace
Weymouth
Birthplace of Presidents John Adams and John Quincy Adams
Holyoke
Ludlow
Spencer
Auburn
Norwood
Randolph
Chicopee
Springfield
Sturbridge
Oxford
Milford
Stoughton
Rockland
Whitman
Agawam
Springfield Armory N.H.S.
Southbridge
Webster
Bellingham
Franklin
Brockton
Bridgewater
Silver Lake
Provincetown
CAPE COD NATIONAL SEASHORE
CONNECTICUT
RHODE ISLAND
North Attleboro
Attleboro
Taunton
TAUNTON NATIONAL WILD & SCENIC RIVER
Plymouth
Plimoth Plantation
Truro
MASSOIT N.W.R.
Wellfleet
Middleboro
Assawompset Pond
Cape Cod Bay
Seekonk
Long Pond
Great Quittacus Pond
Somerset
Buzzards Bay
Cape Cod Canal
Sandwich
Dennis
Orleans
Fall River
New Bedford Whaling N.H.P.
Barnstable
Chatham
New Bedford
Fairhaven
MASHPEE N.W.R.
Hyannis
S. Yarmouth
Monomoy Island
MONOMOY N.W.R.
East Falmouth
Falmouth
Nantucket Sound
Woods Hole
Vineyard Haven
Rhode Island Sound
Elizabeth Islands
Vineyard Sound
Oak Bluffs
NANTUCKET N.W.R.
Edgartown
Chappaquiddick Island
Gay Head WAMPANOAG I.R.
Martha's Vineyard
Nantucket
Nomans Land
NOMANS LAND ISLAND N.W.R.
Nantucket Island

ATLANTIC OCEAN

One of the ten most populous cities in the U.S. in 1790

0   30 miles
0   30 kilometers
Albers Conic Equal-Area Projection

Economy Symbols

- Fishing
- Lobster fishing
- Shellfish
- Poultry/eggs
- Sheep
- Hogs
- Dairy cows/products
- Beef cattle
- Fruits
- Vegetables
- Nursery stock
- Wheat
- Tobacco
- Maple syrup
- Printing/publishing
- Stone/gravel/cement
- Hydro-electricity
- Machinery
- Metal products
- Computers/electronics
- Scientific instruments
- Aerospace
- Tourism

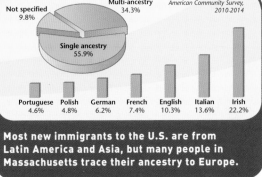

BIG BUSINESS. Cranberries, grown in fields called bogs, are the state's largest agricultural crop. These tiny berries, one of only three fruits native to North America, are consumed mainly in the form of juice or as a tasty accompaniment to holiday dishes. Workers flood fields to make harvesting the floating berries easier.

EUROPEAN ROOTS

American Community Survey, 2010-2014

Not specified 9.8%
Multi-ancestry 34.3%
Single ancestry 55.9%

	%
Portuguese	4.6%
Polish	4.8%
German	6.2%
French	7.4%
English	10.3%
Italian	13.6%
Irish	22.2%

Most new immigrants to the U.S. are from Latin America and Asia, but many people in Massachusetts trace their ancestry to Europe.

New Hampshire

The territory that would become the state of New Hampshire, the ninth state to approve the U.S. Constitution in 1788, began as a fishing colony established along the short 18-mile (29-km)-long coastline in 1623. New Hampshire was named a royal colony in 1679, but as the Revolutionary War approached, it was the first colony to declare its independence from English rule. In the early 19th century, life in New Hampshire followed two very different paths. Near the coast, villages and towns grew up around sawmills, shipyards, and warehouses. But in the forested, mountainous interior, people lived on small, isolated farms, and towns provided only basic services. Today, modern industries such as computer and electronic component manufacturing and other high-tech companies, together with biotech and medical research, have brought prosperity to the state. In addition, the state's natural beauty attracts tourists year-round to hike on forest trails, swim in pristine lakes, and ski on snow-covered mountain slopes.

THE BASICS

Statehood
June 21, 1788; 9th state

Total area (land and water)
9,349 sq mi (24,214 sq km)

Land area
8,953 sq mi (23,187 sq km)

Population
1,330,608

Capital
Concord
Population 42,444 (2014)

Largest city
Manchester
Population 110,229

Racial/ethnic groups
93.9% white; 1.5% African American; 2.6% Asian; 0.3% Native American; 3.4% Hispanic origin (any race)

Foreign born
5.6%

Urban population
60.3% (2010)

Population density
148.6 per sq mi
(57.4 per sq km)

GEO WHIZ

The Granite State boasts more than 200 different kinds of rocks and minerals, making it a great destination for collectors.

The first potato grown in the United States was planted in 1719 in Londonderry on the Common Field, better known as the Commons.

Ben Kilham's unique way of rehabilitating abandoned black bear cubs he finds in the New Hampshire woods has earned him the nickname Bear Man by residents of Lyme.

⬡ **LUMBERING GIANT.** Averaging 6 feet (2 m) tall at the shoulders, moose are the largest of North America's deer. Moose are found throughout New Hampshire.

PURPLE FINCH
PURPLE LILAC

ROARING WINDS

F4 "devastating tornado"
207-260 mph
(333-418 km/h)

Category 5 Hurricane
wind speeds greater
than 155 mph
(249 km/h)

Mt. Washington record:
231 miles an hour
(371 km/h)
April 1934

Mount Washington holds the record for the highest surface wind speed in the U.S., comparable to winds in Category 5 hurricanes and F4 tornadoes.

◗ **ALL ABOARD.** Tourists traveling by train through the White Mountains enjoy the cool autumn weather and the colorful fall foliage of the deciduous trees that cover the mountains.

Economy Symbols

- Fishing
- Lobster fishing
- Shellfish
- Sheep
- Dairy cows/products
- Beef cattle
- Fruits
- Nursery stock
- Corn
- Maple syrup
- Timber/forest products
- Stone/gravel/cements
- Hydro-electricity
- Machinery
- Metal products
- Computers/electronics
- Scientific instruments
- Tourism

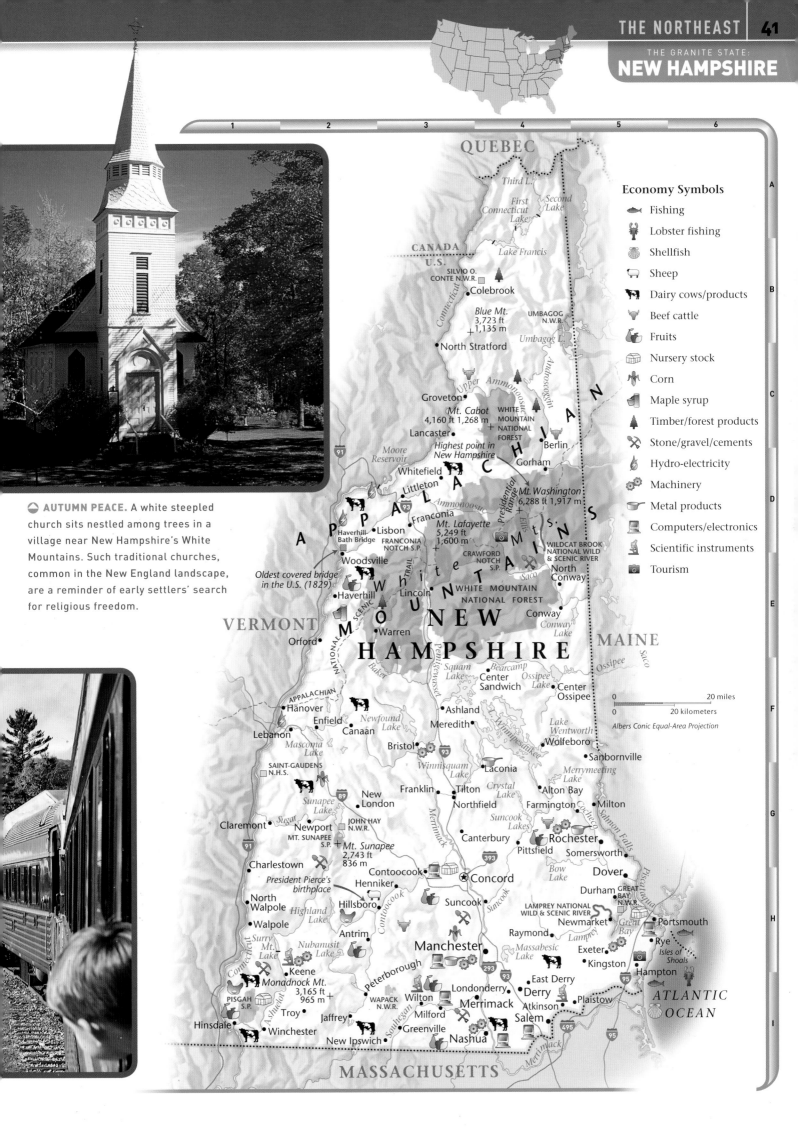

AUTUMN PEACE. A white steepled church sits nestled among trees in a village near New Hampshire's White Mountains. Such traditional churches, common in the New England landscape, are a reminder of early settlers' search for religious freedom.

QUEBEC

CANADA
U.S.

Third L.

First
Connecticut
Lakes

Second
Lake

Lake Francis

SILVIO O.
CONTE N.W.R.

Colebrook

Blue Mt.
3,723 ft
1,135 m

UMBAGOG
N.W.R.

North Stratford

Umbagog L.

Upper Ammonoosuc

Androscoggin

Groveton

Mt. Cabot
4,160 ft 1,268 m

WHITE
MOUNTAIN
NATIONAL
FOREST

Lancaster

Berlin

Whitefield

Highest point in
New Hampshire

Gorham

Moore
Reservoir

Littleton

Presidential
Range

Mt. Washington
6,288 ft 1,917 m

Ammonoosuc

Franconia

Mt. Lafayette
5,249 ft
1,600 m

Ellis

Mts.

Haverhill
Bath Bridge

Lisbon

FRANCONIA
NOTCH S.P.

CRAWFORD
NOTCH
S.P.

WILDCAT BROOK
NATIONAL WILD
& SCENIC RIVER

Woodsville

Saco

North
Conway

Oldest covered bridge
in the U.S. (1829)

TRAIL

White

Lincoln

WHITE MOUNTAIN
NATIONAL FOREST

Haverhill

VERMONT

Orford

Warren

NATIONAL

Baker

Conway

Conway
Lake

MAINE

Saco

Ossipee

**NEW
HAMPSHIRE**

Pemigewasset

Squam
Lake

Bearcamp

Center
Sandwich

Ossipee
Lake

Center
Ossipee

0   20 miles
0   20 kilometers

APPALACHIAN

Hanover

Enfield

Newfound
Lake

Ashland

Meredith

Winnipesaukee

Lake
Wentworth

Albers Conic Equal-Area Projection

Lebanon

Canaan

Bristol

Wolfeboro

Sanbornville

Mascoma
Lake

Winnisquam
Lake

Laconia

Merrymeeting
Lake

SAINT-GAUDENS
N.H.S.

Franklin

Tilton

Crystal
Lake

Alton Bay

Farmington

Milton

New
London

Northfield

Suncook
Lakes

Cochecho

Claremont

Sugar

Newport

JOHN HAY
N.W.R.

Canterbury

Rochester

Salmon Falls

MT. SUNAPEE
S.P.

Pittsfield

Somersworth

Charlestown

Mt. Sunapee
2,743 ft
836 m

Contoocook

Concord

Bow
Lake

Dover

President Pierce's
birthplace

Henniker

Durham

GREAT
BAY
N.W.R.

North
Walpole

Hillsboro

Suncook

LAMPREY NATIONAL
WILD & SCENIC RIVER

Newmarket

Great
Bay

Portsmouth

Walpole

Highland
Lake

Contoocook

Raymond

Lamprey

Piscataqua

Antrim

Manchester

Massabesic
Lake

Exeter

Rye

Isles of
Shoals

Surry
Mt.
Lake

Nubanusit
Lake

Londonderry

Kingston

Hampton

Keene

Peterborough

East Derry

Derry

Plaistow

ATLANTIC

Monadnock Mt.
3,165 ft
965 m

WAPACK
N.W.R.

Wilton

Milford

Atkinson

Salem

OCEAN

PISGAH
S.P.

Ashuelot

Troy

Jaffrey

Greenville

Nashua

Merrimack

Merrimack

Hinsdale

Winchester

New Ipswich

Southegan

MASSACHUSETTS

THE BASICS

Statehood
December 18, 1787; 3rd state

Total area (land and water)
8,723 sq mi (22,591 sq km)

Land area
7,354 sq mi (19,047 sq km)

Population
8,958,013

Capital
Trenton
Population 84,225

Largest city
Newark
Population 281,944

Racial/ethnic groups
72.6% white; 14.8% African American; 9.7% Asian; 0.6% Native American; 19.7% Hispanic origin (any race)

Foreign born
21.5%

Urban population
94.7% (2010)

Population density
1,218.1 per sq mi
(470.3 per sq km)

GEO WHIZ

Site of a one-time trash heap, the Meadowlands, a swampy lowland along the Hackensack River, is now home to a major sports complex.

In 1930 New Jerseyite Charles Darrow developed the game Monopoly. He named Boardwalk and other streets in the game after those in Atlantic City.

Hadrosaurus, the first dinosaur skeleton excavated in North America, was named in honor of Haddonfield, its discovery site.

New Jersey

Long before Europeans settled in New Jersey, the region was home to hunting and farming communities of Delaware Indians. The Dutch set up a trading post in northern New Jersey in 1618, calling it New Netherland, but yielded the land in 1664 to the English, who named it New Jersey after the English Channel Isle of Jersey. New Jersey saw more than 90 battles during the Revolutionary War. It became the third U.S. state in 1787 and the first to sign the Bill of Rights. In the 19th century, southern New Jersey remained largely agricultural, while the northern part of the state rapidly industrialized. Today, highways and railroads link the state to urban centers along the Atlantic seaboard. More than 9,000 farms grow fruits and vegetables for nearby urban markets. Industries as well as services and trade are thriving. Beaches along the Atlantic coast attract thousands of tourists each year.

⊙ **HOLD ON!** New Jersey's Atlantic coast is lined with sandy beaches that attract vacationers from near and far. Amusement parks, such as this one in Wildwood, add to the fun.

**AMERICAN GOLDFINCH
VIOLET**

◐ **HEADED TO MARKET.** New Jersey is a leading producer of fresh fruits and vegetables. These organic vegetables are headed for urban markets in the Northeast.

◐ **SUBURBAN SPRAWL.** With almost 95 percent of the state's population living in urban areas, housing developments with close-set, look-alike houses are a common characteristic of the suburban landscape. Residents commute to jobs in the city.

⬤ **PLAY BALL!** Fans pack the seats at Newark's Bears and Eagles Riverfront Stadium to watch a minor league baseball game. Built in 1999, the stadium is a part of Newark's plan to revitalize the downtown area, drawing people into the city.

Economy Symbols

~	Fishing	🌽	Corn
🐚	Shellfish	🌱	Soybeans
🐔	Poultry/eggs	🖨	Printing/publishing
🐑	Sheep	⚒	Stone/gravel/cement
🐖	Hogs	⚙	Machinery
🐄	Dairy cows/products	🧪	Chemistry
🐂	Beef cattle	📷	Food processing
🍓	Fruits	💻	Computers/electronics
🥬	Vegetables	🚀	Aerospace
🌿	Nursery stock	📷	Tourism
🌾	Wheat		

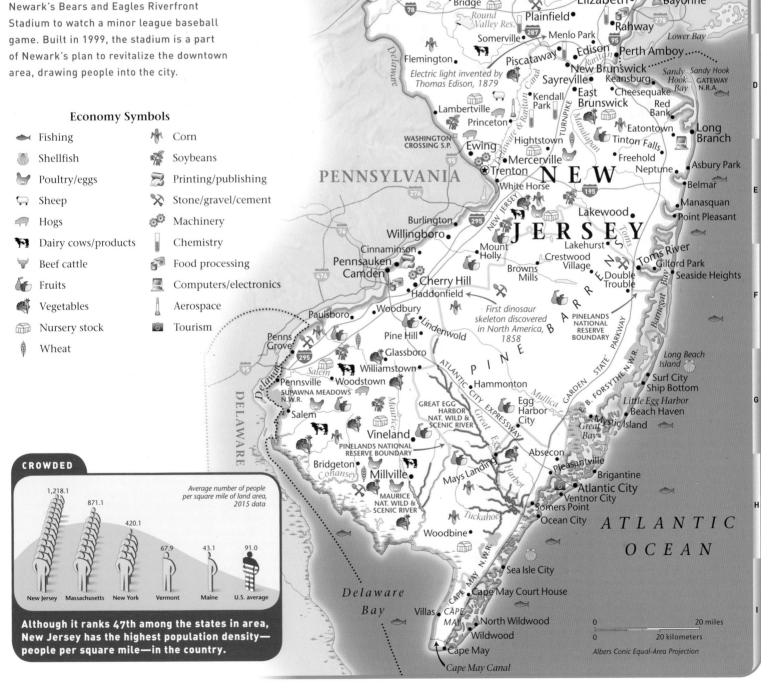

CROWDED

Average number of people per square mile of land area, 2015 data

New Jersey	Massachusetts	New York	Vermont	Maine	U.S. average
1,218.1	871.1	420.1	67.9	43.1	91.0

Although it ranks 47th among the states in area, New Jersey has the highest population density—people per square mile—in the country.

THE BASICS

Statehood
July 26, 1788; 11th state

Total area (land and water)
54,555 sq mi (141,297 sq km)

Land area
47,126 sq mi (122,057 sq km)

Population
19,795,791

Capital
Albany
Population (98,469)

Largest city
New York City
Population (8,550,405)

Racial/ethnic groups
70.1% white; 17.6% African American; 8.8% Asian; 1.0% Native American; 18.8% Hispanic origin (any race)

Foreign born
22.3%

Urban population
87.9% (2010)

Population density
362.9 per sq mi
(140.1 per sq km)

GEO WHIZ

Each year at Halloween, the Headless Horseman rides again through the countryside of Sleepy Hollow, as residents reenact Washington Irving's *The Legend of Sleepy Hollow.*

The Erie Canal, built in the 1820s between Albany and Buffalo, opened the Midwest to development by linking the Hudson River and the Great Lakes.

Cooperstown, home of the National Baseball Hall of Fame, takes its name from a town established in the late 1700s by the father of famed American author James Fenimore Cooper.

New York

When Englishman Henry Hudson explored New York's Hudson River Valley in 1609, the territory was already inhabited by large tribes of Native Americans, including the powerful Iroquois. In 1624 a Dutch trading company established the New Netherland colony, but after just 40 years the colony was taken over by the English and renamed for England's Duke of York. In 1788 New York became the 11th state. The state can be divided into two parts. The powerful port city of New York, center of trade and commerce and gateway to immigrants, is the largest city in the United States. Its metropolitan area, which extends into the surrounding states of Connecticut, New Jersey, and Pennsylvania, has more than 20 million people. Cities such as Buffalo and Rochester are industrial centers, and Ithaca and Syracuse boast major universities. Agriculture is also important, and the state is a major producer of dairy products, fruits, and vegetables.

◒ **LADY LIBERTY.** Standing in New York Harbor, the Statue of Liberty, a gift from the people of France, is a symbol of freedom and democracy.

EASTERN BLUEBIRD
ROSE

◖ **NATURAL WONDER.** Each year more than eight million tourists visit Niagara Falls on the U.S.-Canada border. Visitors in rain slickers trek through the mists below Bridal Veil Falls on the American side.

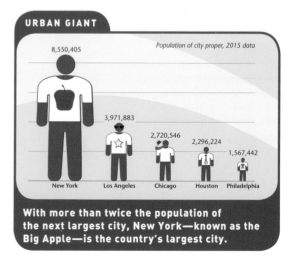

URBAN GIANT

Population of city proper, 2015 data

8,550,405 — New York

3,971,883 — Los Angeles

2,720,546 — Chicago

2,296,224 — Houston

1,567,442 — Philadelphia

With more than twice the population of the next largest city, New York—known as the Big Apple—is the country's largest city.

Economy Symbols

- ⬱ Fishing
- 🦪 Shellfish
- 🐔 Poultry/eggs
- 🐑 Sheep
- 🐷 Hogs
- 🐄 Dairy cows/products
- 🍎 Fruits
- 🌱 Vegetables
- 🌻 Vegetable oil
- Nursery stock
- 🌾 Wheat
- 🌽 Corn
- 🍇 Vineyards
- Maple syrup
- Printing/publishing
- ⚒ Stone/gravel/cement
- Mining
- Oil/gas
- Hydro-electricity
- ⚙ Machinery
- Motor vehicles/parts
- Clothing/textiles
- Electrical equipment
- Scientific instruments
- Motion picture/music industry
- 📷 Tourism
- $ Finance/insurance

Map labels

QUEBEC

CANADA

U.S.

ONTARIO

St. Lawrence

Thousand Islands

ONTARIO

Massena
Malone
Dannemora
ST. REGIS MOHAWK I.R.
Plattsburgh
Ogdensburg
Potsdam
Lake Champlain

Gouverneur
Raquette
Saranac Lake
Lake Placid

Adirondack
Mt. Marcy
Highest point in New York
5,344 ft
1,629 m

Watertown
Black
ADIRONDACK
Mountains
Ticonderoga
FORT TICONDEROGA
Lake George

Lowville
PARK
Hudson

Oswego
Fulton
Oneida Lake
FORT STANWIX NAT. MON.
Rome
Warrensburg
Glens Falls

Greece
Irondequoit
Rochester
Gates
Fairmount
MONTEZUMA N.W.R.
Syracuse
Oneida
ONONDAGA INDIAN RESERVATION
Utica
ONEIDA I.R.
Little Falls
Gloversville
Saratoga Springs
SARATOGA MOUNTAINS
SARATOGA N.H.P.

Geneva
Seneca Falls
Auburn
WOMEN'S RIGHTS N.H.P.
Ilion
Amsterdam
Schenectady
Niskayuna

Canandaigua
Seneca Lake
Finger Lakes
Cayuga Lake
Penn Yan
President Fillmore's birthplace
President Van Buren's birthplace
Cooperstown
Cobleskill
Albany
Troy

Dansville
NEW YORK
Cortland
Norwich
Oneonta
Kinderhook
MARTIN VAN BUREN N.H.S.
NEW YORK STATE THRUWAY
Hudson

GREEN MOUNTAIN & FINGER LAKES NAT. FOREST
Ithaca
Sidney
Susquehanna
Catskill

Keuka Lake
Chemung
Bath
Watkins Glen
APPALACHIAN
Catskill Mountains

Hornell
Horseheads
Endwell
Binghamton
CATSKILL PARK
Slide Mt.
4,180 ft
1,274 m
Kingston
VANDERBILT MANSION N.H.S.

Corning
Elmira
Endicott
W. Branch Delaware
HOME OF FRANKLIN D. ROOSEVELT N.H.S.
ELEANOR ROOSEVELT N.H.S.

PENNSYLVANIA
E. Branch
UPPER DELAWARE SCENIC AND RECREATIONAL RIVER
President Franklin D. Roosevelt's birthplace
SHAWANGUNK GRASSLANDS N.W.R.
New Paltz
Monticello
Poughkeepsie
Beacon

Susquehanna
Delaware
Middletown
Newburgh
West Point
U.S. MILITARY ACADEMY
Peekskill

Port Jervis
New City
NATIONAL
Tarrytown

APPALACHIAN
Tuxedo Park
Spring Valley
Yonkers
White Plains
New Rochelle
Long Island Sound
Block Island Sound
Sag Harbor
Montauk Point

President Theodore Roosevelt's birthplace
ST. PAUL'S CHURCH N.H.S.
Huntington
Coram
Southampton

New York
Levittown
Brentwood
Centereach
FIRE ISLAND NATIONAL SEASHORE
ATLANTIC OCEAN

Ellis Island
STATUE OF LIBERTY NAT. MON.
Freeport
Long Island
SAGAMORE HILL N.H.S.

NEW JERSEY
Staten Island
GATEWAY N.R.A.
Long Beach

VERMONT
Taconic Ranges
MASSACHUSETTS
CONNECTICUT
RHODE ISLAND

◖ SWEET HARVEST. The Finger Lakes region, with its unique combination of soils and climate conditions, is well suited to growing wine grapes. With more than 10,000 acres (4,047 ha) of vineyards, it is the center of New York's wine industry, producing varieties for both domestic and export markets.

Scale

0 — 100 miles
0 — 100 kilometers
Albers Conic Equal-Area Projection

Pennsylvania

Pennsylvania, the 12th of England's 13 American colonies, was established in 1682 by Quaker William Penn and 360 settlers seeking religious freedom and fair government. The colony enjoyed abundant natural resources—dense woodlands, fertile soils, industrial minerals, and water power—that soon attracted Germans, Scotch-Irish, and other immigrants. Pennsylvania played a central role in the move for independence from Britain, and Philadelphia served as the new country's capital from 1790 to 1800. In the 19th century Philadelphia, in the east, and Pittsburgh, in the west, became booming centers of industrial growth. Philadelphia produced ships, locomotives, and textiles, while the iron and steel industry fueled Pittsburgh's growth. Jobs in industry as well as agriculture attracted immigrants from around the world. Today, Pennsylvania's economy has shifted toward information technology, health care, financial services, and tourism, but coal and steel production continue to play a role in the state's economy.

THE BASICS

Statehood
December 12, 1787; 2nd state

Total area (land and water)
46,054 sq mi (119,280 sq km)

Land area
44,743 sq mi (115,883 sq km)

Population
12,802,503

Capital
Harrisburg
Population 49,082 (2014)

Largest city
Philadelphia
Population 1,567,442

Racial/ethnic groups
82.6% white; 11.7% African American; 3.4% Asian; 0.4% Native American; 6.8% Hispanic origin (any race)

Foreign born
6.0%

Urban population
78.7% (2010)

Population density
286.1 per sq mi
(110.5 per sq km)

GEO WHIZ

The Martin Guitar Company in Nazareth has been handcrafting guitars for musicians all over the world for more than 150 years.

For more than a century streets in Philadelphia have been transformed on New Year's Day for the annual Mummers Parade.

⏴ **LET FREEDOM RING.** The Liberty Bell, cast in 1753 by Pennsylvania craftsmen, hangs in Philadelphia. Because of a crack, it is no longer rung.

MOUNTAIN LAUREL
RUFFED GROUSE

LAKE ERIE — Erie — Millcreek — Meadville — Pymatuning Reservoir — Titusville — Greenville — Oil City — Sharon — Grove City — New Castle — Butler — Beaver Falls — OHIO RIVER N.W.R. — Aliquippa — McCandless — Plum — Pittsburgh — Penn Hills — McKeesport — Jeannette — Washington — Monessen — Waynesburg — Uniontown — FRIENDSHIP HILL N.H.S. — FT. NECESSITY NATIONAL BATTLEFIELD — ERIE NATIONAL WILDLIFE REFUGE

OHIO

WEST VIRGINIA

Monongahela — Cheat

⏴ **RIVER TOWN.** Pittsburgh, one of the largest inland ports in the United States, was established in 1758 where the Monongahela and Allegheny Rivers meet to form the Ohio River. Once a booming steel town, Pittsburgh is now a center of finance, medicine, and education.

MAKING COINS

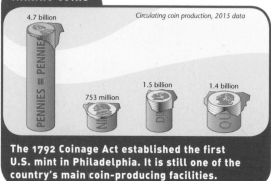

Circulating coin production, 2015 data

PENNIES — 4.7 billion
753 million
1.5 billion
1.4 billion

The 1792 Coinage Act established the first U.S. mint in Philadelphia. It is still one of the country's main coin-producing facilities.

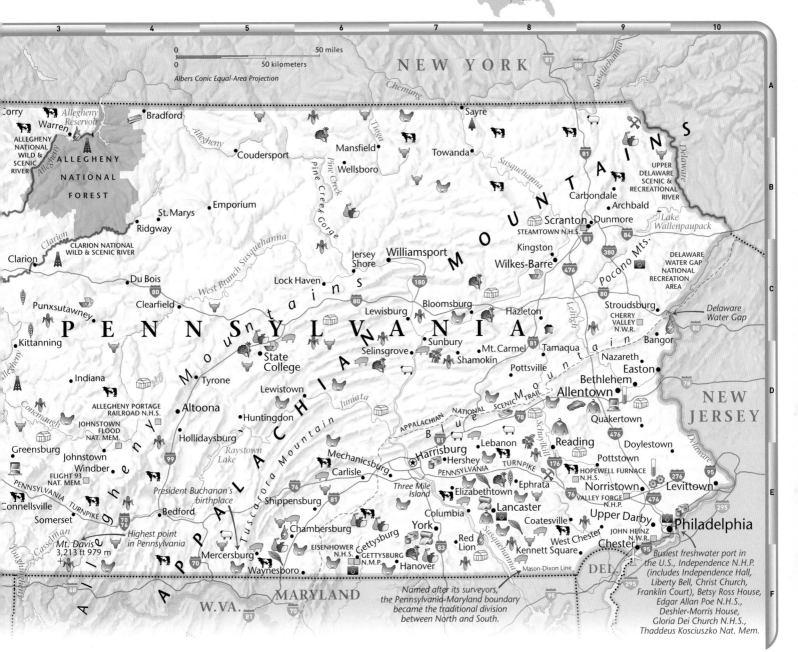

NEW YORK

Corry
Warren
Allegheny Reservoir
Bradford
Sayre

ALLEGHENY NATIONAL WILD & SCENIC RIVER
ALLEGHENY NATIONAL FOREST

Chemung

Coudersport
Mansfield
Towanda

St. Marys
Emporium
Wellsboro

CLARION NATIONAL WILD & SCENIC RIVER
Ridgway

Carbondale
Archbald

UPPER DELAWARE SCENIC & RECREATIONAL RIVER

Clarion
Du Bois

West Branch Susquehanna

Jersey Shore
Williamsport

Scranton
STEAMTOWN N.H.S.
Dunmore

Lake Wallenpaupack

Clarion

Clearfield

Lock Haven

Kingston
Wilkes-Barre

Pocono Mts.

DELAWARE WATER GAP NATIONAL RECREATION AREA

Punxsutawney

Lewisburg
Bloomsburg

Hazleton

Stroudsburg

CHERRY VALLEY N.W.R.

Delaware Water Gap

Kittanning

PENNSYLVANIA

State College

Sunbury
Selinsgrove

Mt. Carmel
Shamokin

Tamaqua

Nazareth

Bangor

Easton

Indiana

Tyrone

Lewistown

Pottsville

Bethlehem
Allentown

NEW JERSEY

ALLEGHENY PORTAGE RAILROAD N.H.S.
JOHNSTOWN FLOOD NAT. MEM.

Altoona

Huntingdon

Juniata

APPALACHIAN NATIONAL SCENIC TRAIL

Quakertown

Greensburg
Johnstown
Windber
FLIGHT 93 NAT. MEM.

Hollidaysburg

Raystown Lake

Mechanicsburg
Harrisburg
Hershey
Lebanon

Reading

Doylestown

Pottstown

HOPEWELL FURNACE N.H.S.

Connellsville

PENNSYLVANIA TURNPIKE

Somerset

Mt. Davis 3,213 ft 979 m
Highest point in Pennsylvania

Casselman

President Buchanan's birthplace

Bedford

Shippensburg

Carlisle

PENNSYLVANIA TURNPIKE

Three Mile Island

Elizabethtown

Ephrata

Lancaster

VALLEY FORGE N.H.P.

Norristown
Levittown

Upper Darby

West Chester
Kennett Square

Philadelphia

Chambersburg

Columbia
York

Coatesville

Chester

JOHN HEINZ N.W.R.

Mercersburg

EISENHOWER N.H.S.
GETTYSBURG N.M.P.
Gettysburg

Hanover

Red Lion

Mason-Dixon Line

DEL.

Busiest freshwater port in the U.S., Independence N.H.P. (includes Independence Hall, Liberty Bell, Christ Church, Franklin Court), Betsy Ross House, Edgar Allan Poe N.H.S., Deshler-Morris House, Gloria Dei Church N.H.S., Thaddeus Kosciuszko Nat. Mem.

Waynesboro

Named after its surveyors, the Pennsylvania-Maryland boundary became the traditional division between North and South.

W.VA.

MARYLAND

Economy Symbols

- Poultry/eggs
- Sheep
- Hogs
- Dairy cows/products
- Beef cattle
- Fruits
- Vegetables
- Nursery stock
- Corn
- Soybeans
- Tobacco
- Vineyards
- Timber/forest products
- Printing/publishing
- Stone/gravel/cement

- Mining
- Coal
- Oil/gas
- Hydro-electricity
- Machinery
- Metal manufacturing
- Railroad equipment
- Motor vehicles/parts
- Rubber/plastics
- Chemistry
- Food processing
- Glass/clay products
- Computers/electronics
- Tourism
- Finance/insurance

TEAMWORK. Amish people in Lancaster County work together to erect a barn. The Amish, who came to Pennsylvania in the early 1700s from Switzerland and Germany, live in traditional farming communities and shun modern technology.

Rhode Island

THE BASICS

Statehood
May 29, 1790; 13th state

Total area (land and water)
1,545 sq mi (4,001 sq km)

Land area
1,034 sq mi (2,678 sq km)

Population
1,056,298

Capital
Providence
Population 179,207

Largest city
Providence
Population 179,207

Racial/ethnic groups
84.8% white; 7.9% African American; 3.6% Asian; 1.0% Native American; 14.4% Hispanic origin (any race)

Foreign born
13.1%

Urban population
90.7% (2010)

Population density
1,021.6 per sq mi
(394.4 per sq km)

GEO WHIZ

Pawtucket is one of several communities in Rhode Island that have become home to a growing number of people from Cape Verde, in West Africa.

Wild coyotes are living and thriving on islands in Narragansett Bay. Researchers have outfitted some with GPS tracking collars so that their numbers and whereabouts can be studied online—even by schoolkids.

In 1524 Italian navigator Giovanni Verrazzano was the first European explorer to visit Rhode Island, but place-names such as Quonochontaug and Narragansett tell of an earlier Native American population. In 1636 Roger Williams, seeking greater religious freedom, left Massachusetts and established the first European settlement in what was to become the colony of Rhode Island. In the years following the Revolutionary War, Rhode Island pressed for fairness in trade, taxes, and representation in Congress as well as greater freedom of worship, before becoming the 13th state. By the 19th century Rhode Island had become an important center of trade and textile factories, attracting many immigrants from Europe. In addition to its commercial activities, Rhode Island's coastline became a popular vacation retreat for the wealthy. Today, Rhode Island, like many other states, has seen its economy shift toward high-tech jobs and service industries. It is also promoting its scenic coastline and bays as well as its rich history to attract tourists.

⬭ **CLUES TO THE PAST.**
Fossils embedded in rocks left behind 10,000 years ago by retreating glaciers tell of Block Island's past.

VIOLET
RHODE ISLAND RED

◖ **SETTING SAIL.** Newport Harbor invites sailors of all ages. From 1930 to 1983 the prestigious America's Cup Yacht Race took place in the waters off Newport. Today, the town provides moorings for boats of all types.

MASSACHUSETTS

CONNECTICUT

RHODE

ISLAND

Wallum Lake
Slatersville
Woonsocket
Pawtucket Reservoir
Union Village
Glendale
Manville
Cumberland Hill
Harrisville
Ashton
Pascoag Lake
Pascoag
Valley Falls
Chepachet
Woonasquatucket Reservoir
Lonsdale
Saylesville
Central Falls
Harmony
Pawtucket
Ponaganset Reservoir
Esmond
Greenville
North Providence
Jerimoth Hill
812 ft 247 m
Highest point in Rhode Island
North Scituate
East Providence
Johnston
Foster Center
Roger Williams National Memorial
Providence
Scituate Reservoir
Cranston
Pawtuxet
Hope
Harris
Barrington
Warren
Rice City
Coventry Center
Anthony
Warwick
Bristol
West Warwick
Mount Hope Bay
Stafford Pond
Flat River Reservoir
Tiogue Lake
East Greenwich
Prudence Island
Island Park
Tiverton
Rhode Island Red Monument
Nonquit Pond
Austin
Wood
Prudence Island
Rhode Island
Portsmouth
Adamsville
Exeter
Wickford
Conanicut Island
Middletown
Little Compton
Hamilton
Allenton
Wyoming
Saunderstown
Hope Valley
Newport
West Kingston
Jamestown
Kingston
SACHUEST POINT N.W.R.
Carolina
Great Swamp
TOURO SYNAGOGUE N.H.S.
Sakonnet Point
Shannock
Wakefield
JOHN H. CHAFEE N.W.R.
Ashaway
Worden Pond
Narragansett Pier
NARRAGANSETT INDIAN RES.
Point Judith Pond
ATLANTIC OCEAN
Bradford
Watchaug Pond
Charlestown
Jerusalem
Galilee
Westerly
Ninigret Pond
NINIGRET N.W.R.
TRUSTOM POND N.W.R.
Point Judith
Napatree Point
Quonochontaug Pond
Quonochontaug

Watch Hill

Block Island Sound

Rhode Island Sound

Narragansett Bay

Sakonnet River

Providence

Seekonk

Blackstone

Woonasquatucket

Moosup

Ponaganset

Queen

Wood

Pawcatuck

OLD AND NEW.
Founded in 1639, the town of Newport on Narragansett Bay is a busy seaport that manages to preserve its historic landscape.

Sandy Point
BLOCK ISLAND N.W.R.
Block Island
Block Island

SIZE EXTREMES

Rhode Island

Tiny Rhode Island, the smallest U.S. state in area, would fit almost 425 times into the giant landmass of Alaska, the country's largest state.

Economy Symbols

Fishing	Metal products
Lobster fishing	Shipbuilding
Shellfish	Rubber/plastics
Poultry/eggs	Chemistry
Hogs	Food processing
Dairy cows/products	Clothing/textiles
Vegetables	Jewelry
Nursery stock	Electrical equipment
Vineyards	Computers/electronics
Printing/publishing	Scientific instruments
Stone/gravel/cement	Tourism
Machinery	Finance/insurance
Metal manufacturing	

Albers Conic Equal-Area Projection

0   10 miles
0   10 kilometers

THE BASICS

Statehood
March 4, 1791; 14th state

Total area (land and water)
9,616 sq mi (24,906 sq km)

Land area
9,217 sq mi (23,871 sq km)

Population
626,042

Capital
Montpelier
Population 7,671 (2014)

Largest city
Burlington
Population 42,211

Racial/ethnic groups
94.8% white; 1.3% African American; 1.6% Asian; 0.4% Native American; 1.8% Hispanic origin (any race)

Foreign born
4.1%

Urban population
38.9% (2010)

Population density
67.9 per sq mi (26.2 per sq km)

GEO WHIZ

The tombstones of President Harry S. Truman, industrialist John D. Rockefeller, Sr., songwriter Stephen Foster, and fast-food-chain founder Col. Harland Sanders are all made of granite from Barre.

Burlington is the home of Ben & Jerry's ice cream. The company gives its leftovers to local farmers, who feed it to their hogs.

From 1777 until it became a state in 1791, Vermont was an independent country.

Vermont is the only state in New England that does not border the Atlantic Ocean.

Vermont

When French explorer Jacques Cartier arrived in Vermont in 1535, Native Americans living in woodland villages had been there for hundreds of years. Settled first by the French in 1666 and then by the English in 1724, the territory of Vermont became an area of conflict between these colonial powers. The French finally withdrew, but conflict continued between New York and New Hampshire, both of which wanted to take over Vermont. The people of Vermont declared their independence in 1777, and Vermont became the 14th U.S. state in 1791. Vermont's name, which means "green mountain," comes from the extensive forests that cover much of the state and provide the basis for furniture and pulp industries. Vermont also boasts the world's largest deep-hole granite quarry and the largest underground marble quarry. Both produce valuable building materials. Tourism and recreation are also important. Lakes, rivers, and mountain trails are popular summer attractions, and snow-covered mountains lure skiers throughout the winter.

⬭ **LIQUID GOLD.** In spring sap from maple trees is collected in buckets by drilling a hole in the tree trunk—called "tapping." The sap is boiled to remove water, then filtered, and finally bottled.

RED CLOVER
HERMIT THRUSH

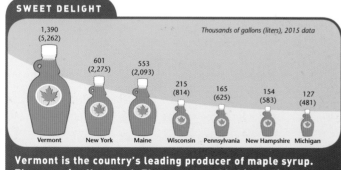

SWEET DELIGHT

Thousands of gallons (liters), 2015 data

1,390 (5,262) Vermont
601 (2,275) New York
553 (2,093) Maine
215 (814) Wisconsin
165 (625) Pennsylvania
154 (583) New Hampshire
127 (481) Michigan

Vermont is the country's leading producer of maple syrup. The syrup is all natural. There are no added ingredients or preservatives, just boiled sap collected from maple trees.

⬭ **WINTER WONDERLAND.** One of the snowiest places in the Northeast, Jay Peak averages 355 inches (900 cm) of snow each year. With 76 trails, the mountain, near Vermont's border with Canada, attracts beginner and expert skiers from near and far.

Economy Symbols

- 🐔 Poultry/eggs
- 🐑 Sheep
- 🐄 Dairy cows/products
- 🐂 Beef cattle
- 🍓 Fruits
- 🥬 Vegetables
- 🏠 Nursery stock
- 🌽 Corn
- 🍁 Maple syrup
- 🌲 Timber/forest products
- 🖨 Printing/publishing
- ⚒ Stone/gravel/cement
- 🔥 Hydro-electricity
- 🍳 Metal products
- 📦 Food processing
- 💻 Computers/electronics
- 📷 Tourism

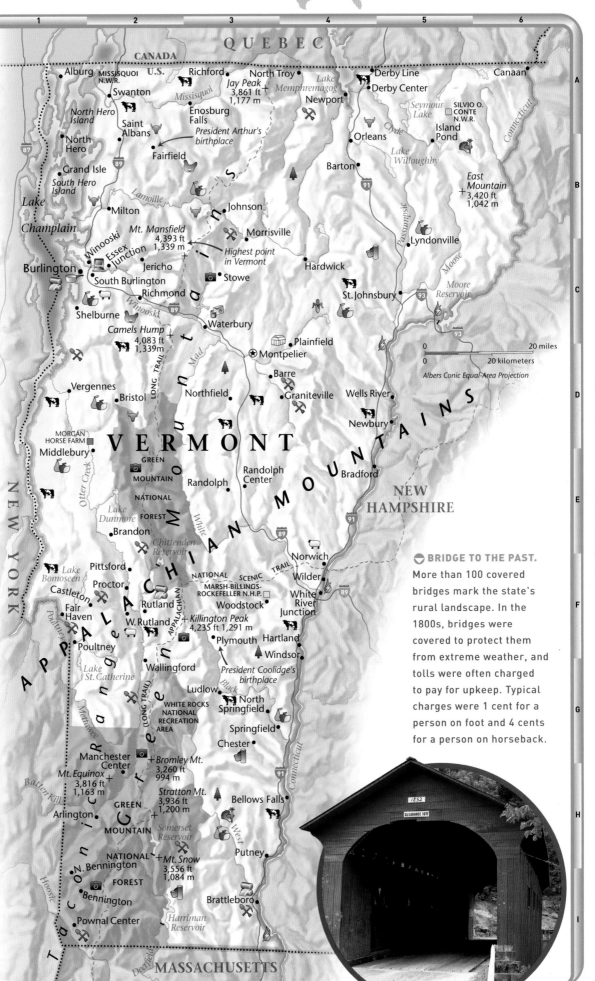

🌉 BRIDGE TO THE PAST.
More than 100 covered bridges mark the state's rural landscape. In the 1800s, bridges were covered to protect them from extreme weather, and tolls were often charged to pay for upkeep. Typical charges were 1 cent for a person on foot and 4 cents for a person on horseback.

QUEBEC

CANADA
U.S.

Alburg
MISSISQUOI N.W.R.
Swanton
Richford
North Troy
Jay Peak 3,861 ft 1,177 m
Derby Line
Derby Center
Canaan
Missisquoi
Lake Memphremagog
Newport
North Hero Island
Enosburg Falls
Saint Albans
President Arthur's birthplace
Fairfield
Orleans
Clyde
Island Pond
SILVIO O. CONTE N.W.R.
Seymour Lake
North Hero
Grand Isle
South Hero Island
Lamoille
Barton
Lake Willoughby
East Mountain 3,420 ft 1,042 m
Milton
Johnson
Lyndonville
Lake Champlain
Morrisville
Mt. Mansfield 4,393 ft 1,339 m
Hardwick
Moose
Winooski
Essex Junction
Jericho
Highest point in Vermont
Burlington
South Burlington
Stowe
St. Johnsbury
Moore Reservoir
Richmond
Winooski
Waterbury
Shelburne
Camels Hump 4,083 ft 1,339 m
Plainfield
Montpelier
Vergennes
Bristol
Northfield
Barre
Graniteville
Wells River
MORGAN HORSE FARM
Middlebury
Mad
Newbury
VERMONT
GREEN MOUNTAIN
Randolph
Randolph Center
Bradford
NEW HAMPSHIRE
NATIONAL
Lake Dunmore
FOREST
White
Brandon
Chittenden Reservoir
Norwich
Pittsford
Otter Creek
Proctor
Wilder
White River Junction
Castleton
Lake Bomoseen
NATIONAL
SCENIC
MARSH-BILLINGS-ROCKEFELLER N.H.P.
Woodstock
Fair Haven
Rutland
TRAIL
Poultney
W. Rutland
Killington Peak 4,235 ft 1,291 m
Plymouth
Hartland
Poultney
Lake St. Catherine
Wallingford
President Coolidge's birthplace
Windsor
Ludlow
Black
North Springfield
WHITE ROCKS NATIONAL RECREATION AREA
Springfield
Chester
Manchester Center
Bromley Mt. 3,260 ft 994 m
Mt. Equinox 3,816 ft 1,163 m
Stratton Mt. 3,936 ft 1,200 m
Bellows Falls
GREEN MOUNTAIN
Somerset Reservoir
Putney
Batten Kill
Arlington
NATIONAL
Mt. Snow 3,556 ft 1,084 m
West
N. Bennington
FOREST
Brattleboro
Bennington
Harriman Reservoir
Pownal Center
Hoosic
Connecticut
Deerfield
MASSACHUSETTS

NEW YORK

APPALACHIAN MOUNTAINS
GREEN Mountain Range
LONG TRAIL
Taconic Range
Mettawee

0 ____ 20 miles
0 ____ 20 kilometers
Albers Conic Equal-Area Projection

THE REGION

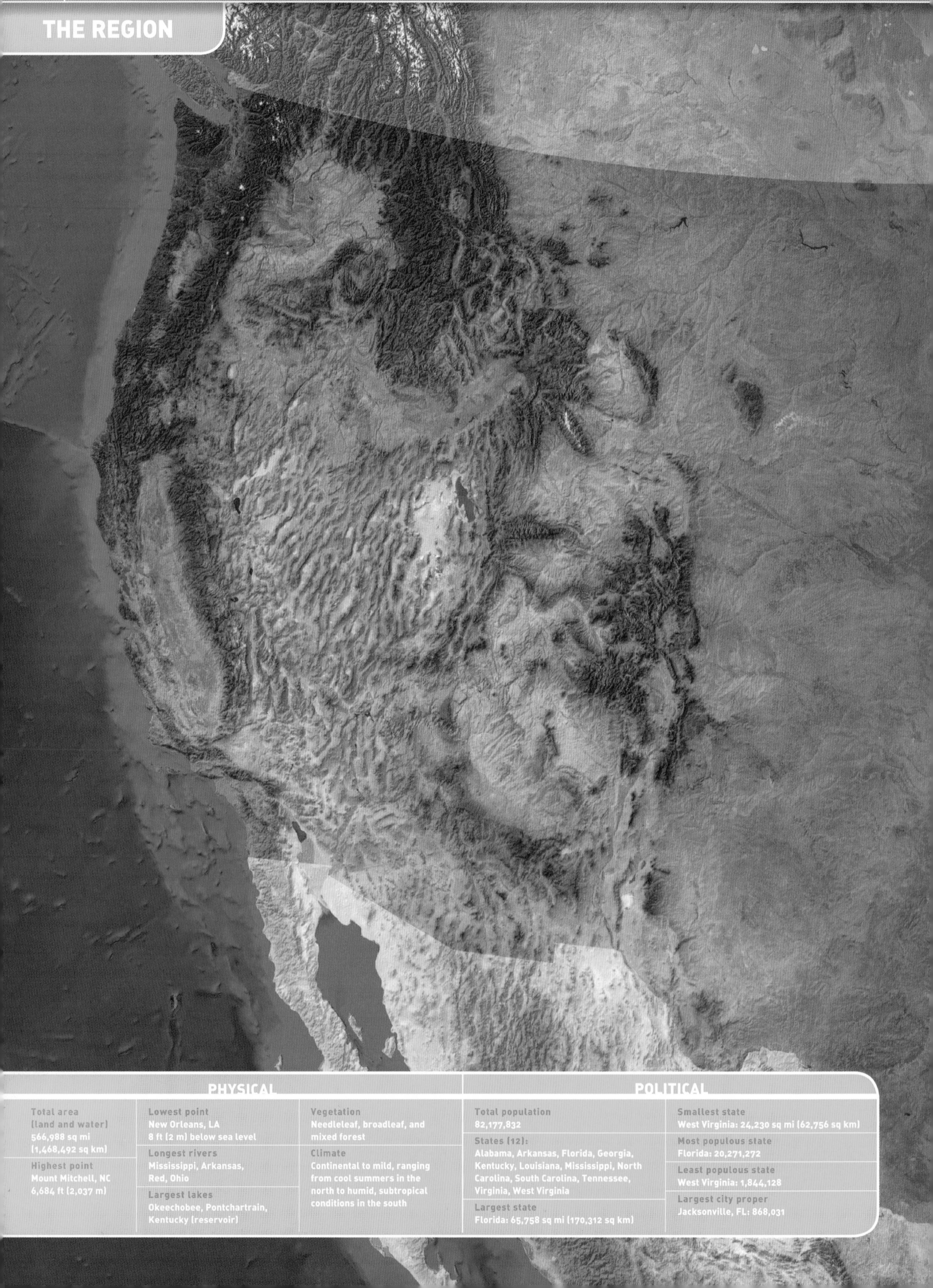

PHYSICAL			POLITICAL	
Total area (land and water) 566,988 sq mi (1,468,492 sq km)	**Lowest point** New Orleans, LA 8 ft (2 m) below sea level	**Vegetation** Needleleaf, broadleaf, and mixed forest	**Total population** 82,177,832	**Smallest state** West Virginia: 24,230 sq mi (62,756 sq km)
	Longest rivers Mississippi, Arkansas, Red, Ohio	**Climate** Continental to mild, ranging from cool summers in the north to humid, subtropical conditions in the south	**States (12):** Alabama, Arkansas, Florida, Georgia, Kentucky, Louisiana, Mississippi, North Carolina, South Carolina, Tennessee, Virginia, West Virginia	**Most populous state** Florida: 20,271,272
Highest point Mount Mitchell, NC 6,684 ft (2,037 m)				**Least populous state** West Virginia: 1,844,128
	Largest lakes Okeechobee, Pontchartrain, Kentucky (reservoir)		**Largest state** Florida: 65,758 sq mi (170,312 sq km)	**Largest city proper** Jacksonville, FL: 868,031

The Southeast

◗ **OPEN WIDE.** An American alligator in Florida's Big Cypress Swamp shows off sharp teeth. These large reptiles live mainly in freshwater swamps and marshes in coastal areas of the Southeast. Adult males average 14 feet (4 m) in length.

The Southeast
TRADITION MEETS TECHNOLOGY

From deeply weathered mountains in West Virginia to warm, humid wetlands in south Florida and the Mississippi River's sprawling delta in southern Louisiana, the Southeast is marked by great physical diversity. The region's historical roots are in agriculture—especially cotton and tobacco. The Civil War brought economic and political upheaval in the mid-19th century, but today the Southeast is part of the Sunbelt, where 5 of the top 20 metropolitan areas of the United States are found and where high-tech industries are redefining the way people earn a living and the way the region is connected to the global economy.

◗ **ENCHANTED KINGDOM.** Fireworks light up the night sky above Cinderella's Castle at Walt Disney World near Orlando, Florida. The park, which accounts for 6 percent of all jobs in central Florida, attracts millions of tourists from around the world each year.

⬣ **SOCIAL CONSCIENCE.** Members of the Big Nine Social Aid and Pleasure Club of New Orleans's Lower Ninth Ward march in a parade through a neighborhood devastated by Hurricane Katrina. Such clubs, which date back to late-19th-century benevolent societies, bring support and hope to communities in need.

WHERE THE PICTURES ARE

Banjo playing p. 67
River rafting p. 81
Coal miner p. 80
Cyclists on outcrop pp. 56-57
Horse race p. 66
Harpers Ferry p. 80
Black bear family p. 76
Luray Caverns p. 78
Motorboats p. 77
Grand Ole Opry p. 77
Cyclists pp. 78-79
Indian Woman p. 73
Dice p. 78
Rocket display p. 58
Race car p. 57
Rockclimber p. 60
Wright Brothers Memorial p. 72
Bird-watchers p. 60
Blackbeard's cannon p. 57
Boys playing basketball p. 72
Diamond hunter p. 61
Beach scene p. 74
Paddleboat p. 70
Wild turkey p. 75
Blues museum p. 70
Historic Charleston pp. 74-75
Catfish p. 71
Atlanta p. 64
Oak Alley Plantation p. 68
Oil rig p. 58
Aerial of Sea Islands p. 64
Peanuts p. 64
Katrina parade p. 56
Manatee p. 62
Rocket launch pp. 62-63
Cinderella's Castle p. 56, Girl in parade p. 62
Shrimp fisherman p. 68
Alligator p. 56

VIEW FROM ABOVE. Cyclists look out from a rocky ledge across West Virginia's Germany Valley. The area took its name from German immigrants who moved there in the mid-1700s from North Carolina and Pennsylvania and established farming villages.

CAR STARS. For more than 50 years, auto racing has been a leading sport in the U.S., especially in the Southeast. The International Motorsports Hall of Fame, located adjacent to the Talladega Superspeedway in Alabama, features racing cars, motorcycles, and vintage cars.

PIRATE'S DEFENSE. This 4.5-foot (1.4-m) cast-iron cannon was recovered from the wreck of the *Queen Anne's Revenge* off North Carolina's coast. The vessel, which probably belonged to Blackbeard, the notorious pirate, grounded on a sand-bar and sank in 1718 near Cape Lookout.

THE NATURAL STATE:
ARKANSAS

THE BASICS

Statehood
June 15, 1836; 25th state

Total area (land and water)
53,179 sq mi (137,732 sq km)

Land area
52,035 sq mi (134,771 sq km)

Population
2,978,204

Capital
Little Rock
Population 197,992

Largest city
Little Rock
Population 197,992

Racial/ethnic groups
79.5% white; 15.7% African American; 1.6% Asian; 1.0% Native American; 7.2% Hispanic (any race)

Foreign born
4.5%

Urban population
56.2% (2010)

Population density
57.2 per sq mi (22.1 per sq km)

GEO WHIZ

In 1924 Arkansas's Crater of Diamonds State Park yielded the largest natural diamond ever found in the United States—a 40.23-carat whopper named "Uncle Sam."

Stuttgart has been the site of the annual World Championship Duck Calling Contest since 1936, when the winner received a hunting coat valued at $6.60. Today, the prize package is worth more than $15,000.

Texarkana is divided by the Arkansas-Texas border. It has two governments, one for each state.

Arkansas

The land that is Arkansas was explored by the Spanish in 1541 and later by the French, but it came under U.S. control with the Louisiana Purchase in 1803. As settlers arrived, Native Americans were pushed out, and cotton fields spread across the fertile valleys of the Arkansas and Mississippi Rivers. Arkansas became the 25th state in 1836, but joined the Confederacy in 1861. Following the war Arkansas faced hard times, and many people moved away in search of jobs. Today, agriculture remains an important part of the economy. Rice has replaced cotton as the state's main crop, and poultry and grain production are also important. Natural gas, in the northwestern part of the state, and petroleum, along the southern border with Louisiana, are key mining products in Arkansas. The state is headquarters for Walmart, the world's largest retail chain, and tourism is growing as visitors are attracted to the natural beauty of the Ozark and Ouachita Mountains.

APPLE BLOSSOM
MOCKINGBIRD

◔ **HOLD ON!** A rock climber clings to a sandstone cliff in northwest Arkansas, where the Ozark and Ouachita Mountains make up the Interior Highlands of the United States. The Ouachita are folded mountains, but the Ozarks are really a deeply eroded plateau.

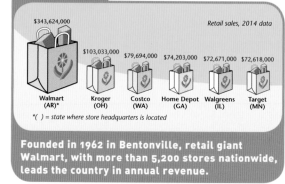

SUPERSTORE

$343,624,000

Retail sales, 2014 data

$103,033,000 $79,694,000 $74,203,000 $72,671,000 $72,618,000

Walmart (AR)*   Kroger (OH)   Costco (WA)   Home Depot (GA)   Walgreens (IL)   Target (MN)

*( ) = state where store headquarters is located

Founded in 1962 in Bentonville, retail giant Walmart, with more than 5,200 stores nationwide, leads the country in annual revenue.

◖ **BIRD-WATCHERS.** Biologists and volunteers scan the treetops for a rare ivory-billed woodpecker in the White River National Wildlife Refuge. Established in 1935 along the White River near where it joins the Mississippi, the refuge provides a protected habitat for migratory birds.

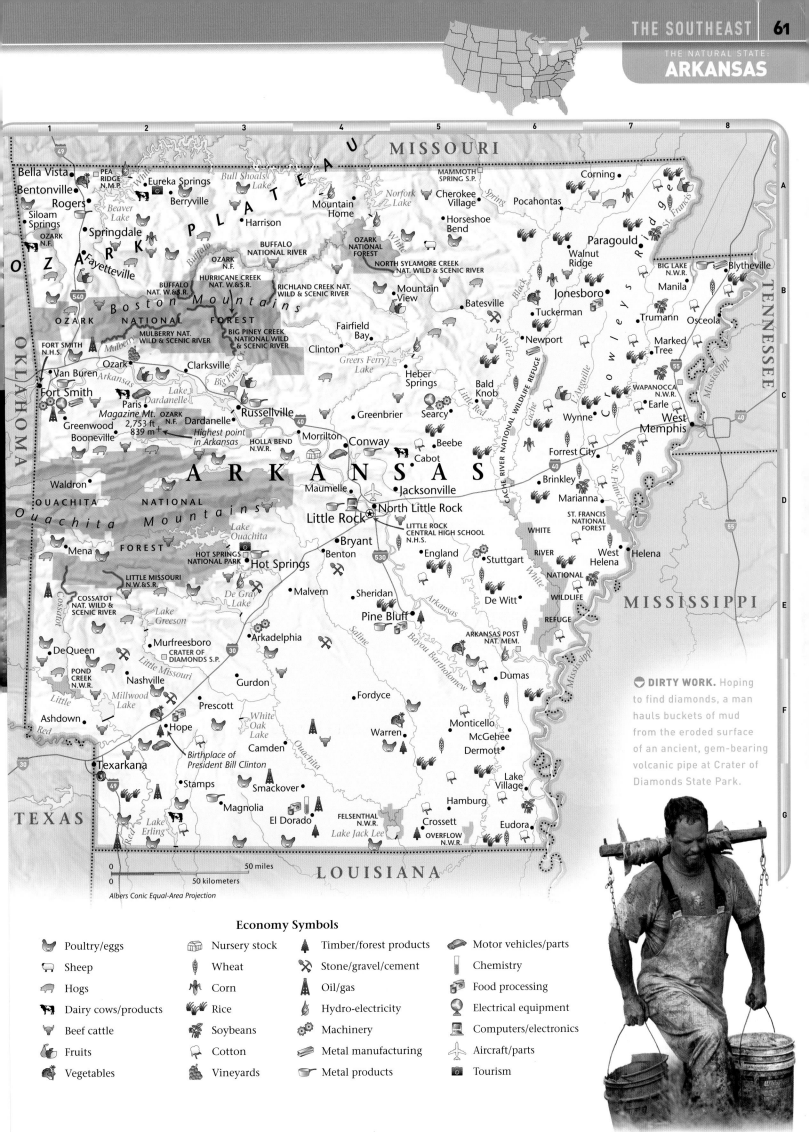

MISSOURI

TENNESSEE

MISSISSIPPI

TEXAS

LOUISIANA

OKLAHOMA

OZARK PLATEAU

Boston Mountains

OZARK NATIONAL FOREST

A R K A N S A S

OUACHITA NATIONAL FOREST

Ouachita Mountains

Bella Vista
Bentonville
Rogers
Siloam Springs
OZARK N.F.
Springdale
Fayetteville
FORT SMITH N.H.S.
Van Buren
Fort Smith
Greenwood
Booneville
Waldron
Mena
DeQueen
POND CREEK N.W.R.
Nashville
Ashdown
Texarkana
Stamps
Magnolia

PEA RIDGE N.M.P.
Beaver Lake
Eureka Springs
Berryville
Harrison
OZARK N.F.
BUFFALO NATIONAL RIVER
BUFFALO NAT. W.&S.R.
HURRICANE CREEK NAT. W.&S.R.
MULBERRY NAT. WILD & SCENIC RIVER
BIG PINEY CREEK NATIONAL WILD & SCENIC RIVER
Ozark
Clarksville
Paris
Magazine Mt. 2,753 ft 839 m
Highest point in Arkansas
OZARK N.F.
Dardanelle
Russellville
Lake Dardanelle
HOLLA BEND N.W.R.
Morrilton
Conway
Maumelle
North Little Rock
Little Rock
LITTLE ROCK CENTRAL HIGH SCHOOL N.H.S.
Bryant
Benton
Hot Springs
HOT SPRINGS NATIONAL PARK
Malvern
LITTLE MISSOURI N.W.&S.R.
COSSATOT NAT. WILD & SCENIC RIVER
Lake Greeson
De Gray Lake
Murfreesboro
CRATER OF DIAMONDS S.P.
Gurdon
Prescott
Hope
Birthplace of President Bill Clinton
Camden
Smackover
El Dorado
FELSENTHAL N.W.R.
Lake Jack Lee
Lake Erling

Bull Shoals Lake
Norfork Lake
Mountain Home
RICHLAND CREEK NAT. WILD & SCENIC RIVER
NORTH SYLAMORE CREEK NAT. WILD & SCENIC RIVER
OZARK NATIONAL FOREST
Mountain View
Fairfield Bay
Clinton
Greers Ferry Lake
Heber Springs
Greenbrier
Searcy
Beebe
Cabot
Jacksonville
England
Sheridan
Pine Bluff
Arkadelphia
Fordyce
Warren
White Oak Lake
Millwood Lake

MAMMOTH SPRING S.P.
Cherokee Village
Horseshoe Bend
Batesville
Tuckerman
Newport
Bald Knob
Stuttgart
De Witt
ARKANSAS POST NAT. MEM.
Dumas
Monticello
McGehee
Dermott
Lake Village
Hamburg
Crossett
OVERFLOW N.W.R.
Eudora

Corning
Pocahontas
Walnut Ridge
Paragould
BIG LAKE N.W.R.
Jonesboro
Manila
Blytheville
Osceola
Trumann
Marked Tree
WAPANOCCA N.W.R.
Wynne
Earle
West Memphis
Forrest City
Brinkley
Marianna
ST. FRANCIS NATIONAL FOREST
West Helena
Helena
WHITE RIVER NATIONAL WILDLIFE REFUGE

Crowleys Ridge

0   50 miles
0   50 kilometers
Albers Conic Equal-Area Projection

DIRTY WORK. Hoping to find diamonds, a man hauls buckets of mud from the eroded surface of an ancient, gem-bearing volcanic pipe at Crater of Diamonds State Park.

Economy Symbols

Poultry/eggs	Nursery stock	Timber/forest products	Motor vehicles/parts
Sheep	Wheat	Stone/gravel/cement	Chemistry
Hogs	Corn	Oil/gas	Food processing
Dairy cows/products	Rice	Hydro-electricity	Electrical equipment
Beef cattle	Soybeans	Machinery	Computers/electronics
Fruits	Cotton	Metal manufacturing	Aircraft/parts
Vegetables	Vineyards	Metal products	Tourism

THE EMPIRE STATE OF THE SOUTH:
GEORGIA

BASICS

Statehood
January 2, 1788; 4th state

Total area
(land and water)
59,425 sq mi
(153,910 sq km)

Land area
57,513 sq mi
(148,959 sq km)

Population
1,056,298

Capital
Atlanta
Population 463,878

Largest city
Atlanta
Population 463,878

Racial/ethnic groups
61.6% white; 31.7% African
American; 4.0% Asian; 0.5%
Native American; 9.4% Hispanic
(any race)

Foreign born
9.7%

Urban population
75.1% (2010)

Population density
171.9 per sq mi (66.4 per sq km)

GEO WHIZ

The Okefenokee Swamp, the largest swamp in North America, has meat-eating plants that capture small animals for food. The swamp was also the setting for the adventures of Pogo the Possum, Albert the Alligator, and other characters created by cartoonist Walt Kelly.

The Georgia Aquarium in Atlanta, the largest in the Western Hemisphere, features thousands of sea creatures in 10 million gallons (37.9 million liters) of water.

Confederate war heroes Robert E. Lee, Stonewall Jackson, and Jefferson Davis are carved into the granite face of Stone Mountain near Atlanta.

Georgia

When Spanish explorers arrived in the mid-1500s in what would become Georgia, they found the land already occupied by Cherokee, Creek, and other native people. Georgia was the frontier separating Spanish Florida and English South Carolina, but in 1733 James Oglethorpe founded a new colony on the site of present-day Savannah. Georgia became the fourth state in 1788 and built an economy based on agriculture and slave labor. The state suffered widespread destruction during the Civil War and endured a long period of poverty in the years that followed. Modern-day Georgia is part of the fast-changing Sunbelt region. Agriculture—especially poultry, cotton, and forest products—remains important. Atlanta has emerged as a regional center of banking, telecommunications, and transportation, and Savannah is a major container port near the Atlantic coast, linking the state to the global economy. Historic sites, sports, and beaches draw thousands of tourists to the state every year.

CASH CROP. Peanuts are a big moneymaker in Georgia, where almost half the U.S. crop is grown—about half of which is used to make peanut butter.

LIGHT SHOW. Busy interstate traffic appears as ribbons of light below Atlanta's nighttime skyline. Atlanta is a center of economic growth, leading all cities in the region with 18 Fortune 500 companies headquartered within the metropolitan area.

CHEROKEE ROSE
BROWN THRASHER

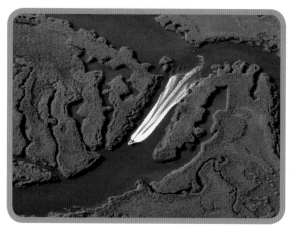

PAST MEETS PRESENT. Georgia's 100-mile (160-km) coastline is laced with barrier islands, wetlands, and winding streams. In the 19th century plantations grew Sea Island cotton here. Today, tourists are attracted to the area's natural beauty and beaches.

FLYING HIGH

Total passengers in millions, 2014 data

- 96.2 Atlanta
- 70.7 Los Angeles
- 70.0 Chicago O'Hare
- 63.6 Dallas–Ft.Worth
- 53.5 Denver

Moving more than 96 million passengers in 2014, Atlanta's Hartsfield-Jackson International Airport is the busiest in the country.

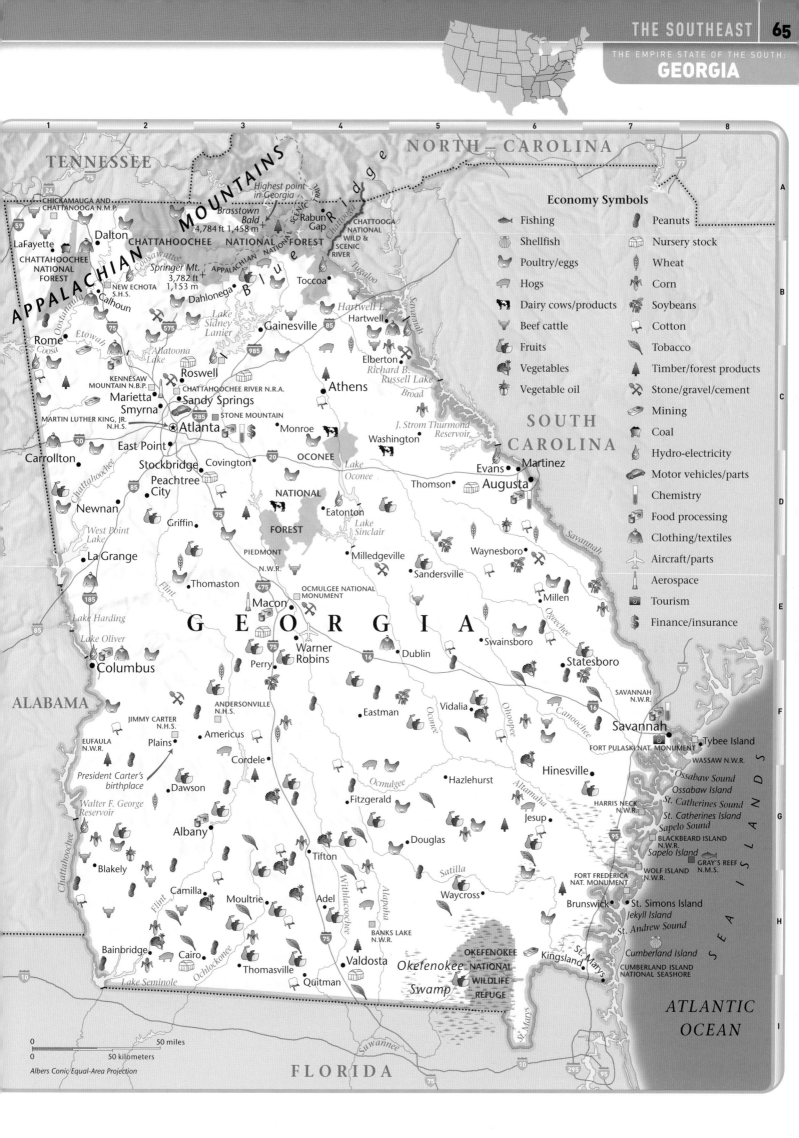

Economy Symbols

Fishing
Shellfish
Poultry/eggs
Hogs
Dairy cows/products
Beef cattle
Fruits
Vegetables
Vegetable oil

Peanuts
Nursery stock
Wheat
Corn
Soybeans
Cotton
Tobacco
Timber/forest products
Stone/gravel/cement
Mining
Coal
Hydro-electricity
Motor vehicles/parts
Chemistry
Food processing
Clothing/textiles
Aircraft/parts
Aerospace
Tourism
Finance/insurance

TENNESSEE
NORTH CAROLINA
SOUTH CAROLINA
GEORGIA
ALABAMA
FLORIDA
ATLANTIC OCEAN

APPALACHIAN MOUNTAINS
CHATTAHOOCHEE NATIONAL FOREST
Blue Ridge

Brasstown Bald 4,784 ft 1,458 m
Highest point in Georgia
Springer Mt. 3,782 ft 1,153 m

CHICKAMAUGA AND CHATTANOOGA N.M.P.
LaFayette
Dalton
CHATTAHOOCHEE NATIONAL FOREST
NEW ECHOTA S.H.S.
Calhoun
Rome
Coosa
Etowah
Allatoona Lake
Lake Sidney Lanier
Dahlonega
Toccoa
Gainesville
Hartwell L.
Hartwell
Elberton
Richard B. Russell Lake
Broad
Roswell
KENNESAW MOUNTAIN N.B.P.
Marietta
Smyrna
MARTIN LUTHER KING, JR. N.H.S.
Atlanta
Sandy Springs
STONE MOUNTAIN
Monroe
Washington
Athens
CHATTAHOOCHEE RIVER N.R.A.
East Point
Carrollton
Stockbridge
Covington
OCONEE
Lake Oconee
J. Strom Thurmond Reservoir
Evans
Martinez
Thomson
Augusta
Peachtree City
Newnan
Griffin
NATIONAL
Eatonton
Lake Sinclair
FOREST
PIEDMONT N.W.R.
Milledgeville
Waynesboro
La Grange
West Point Lake
Thomaston
Sandersville
Lake Harding
Macon
OCMULGEE NATIONAL MONUMENT
Millen
Lake Oliver
Warner Robins
Perry
Dublin
Swainsboro
Statesboro
Columbus
ANDERSONVILLE N.H.S.
Eastman
Vidalia
SAVANNAH N.W.R.
JIMMY CARTER N.H.S.
Americus
Eufaula N.W.R.
Plains
President Carter's birthplace
Cordele
Hazlehurst
Hinesville
Savannah
FORT PULASKI NAT. MONUMENT
Tybee Island
WASSAW N.W.R.
Dawson
Fitzgerald
Ossabaw Sound
Ossabaw Island
HARRIS NECK N.W.R.
St. Catherines Sound
St. Catherines Island
Sapelo Sound
BLACKBEARD ISLAND N.W.R.
Albany
Douglas
Jesup
Sapelo Island
GRAY'S REEF N.M.S.
Blakely
Tifton
WOLF ISLAND N.W.R.
Camilla
Satilla
FORT FREDERICA NAT. MONUMENT
Moultrie
Adel
Waycross
Brunswick
St. Simons Island
Jekyll Island
St. Andrew Sound
Bainbridge
Cairo
BANKS LAKE N.W.R.
OKEFENOKEE NATIONAL WILDLIFE REFUGE
Kingsland
Cumberland Island
CUMBERLAND ISLAND NATIONAL SEASHORE
Thomasville
Valdosta
Quitman
Okefenokee Swamp
St. Marys
Lake Seminole
SEA ISLANDS

Walter F. George Reservoir
Chattahoochee
Flint
Ocmulgee
Oconee
Altamaha
Ocmulgee
Withlacoochee
Alapaha
Satilla
Ochlockonee
Suwannee
St. Marys
Savannah
Ogeechee
Ohoopee
Canoochee
Oostanaula
Coosawattee
Tugaloo
Chattooga
Chattooga NATIONAL WILD & SCENIC RIVER

0   50 miles
0   50 kilometers
Albers Conic Equal-Area Projection

THE BLUEGRASS STATE: KENTUCKY

BASICS

Statehood
June 1, 1792; 15th state

Total area (land and water)
40,408 sq mi (104,656 sq km)

Land area
39,486 sq mi (102,269 sq km)

Population
4,425,092

Capital
Frankfort
Population 27,557 (2014)

Largest city
Louisville/Jefferson County
Population 615,366

Racial/ethnic groups
88.1% white; 8.3% African American; 1.4% Asian; 0.3% Native American; 3.4% Hispanic (any race)

Foreign born
3.3%

Urban population
58.4% (2010)

Population density
112.1 per sq mi (43.3 per sq km)

GEO WHIZ

A favorite Kentucky dessert is Derby Pie, a rich chocolate-and-walnut pastry that was first created by George Kern, manager of the Melrose Inn, in Prospect, in the 1950s. It became so popular that the name was registered with the U.S. Patent Office and the Commonwealth of Kentucky.

Pleasant Hill, near Lexington, was the site of a Shaker religious community. It is now a National Historic Site with a living history museum.

The song "Happy Birthday to You," one of the most popular songs in the English language, was the creation of two Louisville sisters in 1893.

Post-it notes are manufactured exclusively in Cynthiana. Millions of self-stick notes in 27 sizes and 57 colors are produced each year.

Kentucky

The original inhabitants of the area known today as Kentucky were Native American, but a treaty with the Cherokee, signed in 1775, opened the territory to settlers—including the legendary Daniel Boone—from the soon-to-be-independent eastern colonies. In 1776 Kentucky became a western county of the state of Virginia. In 1792 it became the 15th state. Eastern Kentucky is a part of Appalachia, a region rich in soft, bituminous coal but burdened with the environmental problems that often accompany the mining industry. The region is known for crafts and music that can be traced back to Scotch-Irish immigrants who settled there. In central Kentucky, the Bluegrass region produces some of the finest thoroughbred horses in the world, and the Kentucky Derby, held in Louisville, is a part of racing's coveted Triple Crown. In western Kentucky, coal found near the surface is strip mined, leaving scars on the landscape, but federal laws now require that the land be restored after mining.

GOLDENROD
CARDINAL

BENEATH THE SURFACE

Mammoth Cave System, KY	367 miles (591 km)
Jewel Cave, SD	140 miles (225 km)
Wind Cave, SD	125 miles (201 km)
Lechuguilla Cave, NM	121 miles (195 km)
Fisher Ridge Cave System, KY	110 miles (177 km)

Caves, natural openings in Earth's surface extending beyond the reach of sunlight, are often created by water dissolving limestone.

THEY'RE OFF! Riders and horses press for the finish line at Churchill Downs, in Louisville. Kentucky is a major breeder of thoroughbred race horses, and horses are the leading source of farm income in the state.

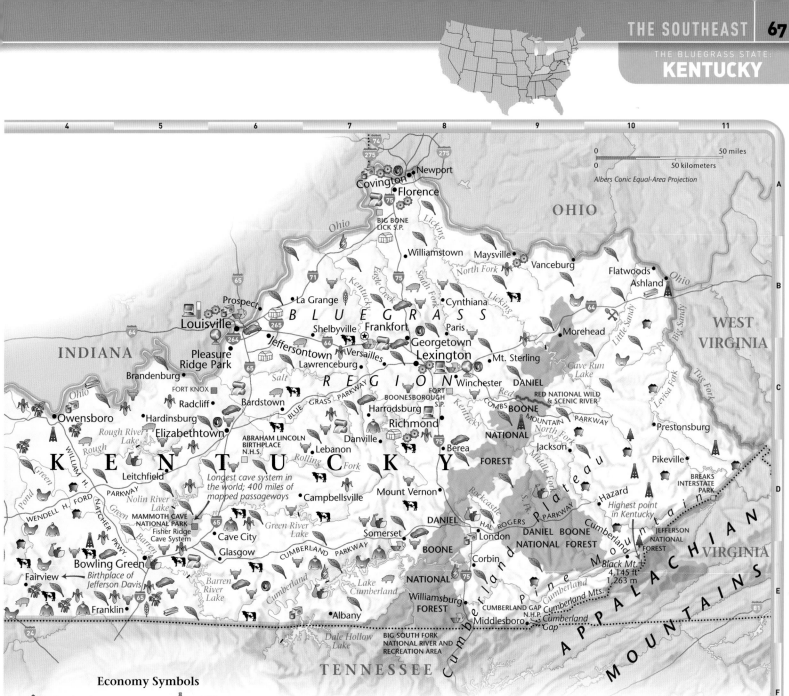

0 ___ 50 miles

0 ___ 50 kilometers

Albers Conic Equal-Area Projection

OHIO

WEST VIRGINIA

INDIANA

KENTUCKY

BLUEGRASS REGION

VIRGINIA

TENNESSEE

APPALACHIAN MOUNTAINS

Newport
Covington
Florence
BIG BONE LICK S.P.
Williamstown
Maysville
Vanceburg
Flatwoods
Ashland
Prospect
La Grange
Cynthiana
Louisville
Shelbyville
Frankfort
Paris
Morehead
Jeffersontown
Georgetown
Lexington
Mt. Sterling
Versailles
Lawrenceburg
Winchester
DANIEL
Cave Run Lake
Pleasure Ridge Park
FORT BOONESBOROUGH S.P.
BOONE
RED NATIONAL WILD & SCENIC RIVER
Brandenburg
FORT KNOX
Harrodsburg
MOUNTAIN PARKWAY
Prestonsburg
Radcliff
Richmond
NATIONAL
Owensboro
Hardinsburg
Danville
FOREST
Jackson
Pikeville
Elizabethtown
ABRAHAM LINCOLN BIRTHPLACE N.H.S.
Lebanon
Berea
BREAKS INTERSTATE PARK
Leitchfield
Longest cave system in the world; 400 miles of mapped passageways
Mount Vernon
Hazard
Highest point in Kentucky
JEFFERSON NATIONAL FOREST
Campbellsville
DANIEL
London
Cave City
Somerset
DANIEL BOONE NATIONAL FOREST
Glasgow
CUMBERLAND PARKWAY
BOONE
Corbin
Black Mt. 4,145 ft 1,263 m
Bowling Green
NATIONAL
Birthplace of Jefferson Davis
Fairview
Barren River Lake
Lake Cumberland
Williamsburg
CUMBERLAND GAP N.H.P.
Cumberland Mts.
Franklin
Albany
FOREST
Middlesboro
Cumberland Gap
Dale Hollow Lake
BIG SOUTH FORK NATIONAL RIVER AND RECREATION AREA
MAMMOTH CAVE NATIONAL PARK Fisher Ridge Cave System

Ohio
Licking
North Fork
Kentucky
Eagle Creek
South Fork
Salt
Green
Rough River Lake
Nolin River Lake
Green River Lake
Rolling Fork
Barren
Cumberland
Rockcastle
Pine Mountain
Little Sandy
Big Sandy
Levisa Fork
Tug Fork
Red
COMBS
North Fork
Middle Fork
WILLIAM H. NATCHER PKWY.
WENDELL H. FORD PARKWAY
HAL ROGERS PARKWAY
Pond
Green

Economy Symbols

Poultry/eggs	Oil/gas
Hogs	Hydro-electricity
Dairy cows/products	Machinery
Beef cattle	Metal manufacturing
Fruits	Motor vehicles/parts
Nursery stock	Rubber/plastics
Wheat	Chemistry
Corn	Food processing
Soybeans	Clothing/textiles
Tobacco	Glass/clay products
Timber/forest products	Electrical equipment
Printing/publishing	Computers/electronics
Stone/gravel/cement	Aerospace
Coal	

STRUMMING A TUNE. Music is an important part of Kentucky's cultural heritage, especially in remote mountain areas where a banjo can become the focus of a family gathering.

THE PELICAN STATE:
LOUISIANA

Louisiana

BASICS

Statehood
April 30, 1812; 18th state

Total area (land and water)
52,378 sq mi (135,659 sq km)

Land area
43,204 sq mi (111,898 sq km)

Population
4,670,724

Capital
Baton Rouge
Population 228,590

Largest city
New Orleans
Population 389,617

Racial/ethnic groups
63.2% white; 32.5% African American; 1.8% Asian; 0.8% Native American; 5.0% Hispanic (any race)

Foreign born
3.9%

Urban population
73.2% (2010)

Population density
108.2 per sq mi (41.7 per sq km)

GEO WHIZ

The brown pelican, the state bird of Louisiana, was placed on the endangered species list in 1970. The species made a remarkable recovery, largely due to a ban of the pesticide DDT by the federal government, and was removed from the endangered list in 2009.

The magnolia, Louisiana's state flower, is the oldest flowering plant in the world. Some species are believed to be 100 million years old.

Cajuns, people whose French-speaking ancestors were exiled by the British from Acadia, in what is now Canada, live primarily in the bayou region of Louisiana. Their distinctive music and spicy food have become popular throughout the country.

TASTY HARVEST. Louisiana produces more than half of all shrimp caught in the U.S. Most comes from Barataria-Terre-bonne, an estuary at the mouth of the Mississippi River.

MAGNOLIA BROWN PELICAN

Louisiana's Native American heritage is evident in place-names such as Natchitoches and Opelousas. Spanish sailors explored the area in 1528, but the French, traveling down the Mississippi River, established permanent settlements in the mid-17th century and named the region for King Louis XIV. The United States gained possession of the territory as part of the Louisiana Purchase in 1803, and Louisiana became the 18th state in 1812. New Orleans and the Port of South Louisiana, located near the delta of the Mississippi River, are Louisiana's main ports. Trade from the interior of the United States moves through these ports and out to world markets. Oil and gas are drilled in the Mississippi Delta area and in the Gulf of Mexico. The explosion of an off-shore oil rig in 2010 brought serious environmental damage to coastal areas still recovering from Hurricane Katrina, a massive storm that roared in off the Gulf in 2005, flooding towns, breaking through levees, and changing the lives of everyone in southern Louisiana.

AVENUE TO THE PAST. Stately live oaks, believed to be 300 years old, frame Oak Alley Plantation on the banks of the Mississippi River west of New Orleans. Built in 1839, the house has been restored to its former grandeur and is open to the public for tours and private events.

Springhill
Vivian
Caddo Lake
Red
KISATCHIE NATIONAL FOREST
49
220
Minden
20
Bossier City
Shreveport
Lake Bistineau
49
Mansfield
Red
Many
Toledo Bend Reservoir
Leesville
Rosepine
De Ridder
TEXAS
Sabine
De Quincy
Sulphur
10
Lake Charles
Intracoastal
CAMERON PRAIRIE N.W.R.
Calcasieu Lake
Sabine Lake
SABINE NAT. WILDLIFE REFUGE

ARKANSAS

KISATCHIE
NATIONAL
FOREST
Homer

UPPER
OUACHITA
N.W.R.

Bastrop

Lake
Providence

POVERTY POINT
NATIONAL
MONUMENT

Bayou D'Arbonne

D'ARBONNE
N.W.R.

Grambling • Ruston
West
Monroe • **Monroe**
Rayville

20

Tallulah

Driskill Mt.
535 ft
163 m
Highest point
in Louisiana

TENSAS
RIVER
N.W.R.

Jonesboro

SALINE BAYOU
NATIONAL WILD &
SCENIC RIVER

Winnsboro

Winnfield

KISATCHIE

Natchitoches

NATIONAL

CANE RIVER CREOLE N.H.P.
AND HERITAGE AREA

FOREST

*Catahoula
Lake*

CATAHOULA
N.W.R.

Ferriday

Vidalia

BAYOU
COCODRIE
N.W.R.

KISATCHIE

Alexandria • Pineville

NATIONAL

LAKE
OPHELIA
N.W.R.

FOREST

Marksville

TUNICA-BILOXI
INDIAN RES.

MISSISSIPPI

Bunkie

L O U I S I A N A

Oakdale
Ville
Platte

COUSHATTA
INDIAN RESERVATION

49

Opelousas

Eunice

ATCHAFALAYA
N.W.R.

CAT ISLAND
N.W.R.

Zachary

55

Amite

Bogalusa

BOGUE
CHITTO
N.W.R.

59

Denham
Springs Hammond Covington

Evangeline
Breaux Bridge
Port Allen
Baton Rouge

Jennings Rayne • **Lafayette**

Crowley

Plaquemine

10

Port Allen

Prairieville

Gonzales

12

Mandeville

Slidell

Lake
Maurepas

Lake
Pontchartrain

10

LACASSINE
N.W.R.

Waterway

Abbeville

New Iberia

Donaldsonville

BAYOU SAUVAGE N.W.R.

Lake Borgne

Laplace

Kenner

Metairie

*Grand
Lake*

Avery Island

Jeanerette

CHITIMACHA
INDIAN RES.

Lowest point in Louisiana;
8 feet below sea level,
JEAN LAFITTE N.H.P. AND PRESERVE,
NEW ORLEANS JAZZ N.H.P.

New Orleans

Chalmette

*White
Lake*

Franklin

Morgan City

Thibodaux

Raceland

Lake
Salvador

*Breton
Sound*

Houma

Larose

*Marsh
Island*

SHELL KEYS
NATIONAL
WILDLIFE
REFUGE

*Atchafalaya
Bay*

Intracoastal

Waterway

Port Sulphur

*Barataria
Bay*

Grand Isle

DELTA
N.W.R.

GULF OF MEXICO

Terrebonne Bay

Timbalier Bay

*Mississippi
River Delta*

Mississippi Sound

*Chandeleur
Islands*

*Chandeleur
Sound*

BRETON

NATIONAL

WILDLIFE

REFUGE

*Breton
Islands*

CARGO PORTS

Port	Tons
South Louisiana, LA	238,585,604
Houston, TX	229,246,833
New York/New Jersey	123,322,644
Beaumont, TX	94,403,631
Long Beach, CA	84,492,739
Hampton Roads, VA	78,664,496
New Orleans, LA	77,159,081
Corpus Christi, TX	76,157,693
Baton Rouge, LA	63,875,439
Los Angeles, CA	57,928,594

Total cargo volume in tons, 2013 data

Container shipping plays a key role in today's global economy,
which involves moving goods around the world. Gulf Coast ports,
led by South Louisiana, dominate U.S. cargo ports.

Economy Symbols

Fishing

Shellfish

Poultry/eggs

Dairy cows/products

Beef cattle

Fruits

Nursery stock

Corn

Rice

Soybeans

Sugarcane

Cotton

Timber/forest products

Stone/gravel/cement

Oil/gas

Hydro-electricity

Chemistry

Food processing

Tourism

---

0   50 miles
0   50 kilometers

Albers Conic Equal-Area Projection

THE MAGNOLIA STATE
MISSISSIPPI

BASICS

Statehood
December 10, 1817; 20th state

Total area (land and water)
48,432 sq mi (125,438 sq km)

Land area
46,923 sq mi (121,531 sq km)

Population
2,992,333

Capital
Jackson
Population 170,674

Largest city
Jackson
Population 170,674

Racial/ethnic groups
59.5% white; 37.6% African American; 1.1% Asian; 0.6% Native American; 3.1% Hispanic (any race)

Foreign born
2.2%

Urban population
49.4% (2010)

Population density
607.8 per sq mi (234.7 per sq km)

GEO WHIZ

The Windsor Ruins, located near Port Gibson, are 23 monolithic columns that once made up the largest antebellum mansion in the state. The mansion survived the Civil War but was destroyed by a fire in 1890.

The Marine Life Oceanarium in Gulfport was almost completely destroyed by Hurricane Katrina in 2005. Eight of its 14 bottlenose dolphins were swept into the Gulf of Mexico by a 40-foot (12-m) wave. These animals and two sea lions named Splash and Elliot were eventually rescued. Others were not so lucky.

Greenville is the birthplace of Jim Henson, creator of Kermit the Frog, Miss Piggy, Big Bird, and other famous Muppets.

Mississippi

Mississippi is named for the river that forms its western boundary. The name comes from the Chippewa words *mici zibi*, meaning "great river." Indeed it is a great river, draining much of the interior United States and providing a trade artery to the world. Explored by the Spanish in 1540 and claimed by the French in 1699, the territory of Mississippi passed to the United States in 1783 and became the 20th state in 1817. For more than a hundred years following statehood, Mississippi was the center of U.S. cotton production and trade. The fertile soils and mild climate of the delta region in northwestern Mississippi provided a perfect environment for cotton, a crop that depended on slave labor. When the Civil War broke out, it took a heavy toll on the state. Today, poverty, especially in rural areas, is a major challenge for the state where agriculture—poultry, cotton, soybeans, and rice—is still the base of the economy.

🡒 **SINGING THE BLUES.** The Gateway to the Blues Museum in Tunica traces the blues, a uniquely American music form, to Mississippi's cotton fields where West Africans, brought on slave ships, toiled in the 1800s.

MOCKINGBIRD
MAGNOLIA

GONE FISHIN'

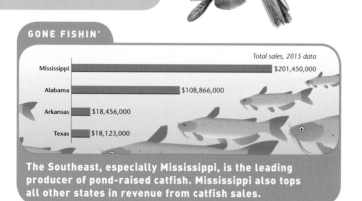

Total sales, 2015 data

Mississippi	$201,450,000
Alabama	$108,866,000
Arkansas	$18,456,000
Texas	$18,123,000

The Southeast, especially Mississippi, is the leading producer of pond-raised catfish. Mississippi also tops all other states in revenue from catfish sales.

DELTA QUEEN

🡒 **BIG WHEEL TURNING.** Now popular with tourists, paddlewheel boats made the Mississippi River a major artery for trade and travel in the 19th century.

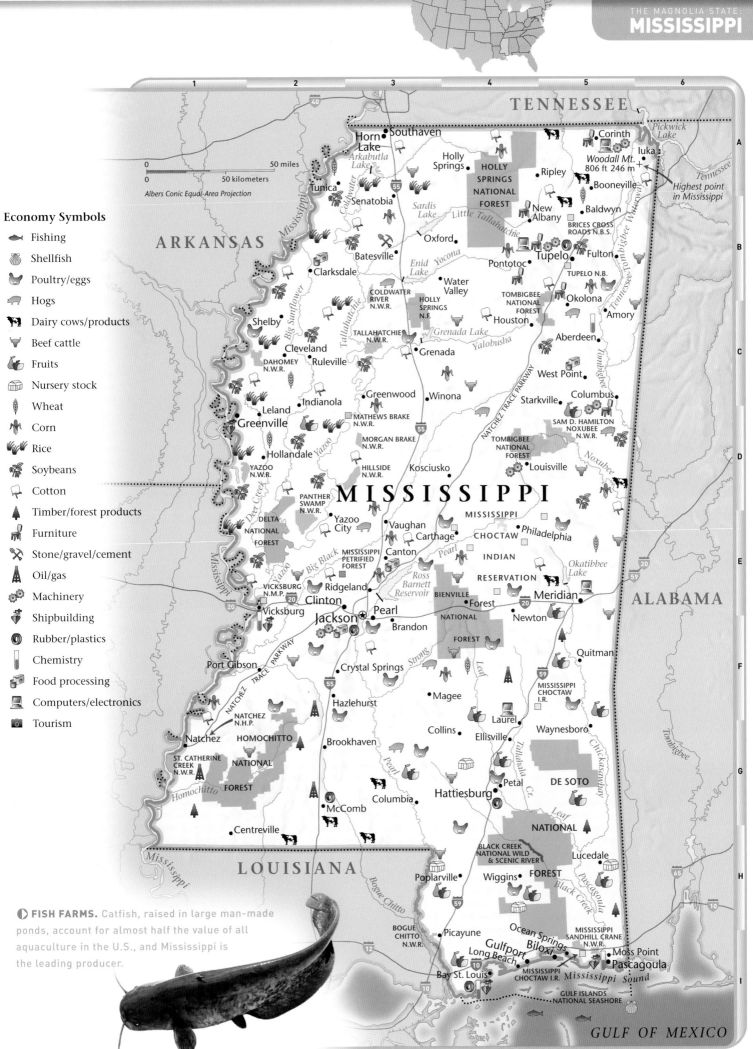

Economy Symbols

- Fishing
- Shellfish
- Poultry/eggs
- Hogs
- Dairy cows/products
- Beef cattle
- Fruits
- Nursery stock
- Wheat
- Corn
- Rice
- Soybeans
- Cotton
- Timber/forest products
- Furniture
- Stone/gravel/cement
- Oil/gas
- Machinery
- Shipbuilding
- Rubber/plastics
- Chemistry
- Food processing
- Computers/electronics
- Tourism

TENNESSEE

ARKANSAS

ALABAMA

LOUISIANA

GULF OF MEXICO

MISSISSIPPI

Southaven
Horn Lake
Holly Springs
Arkabutla Lake
Corinth
Iuka
Woodall Mt. 806 ft 246 m
Ripley
Booneville
Highest point in Mississippi
HOLLY SPRINGS NATIONAL FOREST
Senatobia
Sardis Lake
New Albany
Baldwyn
Tunica
Little Tallahatchie
BRICES CROSS ROADS N.B.S.
Oxford
Pontotoc
Tupelo
Fulton
Batesville
Enid Lake
Yocona
TUPELO N.B.
Clarksdale
Water Valley
TOMBIGBEE NATIONAL FOREST
Okolona
Amory
COLDWATER RIVER N.W.R.
HOLLY SPRINGS N.F.
Houston
Shelby
Grenada Lake
Aberdeen
TALLAHATCHIE N.W.R.
Yalobusha
Cleveland
Ruleville
Grenada
West Point
DAHOMEY N.W.R.
Columbus
Greenwood
Winona
Starkville
Indianola
Leland
MATHEWS BRAKE N.W.R.
SAM D. HAMILTON NOXUBEE N.W.R.
Greenville
MORGAN BRAKE N.W.R.
Noxubee
Hollandale
Yazoo
HILLSIDE N.W.R.
Kosciusko
Louisville
YAZOO N.W.R.
TOMBIGBEE NATIONAL FOREST
Deer Creek
PANTHER SWAMP N.W.R.
DELTA NATIONAL FOREST
Yazoo City
MISSISSIPPI
Vaughan
Philadelphia
Mississippi
CHOCTAW
Carthage
MISSISSIPPI PETRIFIED FOREST
Canton
INDIAN
Okatibbee Lake
Big Black
Ross Barnett Reservoir
RESERVATION
VICKSBURG N.M.P.
Ridgeland
BIENVILLE
Meridian
Clinton
Pearl
Forest
Vicksburg
Jackson
Pearl
Newton
Brandon
NATIONAL
Port Gibson
Strong
FOREST
Quitman
Crystal Springs
NATCHEZ TRACE PARKWAY
Leaf
MISSISSIPPI CHOCTAW I.R.
Hazlehurst
Magee
NATCHEZ N.H.P.
Laurel
Natchez
HOMOCHITTO
Collins
Waynesboro
Brookhaven
Ellisville
DE SOTO
ST. CATHERINE CREEK N.W.R.
NATIONAL
Tallahala Cr.
Petal
Columbia
Hattiesburg
FOREST
Homochitto
McComb
Centreville
NATIONAL
Leaf
Lucedale
BLACK CREEK NATIONAL WILD & SCENIC RIVER
Chickasawhay
Poplarville
Wiggins
FOREST
BOGUE CHITTO N.W.R.
Picayune
Ocean Springs
MISSISSIPPI SANDHILL CRANE N.W.R.
Moss Point
Gulfport
Biloxi
Pascagoula
Long Beach
MISSISSIPPI CHOCTAW I.R.
Mississippi Sound
Bay St. Louis
GULF ISLANDS NATIONAL SEASHORE
Pickwick Lake
Tennessee
Coldwater
Tallahatchie
Big Sunflower
Mississippi
Yazoo
Pearl
Bogue Chitto
Black Creek
Pascagoula
Tombigbee
Tennessee-Tombigbee Waterway
Natchez Trace Parkway

0 — 50 miles
0 — 50 kilometers
Albers Conic Equal-Area Projection

FISH FARMS. Catfish, raised in large man-made ponds, account for almost half the value of all aquaculture in the U.S., and Mississippi is the leading producer.

BASICS

Statehood
November 21, 1789; 12th state

Total area (land and water)
53,819 sq mi (139,391 sq km)

Land area
48,618 sq mi (125,920 sq km)

Population
10,042,802

Capital
Raleigh
Population 451,066

Largest city
Charlotte
Population 827,097

Racial/ethnic groups
71.2% white; 22.1% African American; 2.8% Asian; 1.6% Native American; 9.1% Hispanic (any race)

Foreign born
7.6%

Urban population
66.1% (2010)

Population density
2,174.7 per sq mi
(839.7 per sq km)

GEO WHIZ

The University of North Carolina at Chapel Hill, which opened its doors in 1795, is the oldest public university in the United States.

The Biltmore estate in Asheville is the largest private residence in the United States. It was built by Cornelius Vanderbilt to resemble a French chateau.

At 208 feet (63 m) high, Cape Hatteras Light is the tallest lighthouse in the U.S. Its beacon can be seen some 20 miles (32 km) out to sea and has warned sailors for more than a century.

North Carolina

1   2   3

Before European contact, the land that became North Carolina was inhabited by numerous Native American groups. Early attempts to settle the area met with strong resistance, and one early colony established in 1587 on Roanoke Island disappeared without a trace. More attempts at settlement came in 1650, and in 1663 King Charles granted a charter for the Carolina colony, which included present-day North Carolina, South Carolina, and part of Georgia. In 1789 North Carolina became the 12th state, but in 1861 it joined the Confederacy, supplying more men and equipment to the Southern cause than any other state. In 1903 the Wright brothers piloted the first successful airplane near Kitty Hawk, foreshadowing the change and growth coming to the Tar Heel State. Traditional

CARDINAL
FLOWERING
DOGWOOD

industries included agriculture, textiles, and furniture making. Today, these plus high-tech industries and education in the Raleigh-Durham Research Triangle area as well as banking and finance in Charlotte are important to the economy.

Highest point in North Carolina and east of the Mississippi

FAVORITE PASTIME.
With four of the state's major schools represented in the powerful Atlantic Coast Conference, it is not surprising that basketball is a popular sport among all ages, whether on the court or in the backyard.

TAKING FLIGHT.
The Wright Brothers Memorial on Kill Devil Hill, near Kitty Hawk on North Carolina's Outer Banks, marks the site of the first successful airplane flight in 1903.

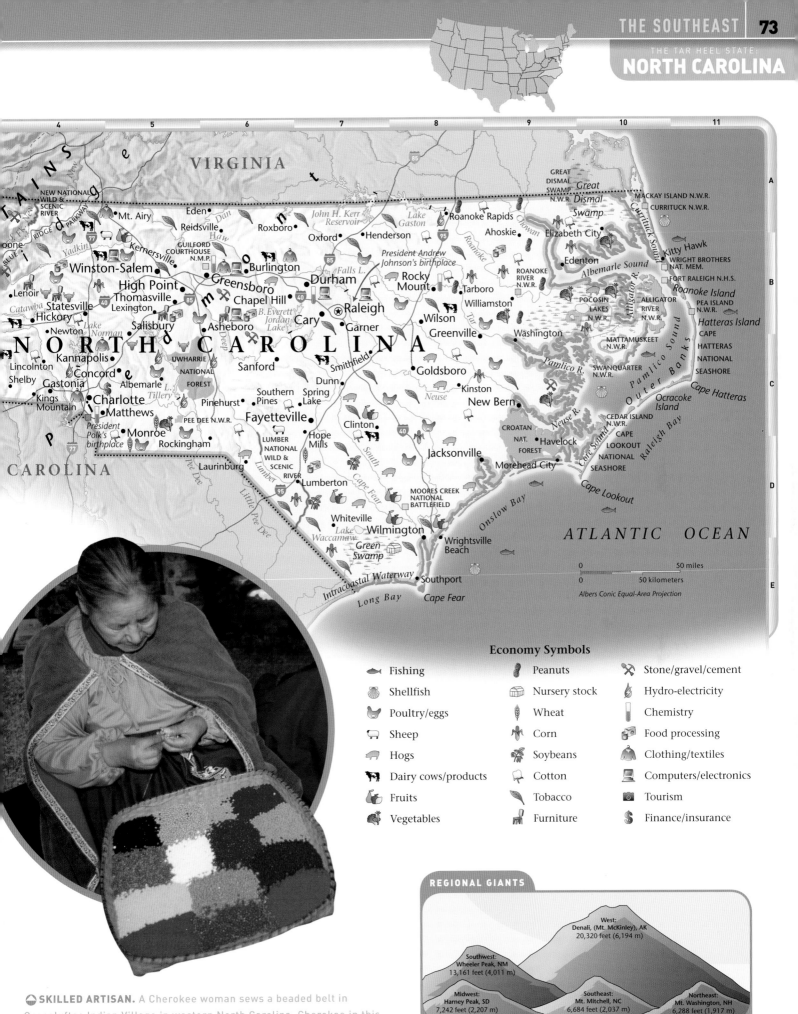

VIRGINIA

NORTH CAROLINA

CAROLINA

ATLANTIC OCEAN

0   50 miles
0   50 kilometers
Albers Conic Equal-Area Projection

Economy Symbols

Fishing	Peanuts	Stone/gravel/cement
Shellfish	Nursery stock	Hydro-electricity
Poultry/eggs	Wheat	Chemistry
Sheep	Corn	Food processing
Hogs	Soybeans	Clothing/textiles
Dairy cows/products	Cotton	Computers/electronics
Fruits	Tobacco	Tourism
Vegetables	Furniture	Finance/insurance

SKILLED ARTISAN. A Cherokee woman sews a beaded belt in Oconaluftee Indian Village in western North Carolina. Cherokee in this mountainous region are descendants of Indians who hid in the hills to avoid the forced migration known as the Trail of Tears. The village preserves traditional 18th-century crafts, customs, and lifestyles.

REGIONAL GIANTS

West:
Denali, (Mt. McKinley), AK
20,320 feet (6,194 m)

Southwest:
Wheeler Peak, NM
13,161 feet (4,011 m)

Midwest:
Harney Peak, SD
7,242 feet (2,207 m)

Southeast:
Mt. Mitchell, NC
6,684 feet (2,037 m)

Northeast:
Mt. Washington, NH
6,288 feet (1,917 m)

Mount Mitchell in the Southeast is the highest peak east of the Mississippi, but young mountains in the West and Southwest tower above older eastern peaks.

THE PALMETTO STATE:
SOUTH CAROLINA

BASICS

Statehood
May 23, 1788; 8th state

Total area (land and water)
32,020 sq mi (82,933 sq km)

Land area
30,061 sq mi
(77,857 sq km)

Population
4,896,146

Capital
Columbia
Population 133,803

Largest city
Columbia
Population 133,803

Racial/ethnic groups
68.4% white; 27.6% African American; 1.6% Asian; 0.5% Native American; 5.5% Hispanic (any race)

Foreign born
4.8%

Urban population
66.3% (2010)

Population density
162.9 per sq mi (62.8 per sq km)

GEO WHIZ

The loggerhead sea turtle, South Carolina's state reptile, is threatened throughout its range.

Congaree National Park, on the Congaree River, protects North America's largest remaining area of primary lowland hardwood forest.

Sweetgrass basketmaking, a traditional art form of African origin, has been a part of the Mount Pleasant community for more than 300 years. The baskets were originally used by slaves in the planting and processing of rice in coastal lowlands.

Bobcats are thriving on Kiawah Island, a resort community near Charleston. These elusive, nocturnal cats, which are about twice the size of an average house cat, help control the island's deer population.

South Carolina

Attempts in the 16th century by the Spanish and the French to colonize the area that would become South Carolina met fierce resistance from local Native American groups, but in 1670 the English were the first to establish a permanent European settlement at present-day Charleston. The colony prospered by relying on slave labor to produce first cotton, then rice and indigo. South Carolina became the eighth state in 1788 and the first to leave the Union just months before the first shots of the Civil War were fired on Fort Sumter in 1861. After the war South Carolina struggled to rebuild its economy. Early in the 20th century, textile mills introduced new jobs. Today, agriculture remains important, manufacturing and high-tech industries are expanding along interstate highway corridors, and tourists and retirees are drawn to the state's Atlantic coastline. But these coastal areas are not without risk. In 1989 Hurricane Hugo's 135-mile-an-hour (217-km/h) winds left a trail of destruction.

🌅 **GLOW OF DAWN.**
The rising sun reflects off the water along the Atlantic coast. Beaches attract visitors year-round, contributing to tourism, the state's largest industry.

YELLOW JESSAMINE
CAROLINA WREN

🏛 **SOUTHERN CHARM.** Established in 1670, Charleston is famous for its stately antebellum homes. The city is an important port, located where the Ashley and Cooper Rivers merge before flowing to the Atlantic Ocean.

Highest point
South Carolina

CHATTOOGA
NATIONAL
WILD &
SCENIC
RIVER
Sassafras Mt.
3,560 ft
1,085 m
SUMTER
NATIONAL
FOREST
Lake Keowee
Greenville
Easley
Gantt
Seneca
Clemson
Belton
Anderson
Hartwell Lake
Richard B.
Russell Lake
Abbeville
85

TRADE PARTNERS

South Korea 2.1%
Netherlands 2.1%
Brazil 2.0%
Belgium 2.4%
Australia 3.0%
Japan 3.1%
Algeria 3.6%
United Kingdom 6.3%
Mexico 7.1%
Canada 12.2%
Germany 13.1%
China 14.3%

Top shares of state export trade, 2014 data (Other countries account for 28.7 percent.)

With more than $29 billion in export goods in 2014, export industries supported almost 25 percent of South Carolina's manufacturing jobs. Transportation equipment is the leading manufactured export.

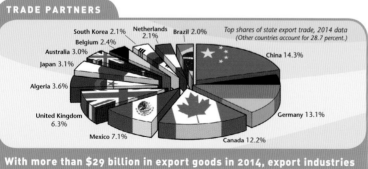

3　　　4　　　5　　　6　　　7　　　8　　　9　　　10

0 — 50 miles
0 — 50 kilometers
Albers Conic Equal-Area Projection

SHOWING OFF. Feathers extended, a male wild turkey struts through Francis Beidler Forest, a wildlife sanctuary and the world's largest virgin cypress–tupelo swamp forest.

NORTH CAROLINA

COWPENS N.B.
Gaffney
KINGS MOUNTAIN N.M.P.
Wylie Lake
York
Fort Mill
Greer
Spartanburg
Rock Hill
CATAWBA I.R.
Taylors
Mauldin
Simpsonville
Union
Chester
Lancaster
Cheraw
SUMTER
Bennettsville
CAROLINA SANDHILLS N.W.R.
Laurens
NATIONAL
Wateree Lake
Hartsville
Dillon
Clinton
FOREST
Winnsboro
Newberry
Camden
Darlington
Mullins
Greenwood
Lake Murray
Florence
Marion
NINETY SIX N.H.S.
Saluda
Irmo
SUMTER
Loris
Forest Acres
Columbia
SOUTH
West Columbia
Cayce
Sumter
Conway
NATIONAL
Batesburg-Leesville
Lake City
WACCAMAW N.W.R.
Intracoastal Waterway
Edgefield
CONGAREE NATIONAL PARK
Manning
North Myrtle Beach
FOREST
J. Strom Thurmond Reservoir
CAROLINA
Kingstree
Myrtle Beach
Socastee
North Augusta
Aiken
Clearwater
Orangeburg
Georgetown
Surfside Beach
Garden City
Williston
S. Fork Edisto
N. Fork Edisto
SANTEE N.W.R.
Lake Marion
Santee Dam
North Island
ATLANTIC
Bamberg
Lake Moultrie
OCEAN
Barnwell
FRANCIS MARION NATIONAL FOREST
Francis Beidler Forest
Moncks Corner
Cape Island
GEORGIA
Savannah
Edisto
Summerville
Goose Creek
CAPE ROMAIN N.W.R.
Allendale
Ladson
Hanahan
Hampton
Walterboro
North Charleston
CHARLES PINCKNEY N.H.S.
Charleston
Mt. Pleasant
FT. SUMTER NAT. MON.
ERNEST F. HOLLINGS ACE BASIN N.W.R.
Edisto Island
Burton
Beaufort
St. Helena Sound
Port Royal
St. Helena Island
SAVANNAH NATIONAL WILDLIFE REFUGE
PINCKNEY ISLAND N.W.R.
Parris Island
Hilton Head Island
Hilton Head Island
Daufuskie Island
SEA ISLANDS
Long Bay

Broad
Catawba
Great Pee Dee
Little Pee Dee
Lynches
Black
Waccamaw
Congaree
Wateree
Cooper
Santee
Combahee
Edisto
Coosawhatchie
Port Royal Sound

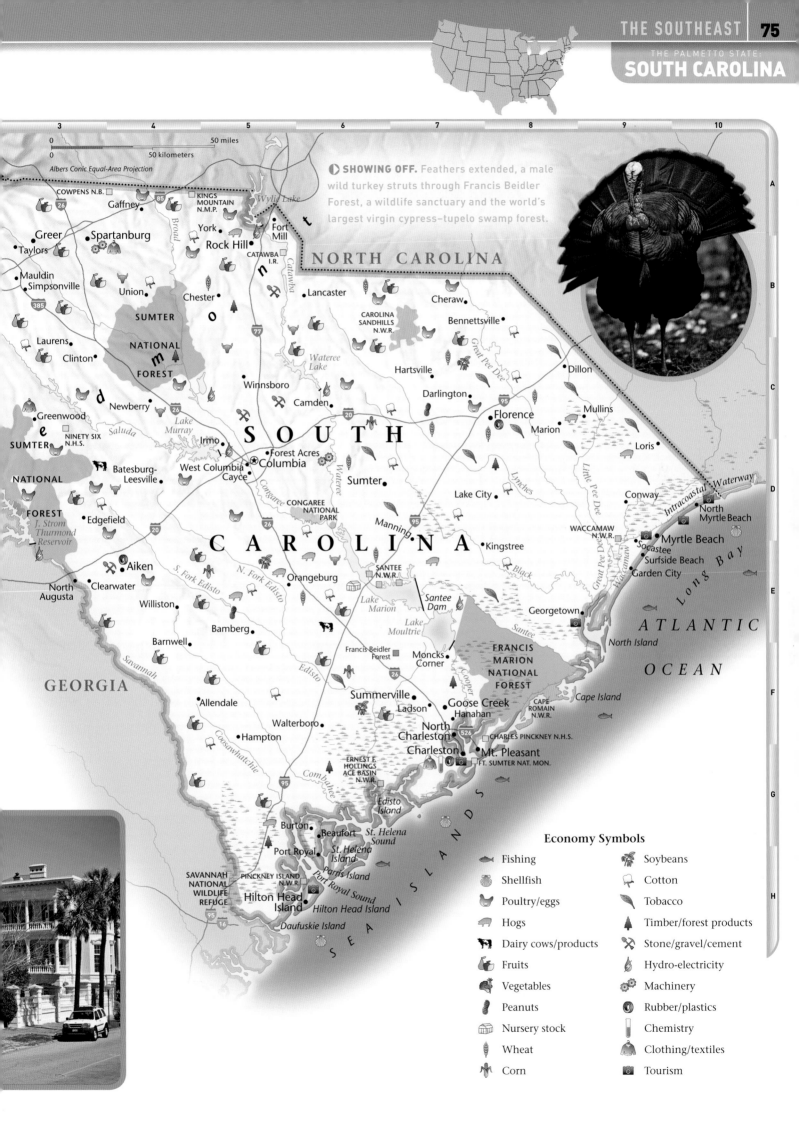

Economy Symbols

Fishing		Soybeans	
Shellfish		Cotton	
Poultry/eggs		Tobacco	
Hogs		Timber/forest products	
Dairy cows/products		Stone/gravel/cement	
Fruits		Hydro-electricity	
Vegetables		Machinery	
Peanuts		Rubber/plastics	
Nursery stock		Chemistry	
Wheat		Clothing/textiles	
Corn		Tourism	

THE VOLUNTEER STATE:
TENNESSEE

BASICS

Statehood
June 1, 1796; 16th state

Total area (land and water)
42,144 sq mi (109,153 sq km)

Land area
41,235 sq mi (106,798 sq km)

Population
6,600,299

Capital
Nashville-Davidson County
Population 654,610

Largest city
Memphis
Population 655,770

Racial/ethnic groups
78.8% white; 17.1% African American; 1.8% Asian; 0.4% Native American; 5.2% Hispanic (any race)

Foreign born
4.6%

Urban population
66.4% (2010)

Population density
160.1 per sq mi (61.8 per sq km)

GEO WHIZ

Great Smoky Mountains National Park is known as the Salamander Capital of the world for the 27 species of salamanders that live there, including the five-foot (1.5-m)-long hellbender.

The New Madrid Earthquakes of 1811–1812, some of the largest earthquakes in U.S. history, created Reelfoot Lake in northwestern Tennessee. It is the state's only large, natural lake; others were created by damming waterways.

The Tennessee-Tombigbee Waterway is a 234-mile (376-km) artificial waterway that connects the Tennessee and Tombigbee Rivers. This water transportation route provides inland ports with an outlet to the Gulf of Mexico.

Tennessee

Following the last ice age, Native Americans moved onto the fertile lands of Tennessee. The earliest Europeans in Tennessee were Spanish explorers who passed through in 1541. In 1673 both the English and French made claims on the land, hoping to develop trade with the powerful Cherokee, whose town, called *Tanasi*, gave the state its name. Originally part of North Carolina, Tennessee was ceded to the federal government and became the 16th state in 1796.

Tennessee was the last state to join the Confederacy and endured years of hardship after the war. Beginning in the 1930s, the federally funded Tennessee Valley Authority (TVA) set a high standard in water management in the state, and the hydropower it generated supported major industrial development. Tennessee played a key role in the civil rights movement of the 1960s. Today, visitors to Tennessee are drawn to national parks, Nashville's country music, and the mournful sound of the blues in Memphis.

MOCKINGBIRD IRIS

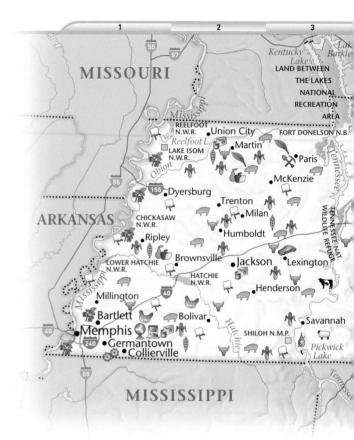

◑ **OUT FOR A STROLL.**
Black bear cubs are usually born in January and remain with their mother for about 18 months. The Great Smoky Mountains National Park is one of the few remaining natural habitats for black bears in the eastern United States.

NATURE'S PLAYGROUND

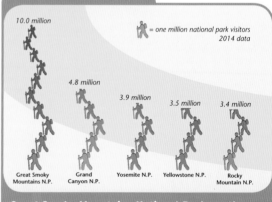

10.0 million

🚶 = one million national park visitors
2014 data

4.8 million

3.9 million

3.5 million

3.4 million

Great Smoky Mountains N.P.

Grand Canyon N.P.

Yosemite N.P.

Yellowstone N.P.

Rocky Mountain N.P.

Great Smoky Mountains National Park, on the Tennessee–North Carolina border, attracts more visitors than any other U.S. national park.

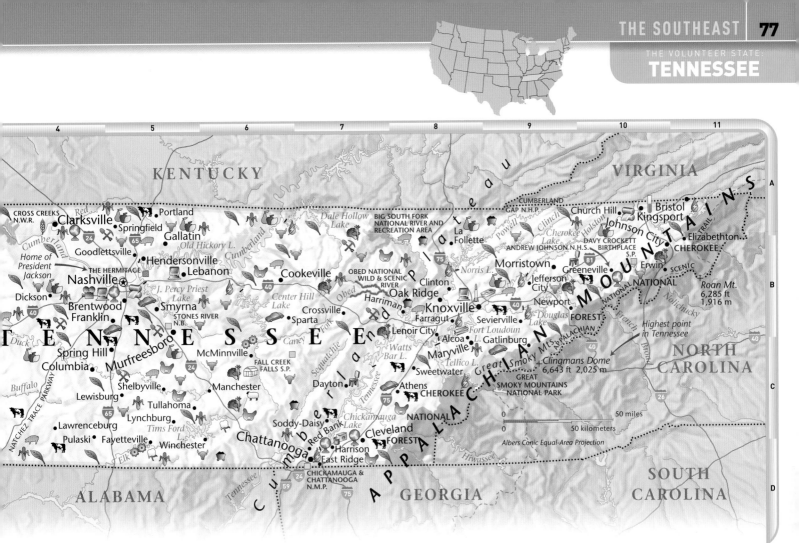

Map labels:

KENTUCKY

VIRGINIA

CROSS CREEKS N.W.R.
Clarksville
Portland
Springfield
Gallatin
Goodlettsville
Old Hickory L.
Hendersonville
Lebanon
Home of President Jackson
THE HERMITAGE
Nashville
Dickson
Brentwood
Franklin
Smyrna
STONES RIVER N.B.
J. Percy Priest Lake
Center Hill Lake
Cookeville
Crossville
Sparta
Dale Hollow Lake
BIG SOUTH FORK NATIONAL RIVER AND RECREATION AREA
OBED NATIONAL WILD & SCENIC RIVER
La Follette
CUMBERLAND GAP N.H.P.
Church Hill
Bristol
Kingsport
Johnson City
Elizabethton
ANDREW JOHNSON N.H.S.
DAVY CROCKETT BIRTHPLACE S.P.
CHEROKEE
Morristown
Greeneville
Erwin
SCENIC
NATIONAL
Jefferson City
Newport
FOREST
Roan Mt. 6,285 ft 1,916 m
Highest point in Tennessee
Clinton
Oak Ridge
Harriman
Knoxville
Farragut
Sevierville
Alcoa
Maryville
Lenoir City
Fort Loudoun L.
Gatlinburg
Tellico L.
Douglas Lake
NORTH CAROLINA
Clingmans Dome 6,643 ft 2,025 m
GREAT SMOKY MOUNTAINS NATIONAL PARK
Watts Bar L.
Athens
Sweetwater
CHEROKEE
NATIONAL
FOREST

TENNESSEE

Spring Hill
Columbia
Murfreesboro
McMinnville
FALL CREEK FALLS S.P.
Shelbyville
Manchester
Dayton
Lewisburg
Tullahoma
Lynchburg
Tims Ford L.
Lawrenceburg
Pulaski
Fayetteville
Winchester
Soddy-Daisy
Red Bank
Chickamauga Lake
Cleveland
Chattanooga
Harrison
East Ridge
CHICKAMAUGA & CHATTANOOGA N.M.P.

ALABAMA

GEORGIA

SOUTH CAROLINA

NATCHEZ TRACE PARKWAY

Cumberland
Duck
Buffalo
Elk
Tennessee
Hiwassee
Nolichucky
French Broad

0   50 miles
0   50 kilometers
Albers Conic Equal-Area Projection

WATTS BAR DAM is one of nine TVA dams built on the Tennessee River to aid navigation and flood control and to supply power. The large reservoir behind the dam provides a recreation area that attracts millions of vacationers each year. Without the dam, cities such as Chattanooga would face devastating floods.

SOUTHERN TRADITION. Nashville's Grand Ole Opry is the home of country music. Originally a 1925 radio show called *WSM Barn Dance*, the Opry now occupies a theater with a seating capacity of 4,400 and the largest broadcasting studio in the world. Country music, using mainly stringed instruments, evolved from traditional folk tunes of the Appalachians.

Economy Symbols

Poultry/eggs		Printing/publishing	
Sheep		Stone/gravel/cement	
Hogs		Mining	
Dairy cows/products		Coal	
Beef cattle		Hydro-electricity	
Fruits		Machinery	
Vegetables		Metal manufacturing	
Nursery stock		Motor vehicles/parts	
Wheat		Chemistry	
Corn		Food processing	
Soybeans		Electrical equipment	
Cotton		Computers/electronics	
Tobacco		Aerospace	
Furniture		Motion picture/music industry	

BASICS

Statehood
June 25, 1788; 10th state

Total area (land and water)
42,775 sq mi (110,787 sq km)

Land area
39,490 sq mi (102,279 sq km)

Population
8,382,993

Capital
Richmond
Population 220,289

Largest city
Virginia Beach
Population 452,745

Racial/ethnic groups
70.2% white; 19.7% African American; 6.5% Asian; 0.5% Native American; 9.0% Hispanic (any race)

Foreign born
11.3%

Urban population
75.5% (2010)

Population density
212.3 per sq mi (82.0 per sq km)

GEO WHIZ

In the early 1700s, the bustling port of Hampton was a major target for pirates, including the notorious Blackbeard. Today, the city hosts the Blackbeard Festival each spring, complete with pirate re-enactors, live music, games, and fireworks.

During the Battle of Hampton Roads in 1862, the USS *Monitor* and the CSS *Virginia* (a rebuilt version of the USS *Merrimac*) met in one of the most famous naval engagements in U.S. history. The battle marked the dawn of a new era of naval warfare.

More than 200,000 telephone calls are made each day at the Pentagon, the headquarters for the U.S. Department of Defense, through phones connected by 100,000 miles (160,000 km) of telephone cable. The Pentagon is one of the world's largest office buildings.

FLOWERING DOGWOOD

CARDINAL

Virginia

Long before Europeans arrived in present-day Virginia, Native Americans populated the area. Early Spanish attempts to establish a colony failed, but in 1607 merchants established the first permanent English settlement in North America at Jamestown. Virginia became a prosperous colony, growing tobacco using slave labor. Virginia played a key role in the drive for independence, and the final battle of the Revolutionary War was at Yorktown, near Jamestown. In 1861 Virginia joined the Confederacy and became a major battleground of the Civil War, which left the state in financial ruin.

EARLY ENTERTAINMENT. Dice made of bone, ivory, and lead, dating to 1607, were excavated at Jamestown, providing evidence of a popular form of entertainment during colonial times.

Today, Virginia has a diversified economy. Farmers still grow tobacco, along with other crops. The Hampton Roads area, near the mouth of Chesapeake Bay, is a center for shipbuilding and home to major U.S. naval bases. Northern Virginia, across the Potomac River from Washington, D.C., boasts federal government offices and high-tech businesses. And the state's natural beauty and many historic sites attract tourists from around the world.

KENTUCKY

Bluefield
Tazewell
Richlands APPALACHIA
Norton Lebanon Clinch Wytheville
Mountain
CUMBERLAND GAP N.H.P. Big Stone Gap JEFFERSON NATIONAL FOREST
Powell Clinch Marion
North Fork 81 Mt. Rogers
Bristol Abingdon 5,729 ft 1,746 m
A P P A L A
Holston
J. Fork
TENNESSEE

Highest point in Virginia

NATURAL WONDER. Winding under the Appalachian Mountains, Luray Caverns formed as water dissolved limestone rocks and precipitated calcium deposits to form stalactites and stalagmites.

PAST AND PRESENT. Cyclists speed past a statue of Confederate General Robert E. Lee on Richmond's Monument Avenue. The street has drawn criticism for recognizing leaders of the Confederacy.

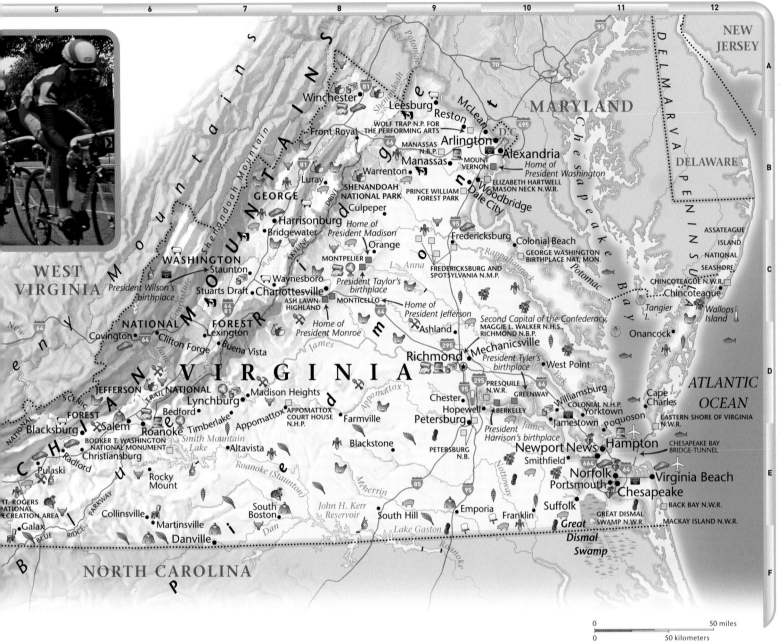

5 6 7 8 9 10 11 12

NEW JERSEY

MARYLAND

DELAWARE

WEST VIRGINIA

Winchester
Leesburg
Reston
McLean
Front Royal
WOLF TRAP N.P. FOR THE PERFORMING ARTS
MANASSAS N.B.P.
Arlington
D.C.
Alexandria
Manassas
MOUNT VERNON
Home of President Washington
Warrenton
Luray
ELIZABETH HARTWELL MASON NECK N.W.R.
GEORGE
SHENANDOAH NATIONAL PARK
PRINCE WILLIAM FOREST PARK
Woodbridge
Dale City
Culpeper
Harrisonburg
Bridgewater
Home of President Madison
Orange
Fredericksburg
Colonial Beach
GEORGE WASHINGTON BIRTHPLACE NAT. MON.
MONTPELIER
FREDERICKSBURG AND SPOTSYLVANIA N.M.P.
WASHINGTON
Staunton
President Wilson's birthplace
Waynesboro
President Taylor's birthplace
ASSATEAGUE ISLAND NATIONAL SEASHORE
Stuarts Draft
Charlottesville
ASH LAWN-HIGHLAND
MONTICELLO
Home of President Jefferson
L. Anna
Ashland
Second Capital of the Confederacy
MAGGIE L. WALKER N.H.S.,
RICHMOND N.B.P.
CHINCOTEAGUE N.W.R.
Chincoteague
Tangier I.
Wallops Island
NATIONAL FOREST
Lexington
Home of President Monroe
Covington
Clifton Forge
Buena Vista
James
Richmond
Mechanicsville
President Tyler's birthplace
West Point
Onancock
JEFFERSON
NATIONAL
Lynchburg
Madison Heights
Appomattox
PRESQUILE N.W.R.
GREENWAY
Williamsburg
Cape Charles
ATLANTIC OCEAN
Chester
Hopewell
COLONIAL N.H.P.
Yorktown
EASTERN SHORE OF VIRGINIA N.W.R.
FOREST
Blacksburg
Salem
Roanoke
Bedford
Timberlake
APPOMATTOX COURT HOUSE N.H.P.
Farmville
Petersburg
BERKELEY
Jamestown
Poquoson
Smith Mountain Lake
Altavista
Blackstone
PETERSBURG N.B.
President Harrison's birthplace
Newport News
Hampton
CHESAPEAKE BAY BRIDGE-TUNNEL
BOOKER T. WASHINGTON NATIONAL MONUMENT
Christiansburg
Smithfield
Norfolk
Virginia Beach
Pulaski
Radford
Rocky Mount
Roanoke (Staunton)
Portsmouth
Chesapeake
MT. ROGERS NATIONAL RECREATION AREA
Collinsville
John H. Kerr Reservoir
South Hill
Emporia
Franklin
Suffolk
Great Dismal Swamp
GREAT DISMAL SWAMP N.W.R.
BACK BAY N.W.R.
MACKAY ISLAND N.W.R.
Galax
Martinsville
Danville
South Boston
Lake Gaston
NORTH CAROLINA

0 50 miles
0 50 kilometers

Albers Conic Equal-Area Projection

Economy Symbols

- Fishing
- Shellfish
- Poultry/eggs
- Sheep
- Hogs
- Dairy cows/products
- Beef cattle
- Fruits
- Vegetables
- Peanuts
- Wheat

- Corn
- Soybeans
- Cotton
- Tobacco
- Furniture
- Printing/publishing
- Stone/gravel/cement
- Coal
- Hydro-electricity
- Machinery
- Ship Building

- Motor vehicles/parts
- Chemistry
- Food processing
- Clothing/textiles
- Electrical equipment
- Computers/electronics
- Aircraft/parts
- Aerospace
- Tourism

MODERN CONNECTORS

17.6 mi (28.3 km)	Chesapeake Bay Bridge-Tunnel (Virginia Beach to Kiptopeke, VA)
15.8 miles (25.5 km)	Shanghai Yangtze Tunnel and Bridge (Pudong District to Chongming Island, China)
9.9 mi (15.0 km)	Oresund Connection (Sweden to Denmark)
8.7 mi (14.0 km)	Tokyo Bay Aqua Line (Kawasaki to Kisarazu, Japan)
5.1 miles (8.2 km)	Busan-Geoje Fixed Link (Busan to Geoje Island, South Korea)

Advanced engineering has made it possible to span wide expanses of water. The longest bridge-tunnel in the world is in Virginia.

BASICS

Statehood
June 20, 1863; 35th state

Total area (land and water)
24,230 sq mi (62,756 sq km)

Land area
24,038 sq mi (62,259 sq km)

Population
1,844,128

Capital
Charleston
Population 49,736

Largest city
Charleston
Population 49,736

Racial/ethnic groups
93.6% white; 3.6% African
American; 0.8% Asian; 0.2%
Native American; 1.5%
Hispanic (any race)

Foreign born
1.4%

Urban population
48.7% (2010)

Population density
76.7 per sq mi (29.6 per sq km)

GEO WHIZ

The FBI Criminal Justice
Information Center (CJIS) near
Clarksburg has the largest
collection of criminal finger-
prints in the world. The center
handles about 12 million
inquiries each day.

The city of Weirton is nestled in
the panhandle between Ohio and
Pennsylvania. It is the only city
in the U.S. that sits in one state
and borders two others.

The first rural free mail
delivery in the United States
started in Charles Town on
October 1, 1896.

West Virginia

Mountainous West Virginia was first settled by Native Americans who favored the wooded region for hunting. The first Europeans to settle in what originally was an extension of Virginia were Germans and Scotch-Irish, who came through mountain valleys of Pennsylvania in the early 1700s. Because farms in West Virginia did not depend on slaves, residents opposed secession during the Civil War and broke away from Virginia, becoming the 35th state in 1863. In the early 1800s West Virginia harvested forest products and mined salt, but it was the exploitation of vast coal deposits that brought industrialization to the state. Coal fueled steel mills, steamboats, and trains, and jobs in the mines attracted immigrants from far and near. However, poor work conditions resulted in a legacy of poverty, illness, and environmental degradation—problems the state continues to face. Today, the state is working to build a tourist industry based on its natural beauty and mountain crafts and culture.

🪨 **HARD LABOR.**
Coal miners work under difficult conditions—some in underground mines; others in surface mines. In 2013 West Virginia's mines employed more than 20,000 people.

**CARDINAL
RHODODENDRON**

O H I O

Point Pleasant

Ohio

Kanawha

Hurricane

Huntington

Kenova

Big Sandy

Tug Fork

Guyandotte

Loga

Williamson

KENTUCKY

◖**STRATEGIC
LOCATION.**
Founded in 1751 by Robert Harper, who built a ferry to cross the Shenandoah River, Harpers Ferry was the focus of John Brown's historic 1859 raid on the town's U.S. arsenal as a first step in a planned slave uprising.

A

Economy Symbols

- Poultry/eggs
- Sheep
- Hogs
- Dairy cows/products
- Beef cattle
- Fruits
- Corn
- Tobacco
- Timber/forest products
- Printing/publishing
- Stone/gravel/cement
- Coal
- Oil/gas
- Hydro-electricity
- Machinery
- Metal manufacturing
- Motor vehicles/parts
- Rubber/plastics
- Chemistry
- Clothing/textiles
- Glass/clay products
- Computers/electronics
- Aircraft/parts
- Tourism

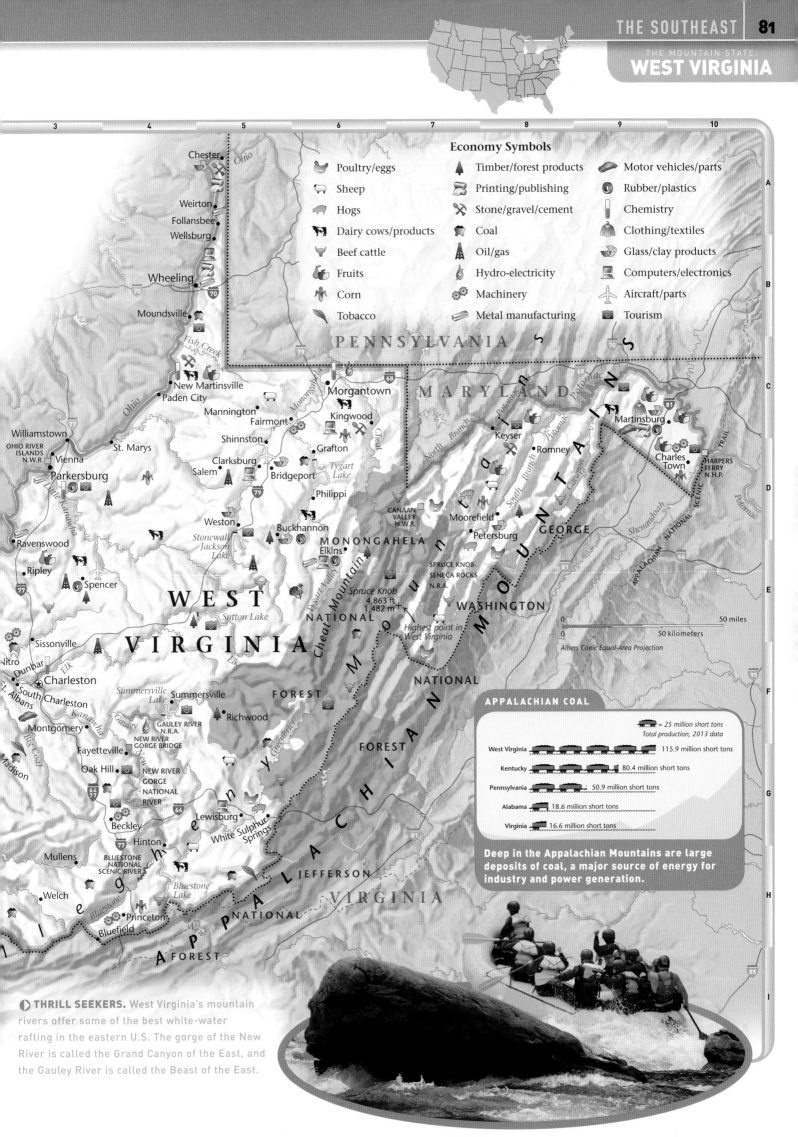

PENNSYLVANIA

MARYLAND

Chester
Weirton
Follansbee
Wellsburg
Wheeling
Moundsville
New Martinsville
Paden City
Mannington
Fairmont
Morgantown
Kingwood
Shinnston
Grafton
Clarksburg
Salem
Bridgeport
Philippi
Williamstown
OHIO RIVER ISLANDS N.W.R.
Vienna
Parkersburg
St. Marys
Weston
Buckhannon
Ravenswood
MONONGAHELA
Elkins
Ripley
Stonewall Jackson Lake
Spencer
NATIONAL
Keyser
Romney
Martinsburg
Charles Town
HARPERS FERRY N.H.P.
Moorefield
Petersburg
GEORGE
CANAAN VALLEY N.W.R.
SPRUCE KNOB-SENECA ROCKS N.R.A.
WASHINGTON
APPALACHIAN NATIONAL SCENIC TRAIL
Sissonville
Nitro
Dunbar
Charleston
St. Albans
South Charleston
Montgomery
Fayetteville
Oak Hill
Summersville Lake
Summersville
Richwood
GAULEY RIVER N.R.A.
NEW RIVER GORGE BRIDGE
NEW RIVER GORGE NATIONAL RIVER
Beckley
Hinton
Lewisburg
White Sulphur Springs
Mullens
BLUESTONE NATIONAL SCENIC RIVER
Welch
Bluestone Lake
Princeton
Bluefield
JEFFERSON
VIRGINIA
NATIONAL
FOREST

WEST
VIRGINIA

Cheat Mountain
Spruce Knob
4,863 ft
1,482 m
Highest point in West Virginia

Sutton Lake

NATIONAL

FOREST

FOREST

APPALACHIAN COAL

= 25 million short tons
Total production, 2013 data

West Virginia	115.9 million short tons
Kentucky	80.4 million short tons
Pennsylvania	50.9 million short tons
Alabama	18.6 million short tons
Virginia	16.6 million short tons

Deep in the Appalachian Mountains are large deposits of coal, a major source of energy for industry and power generation.

0   50 miles
0   50 kilometers
Albers Conic Equal-Area Projection

THRILL SEEKERS. West Virginia's mountain rivers offer some of the best white-water rafting in the eastern U.S. The gorge of the New River is called the Grand Canyon of the East, and the Gauley River is called the Beast of the East.

THE REGION

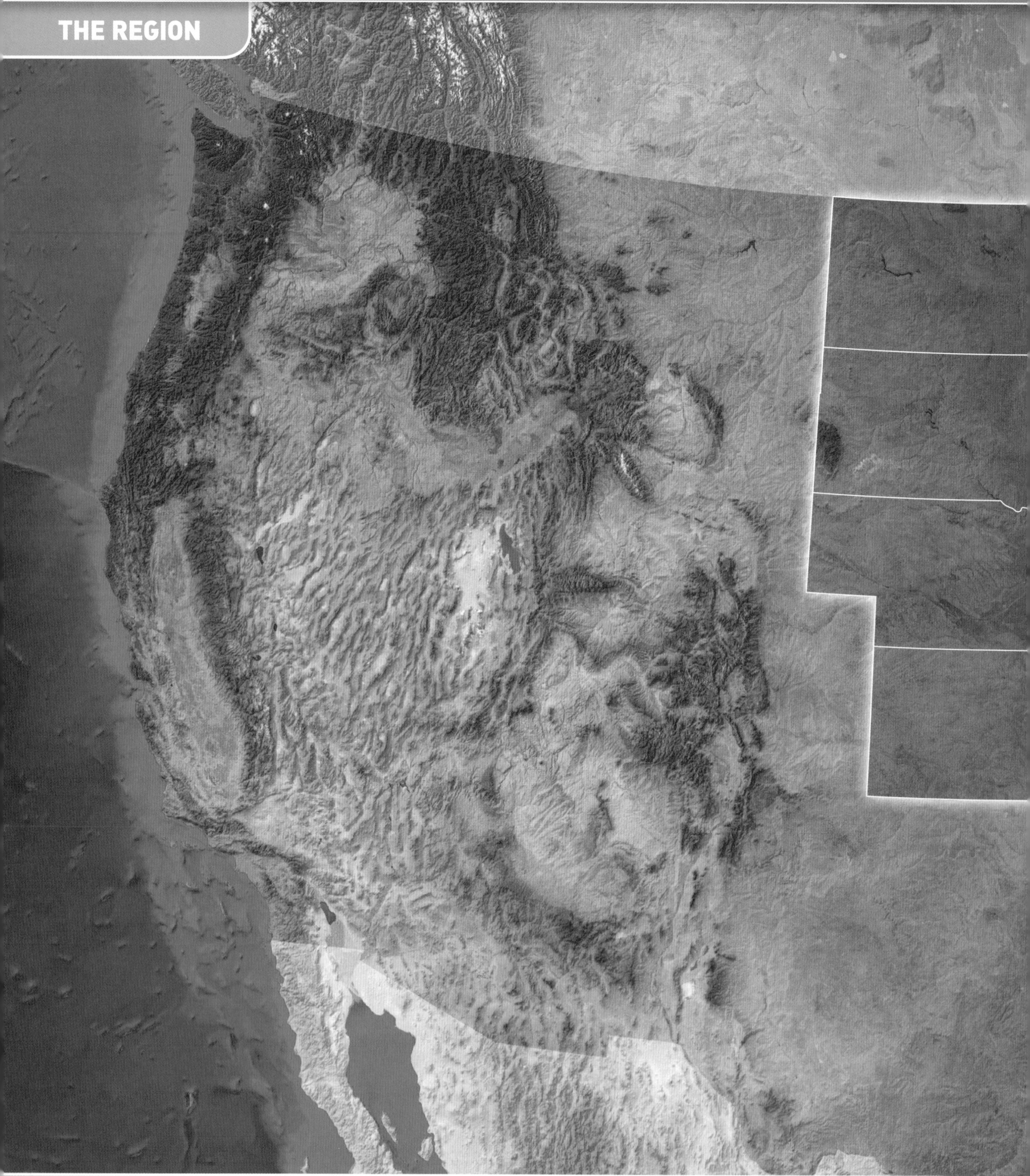

PHYSICAL

Total area (land and water) 821,726 sq mi (2,128,257 sq km)	**Lowest point** St. Francis River, MO 230 ft (70 m)	**Vegetation** Grassland; broadleaf, needleleaf, and mixed forest
Highest point Harney Peak, SD 7,242 ft (2,207 m)	**Longest rivers** Mississippi, Missouri, Arkansas, Ohio	**Climate** Continental to mild, ranging from cold winters and cool summers in the north to mild winters and humid summers in the south
	Largest lakes Superior, Michigan, Huron, Erie	

POLITICAL

Total population 67,907,403	**Smallest state** Indiana: 36,420 sq mi (94,326 sq km)
States (12): Illinois, Indiana, Iowa, Kansas, Michigan, Minnesota, Missouri, Nebraska, North Dakota, Ohio, South Dakota, Wisconsin	**Most populous state** Illinois: 12,859,995
	Least populous state North Dakota: 756,927
Largest state Michigan: 96,714 sq mi (250,487 sq km)	**Largest city proper** Chicago, IL: 2,720,546

The Midwest

◐ **FIERCE GIANT.** Students in Chicago's Field Museum eye the skeleton of *Tyrannosaurus rex*, a dinosaur that roamed North America's plains 65 million years ago.

The Midwest
GREAT LAKES, GREAT RIVERS

The Midwest's early white settlers emigrated from eastern states or Europe, but recent immigrants come from all parts of the world. Hispanics, for example, are settling in communities large and small throughout the region, and many Arabs reside in Detroit and Dearborn, Michigan. Drained by three mighty rivers— the Mississippi, Missouri, and Ohio—the Midwestern lowlands and plains are one of the world's most bountiful farmlands. Though the number of farmers has declined, new technologies and equipment have made farms larger and more productive. Meanwhile, industrial cities of the Rust Belt are adjusting to an economy focused more on information and services than on manufacturing.

◐ **CROP CIRCLES.** Much of the western part of the region receives less than 20 inches (50 cm) of rain yearly—not enough to support agriculture. Large, circular, center-pivot irrigation systems draw water from underground reserves called aquifers to provide life-giving water to crops.

◐ **DAIRY HEARTLAND.** Dairy cows, such as these in Wisconsin, are sometimes treated with growth hormones to increase milk production. These animals play an important role in the economy of the Midwest, which supplies much of the country's milk, butter, and cheese.

MIDWEST URBAN HUB. Chicago, the third largest metropolitan area in the U.S., with almost 10 million people, is the economic and cultural core of the Midwest and a major transportation hub.

PRESERVING THE PAST.
A young Cherokee man, dressed in beaded costume and feathered headband, dances at a powwow in Milwaukee. Such gatherings provide Indians from across the country with a chance to share their traditions.

NATURE'S MOST VIOLENT STORMS.
Parts of the midwestern U.S. have earned the nickname Tornado Alley because these destructive, swirling storms, which develop in association with thunderstorms along eastward-moving cold fronts, occur here more than any other place on Earth.

WHERE THE PICTURES ARE

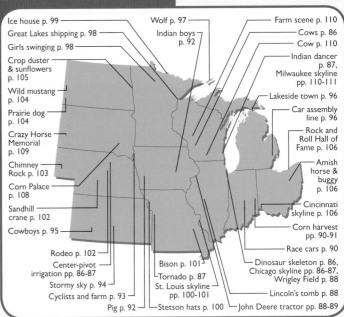

Ice house p. 99
Great Lakes shipping p. 98
Girls swinging p. 98
Crop duster & sunflowers p. 105
Wild mustang p. 104
Prairie dog p. 104
Crazy Horse Memorial p. 109
Chimney Rock p. 103
Corn Palace p. 108
Sandhill crane p. 102
Cowboys p. 95
Rodeo p. 102
Center-pivot irrigation pp. 86-87
Stormy sky p. 94
Cyclists and farm p. 93
Pig p. 92

Wolf p. 97
Indian boys p. 92
Bison p. 101
Tornado p. 87
St. Louis skyline pp. 100-101
Stetson hats p. 100

Farm scene p. 110
Cows p. 86
Cow p. 110
Indian dancer p. 87, Milwaukee skyline pp. 110-111
Lakeside town p. 96
Car assembly line p. 96
Rock and Roll Hall of Fame p. 106
Amish horse & buggy p. 106
Cincinnati skyline p. 106
Corn harvest pp. 90-91
Race cars p. 90
Dinosaur skeleton p. 86, Chicago skyline pp. 86-87, Wrigley Field p. 88
Lincoln's tomb p. 88
John Deere tractor pp. 88-89

THE LAND OF LINCOLN:
ILLINOIS

ILLINOIS

THE BASICS

Statehood
December 3, 1818; 21st state

Total area (land and water)
57,914 sq mi (149,995 sq km)

Land area
55,519 sq mi (143,793 sq km)

Population
12,859,995

Capital
Springfield
Population 116,565

Largest city
Chicago
Population 2,720,546

Racial/ethnic groups
77.3% white; 14.7% African American; 5.5% Asian; 0.6% Native American; 16.9% Hispanic (any race)

Foreign born
13.8%

Urban population
88.5% (2010)

Population density
231.6 per sq mi (89.4 per sq km)

GEO WHIZ

A giant fossilized rain forest has been unearthed in an eastern Illinois coal mine near the town of Danville. Scientists believe an earthquake buried the entire forest 300 million years ago.

The Great Chicago fire of 1871 destroyed the city's waterworks, so firemen had to drag water in buckets from Lake Michigan and the Chicago River. The fire burned out of control for two days until rain finally put it out.

Illinois

Two rivers that now form the borders of Illinois aided the state's early white settlement. Frenchmen first explored the area in 1673 by traveling down the Mississippi, and the Ohio brought many 19th-century settlers to southern Illinois. Most Indians were forced out by the 1830s, more than a decade after Illinois became the 21st state. Ethnically diverse Chicago, the most populous city in the Midwest, is an economic giant and one of the country's busiest rail, highway, and air transit hubs. Barges from its port reach the Gulf of Mexico via rivers and canals, and ships reach the Atlantic Ocean via the Great Lakes and St. Lawrence Seaway. Flat terrain and fertile prairie soils in the northern and central regions help make the state a top producer of corn and soybeans. The more rugged, forested south has deposits of bituminous coal. Springfield, capital of the Land of Lincoln, welcomes tourists visiting the home and tomb of the country's 16th president.

REMEMBERING A PRESIDENT. Dedicated in 1874, the National Lincoln Monument in Springfield honors Abraham Lincoln, who was assassinated in 1865. A special vault holds the remains of the slain president, who led the country during the Civil War.

VIOLET CARDINAL

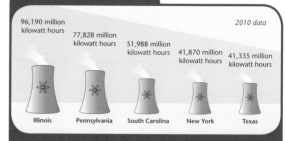

ALTERNATIVE ENERGY

2010 data

96,190 million kilowatt hours — Illinois
77,828 million kilowatt hours — Pennsylvania
51,988 million kilowatt hours — South Carolina
41,870 million kilowatt hours — New York
41,335 million kilowatt hours — Texas

Illinois ranks first among the 30 states that produce nuclear power. The state has six nuclear power plants with 11 reactors.

PLAY BALL! Wrigley Field, home to the Chicago Cubs baseball team, is affected by wind conditions more than any other Major League park due to its location near Lake Michigan.

FIELDS OF GRAIN. Illinois has long been a major grain producer, but farming today is highly mechanized. Above, a tractor with a front loader moves bales of rolled hay.

Economy Symbols

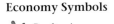 Poultry/eggs

Sheep

Hogs

Dairy cows/products

Beef cattle

Vegetables

Nursery stock

Wheat

Corn

Soybeans

Printing/publishing

Stone/gravel/cement

Mining

Coal

Oil/gas

Machinery

Metal products

Motor vehicles/parts

Rubber/plastics

Chemistry

Food processing

Computers/electronics

Motion picture/music industry

Tourism

$ Finance/insurance

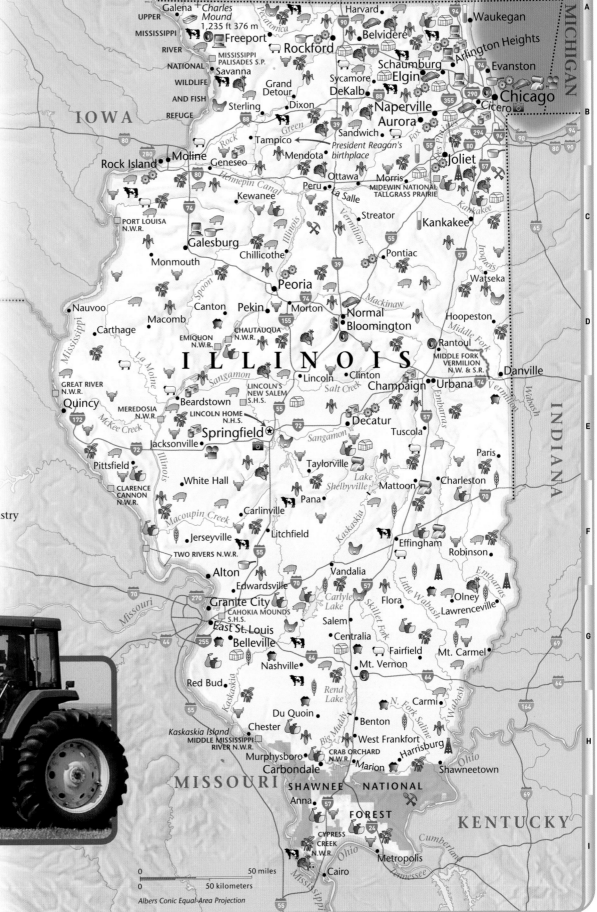

WISCONSIN

LAKE MICHIGAN

MICHIGAN

Highest point in Illinois

Mississippi River

Galena
Charles Mound
1,235 ft 376 m

UPPER

MISSISSIPPI

RIVER

NATIONAL

WILDLIFE

AND FISH

REFUGE

Pecatonica

Harvard

Waukegan

Freeport
Belvidere
Rockford

Arlington Heights

Schaumburg

Evanston

MISSISSIPPI PALISADES S.P.

Savanna

Sycamore
Elgin

DeKalb

Chicago

Grand Detour

Cicero

IOWA

Sterling
Dixon

Naperville
Aurora

Sandwich

Tampico

Green

President Reagan's birthplace

Rock

Mendota

Moline
Rock Island

Geneseo

Ottawa

Joliet

Hennepin Canal

Morris

Kewanee

Peru
La Salle

MIDEWIN NATIONAL TALLGRASS PRAIRIE

PORT LOUISA N.W.R.

Illinois

Streator

Kankakee

Galesburg

Chillicothe

Pontiac

Watseka

Monmouth

Peoria

Spoon

Canton
Pekin
Morton

Mackinaw

Normal
Bloomington

Hoopeston

Nauvoo

Macomb

Rantoul

Carthage

CHAUTAUQUA N.W.R.

MIDDLE FORK VERMILION N.W. & S.R.

Danville

EMIQUON N.W.R.

La Moine

ILLINOIS

Sangamon

Lincoln

Clinton
Champaign
Urbana

GREAT RIVER N.W.R.

Salt Creek

Lincoln's New Salem S.H.S.

Beardstown

MEREDOSIA N.W.R.

LINCOLN HOME N.H.S.

Quincy

McKee Creek

Springfield

Jacksonville

Sangamon

Decatur

Tuscola

Paris

Illinois

Taylorville

Charleston

Pittsfield

Lake Shelbyville

Mattoon

CLARENCE CANNON N.W.R.

White Hall

Pana

Macoupin Creek

Carlinville

Kaskaskia

Effingham

Robinson

Jerseyville

Litchfield

TWO RIVERS N.W.R.

Vandalia

Flora

Olney

Alton

Edwardsville

Lawrenceville

Missouri

Granite City

Carlyle Lake

Salem

Little Wabash

CAHOKIA MOUNDS S.H.S.

East St. Louis

Centralia

Fairfield

Mt. Carmel

Belleville

Nashville

Mt. Vernon

Red Bud

Rend Lake

Carmi

Kaskaskia

Du Quoin

Benton

Chester

West Frankfort

Harrisburg

Kaskaskia Island
MIDDLE MISSISSIPPI RIVER N.W.R.

CRAB ORCHARD N.W.R.

Murphysboro

Marion

Shawneetown

Carbondale

Ohio

MISSOURI

SHAWNEE NATIONAL FOREST

Anna

KENTUCKY

CYPRESS CREEK N.W.R.

Cumberland

Metropolis

Mississippi

Cairo

Tennessee

INDIANA

Wabash

0   50 miles
0   50 kilometers
Albers Conic Equal-Area Projection

THE BASICS

Statehood
December 11, 1816; 19th state

Total area (land and water)
36,420 sq mi (94,326 sq km)

Land area
35,826 sq mi (92,789 sq km)

Population
6,619,680

Capital
Indianapolis
Population 853,173

Largest city
Indianapolis
Population 853,173

Racial/ethnic groups
85.8% white; 9.6% African American; 2.1% Asian; 0.4% Native American; 6.7% Hispanic (any race)

Foreign born
4.7%

Urban population
72.4% (2010)

Population density
184.8 per sq mi (71.3 per sq km)

GEO WHIZ

Every July during Circus Festival in Peru, a couple hundred local kids and a couple thousand volunteers put on a three-ring circus complete with clowns, snow cones, and standing ovations from sellout crowds. The city is home to the International Circus Hall of Fame.

Every year Fort Wayne hosts the Johnny Appleseed Festival to honor John Chapman, the man who planted apple orchards from Pennsylvania to Illinois.

The Children's Museum of Indianapolis, the largest children's museum in the world, features life-size dinosaur replicas, a planetarium, hands-on science labs, and much more. About one million people visit the museum each year.

Indiana

Indiana's name, meaning "Land of the Indians," honors the tribes who lived in the region before the arrival of Europeans. The first permanent white settlement was Vincennes, established by the French in the early 1700s. Following statehood in 1816, most Indians were forced out to make way for white settlement. Lake Michigan, in the state's northwest corner, brings economic and recreational opportunities. The lakefront city of Gary anchors a major industrial region. Nearby, the natural beauty and shifting sands of the Indiana Dunes National Lakeshore attract many visitors. Corn, soybeans, and hogs are the most important products from Indiana's many farms. True to the state motto, "The Crossroads of America," highways from all directions converge at Indianapolis. Traveling at a much higher speed are cars on that city's famed Motor Speedway, home to the Indy 500 auto race since 1911. Cheering for a favorite high school or college team is a favorite pastime for many Hoosiers who catch basketball fever.

⬤ **START YOUR ENGINES.** The Indianapolis Motor Speedway seats up to 250,000 sports fans. Nicknamed the Brickyard, its track was once paved with 3.2 million bricks.

CARDINAL PEONY

◗ **FUEL FARMING.** Indiana farmers grow corn for many uses—livestock feed, additives used in human food products, and production of ethanol, a non-fossil fuel energy source.

HEAVY INDUSTRY

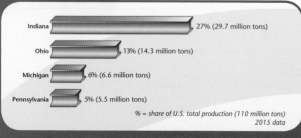

Indiana		27% (29.7 million tons)
Ohio		13% (14.3 million tons)
Michigan		6% (6.6 million tons)
Pennsylvania		5% (5.5 million tons)

% = share of U.S. total production (110 million tons)
2015 data

Steel production was the core of early industrialization in the United States. Indiana and Ohio lead in steel production, but the U.S. also imports much of the steel it uses.

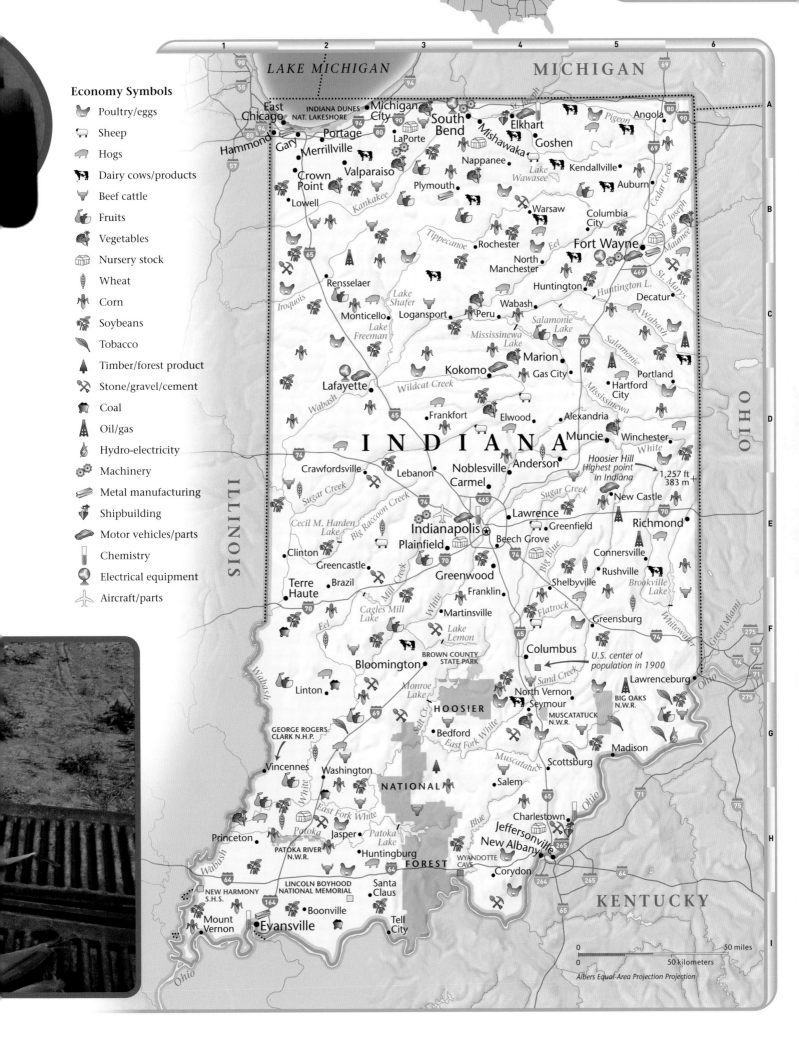

Economy Symbols

- Poultry/eggs
- Sheep
- Hogs
- Dairy cows/products
- Beef cattle
- Fruits
- Vegetables
- Nursery stock
- Wheat
- Corn
- Soybeans
- Tobacco
- Timber/forest product
- Stone/gravel/cement
- Coal
- Oil/gas
- Hydro-electricity
- Machinery
- Metal manufacturing
- Shipbuilding
- Motor vehicles/parts
- Chemistry
- Electrical equipment
- Aircraft/parts

LAKE MICHIGAN

MICHIGAN

INDIANA

ILLINOIS

OHIO

KENTUCKY

East Chicago
INDIANA DUNES NAT. LAKESHORE
Michigan City
South Bend
Mishawaka
Elkhart
Goshen
Angola
Pigeon
Hammond
Gary
Portage
LaPorte
Merrillville
Nappanee
Kendallville
Auburn
Crown Point
Valparaiso
Lake Wawasee
Lowell
Plymouth
Warsaw
Columbia City
Kankakee
Tippecanoe
Rochester
Eel
Fort Wayne
North Manchester
Huntington
Huntington L.
Maumee
Rensselaer
Lake Shafer
Logansport
Peru
Wabash
Salamonie Lake
Decatur
St. Marys
Iroquois
Monticello
Lake Freeman
Mississinewa Lake
Salamonie
Wabash
Kokomo
Marion
Gas City
Portland
Hartford City
Lafayette
Wildcat Creek
Mississinewa
Wabash
Frankfort
Elwood
Alexandria
Muncie
Winchester
White
I N D I A N A
Crawfordsville
Lebanon
Noblesville
Anderson
Hoosier Hill Highest point in Indiana 1,257 ft 383 m
Carmel
New Castle
Sugar Creek
Cecil M. Harden Lake
Big Raccoon Creek
Indianapolis
Lawrence
Greenfield
Richmond
Clinton
Plainfield
Beech Grove
Big Blue
Connersville
Greencastle
Brazil
Greenwood
Rushville
Brookville Lake
Terre Haute
Mill Creek
Franklin
Shelbyville
Flatrock
Greensburg
Cagles Mill Lake
White
Martinsville
Lake Lemon
Eel
Columbus
U.S. center of population in 1900
Lawrenceburg
Bloomington
BROWN COUNTY STATE PARK
Sand Creek
Linton
Monroe Lake
North Vernon
Seymour
MUSCATATUCK N.W.R.
BIG OAKS N.W.R.
Wabash
HOOSIER
Bedford
East Fork White
Muscatatuck
Madison
GEORGE ROGERS CLARK N.H.P.
Salt Cr.
Scottsburg
Vincennes
Washington
NATIONAL
Salem
White
Charlestown
Blue
Jeffersonville
New Albany
Princeton
East Fork White
Jasper
Patoka Lake
FOREST
WYANDOTTE CAVE
Corydon
Patoka
PATOKA RIVER N.W.R.
Huntingburg
Wabash
NEW HARMONY S.H.S.
LINCOLN BOYHOOD NATIONAL MEMORIAL
Santa Claus
Mount Vernon
Evansville
Boonville
Tell City
Ohio

0   50 miles
0   50 kilometers
Albers Equal-Area Projection Projection

IOWA

THE BASICS

Statehood
December 28, 1846; 29th state

Total area (land and water)
56,273 sq mi (145,746 sq km)

Land area
55,857 sq mi (144,669 sq km)

Population
3,123,899

Capital
Des Moines
Population 210,330

Largest city
Des Moines
Population 210,330

Racial/ethnic groups
91.8% white; 3.5%
African American; 2.4%
Asian; 0.5% Native
American; 5.7% Hispanic
(any race)

Foreign born
4.5%

Urban population
64.0% (2010)

Population density
55.9 per sq mi (21.6 per sq km)

GEO WHIZ

One of the most famous houses in America is in Eldon. It was immortalized in Grant Wood's famous painting "American Gothic." The pitchfork-holding man and his wife shown in the art were not farmers at all. Wood's sister and his dentist posed for the painting.

Effigy Mounds National Monument, in northeast Iowa, is the only place in the country with such a large collection of mounds in the shapes of birds, mammals, and reptiles. Eastern Woodland Indians built these mounds from about 500 B.C. to A.D. 1300.

Iowa ranks second, after Texas, among wind energy producers. Just 12 states produce 80 percent of energy generated in the U.S. by wind.

Iowa

Iowa's prehistoric inhabitants built earthen mounds—some shaped like birds and bears—that are visible in the state's northeast. Nineteenth-century white settlers found rolling prairies covered by a sea of tall grasses that soon yielded to the plow. A decade after statehood in 1846, a group of religious German immigrants established the Amana Colonies, a communal society that still draws visitors. Blessed with ample precipitation and rich soils, Iowa is the heart of one of the world's most productive farming regions. The state is the country's top producer of corn, soybeans, hogs, and eggs. Food processing and manufacturing machinery are two of the biggest industries. Much of the grain crop feeds livestock destined to reach dinner plates in the United States and around the world.

An increasing amount of corn is used to make ethanol, which is mixed with gasoline to fuel cars and trucks. Des Moines, the capital and largest city, is a center of insurance and publishing.

⬤ PIG BUSINESS.
Hogs outnumber people almost seven to one in Iowa. The state raises nearly one third of the country's hogs, making it the leading producer.

WILD ROSE

AMERICAN GOLDFINCH

GREEN ENERGY

Ethanol production in millions of gallons (liters) 2015 data

Iowa	Nebraska	Illinois	Minnesota	Indiana
3,785 (14,328)	1,780 (6,738)	1,480 (5,602)	1,166 (4,414)	1,150 (4,353)

Iowa is the leading producer of ethanol fuel, a clean-burning, renewable, non-fossil fuel energy source made mainly from corn.

◗ LEGACY OF THE PAST. Young boys dressed in colorful outfits participate in a traditional dance ceremony, calling to mind Iowa's rich Native American heritage.

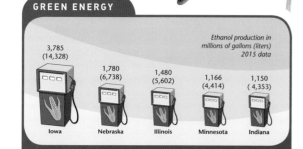

SOUTH DAKOTA

Hawkeye Point
1,670 ft
509 m
Highest point
in Iowa

Sioux Center
Sheldo

Orange City

Le Mars

Sioux City

Big Sioux
Missouri
Floyd
Little Sioux

Onawa

NEBRASKA

DESOTO N.W.R

Council Bluffs

Glenwoo

Missouri

680
80
29

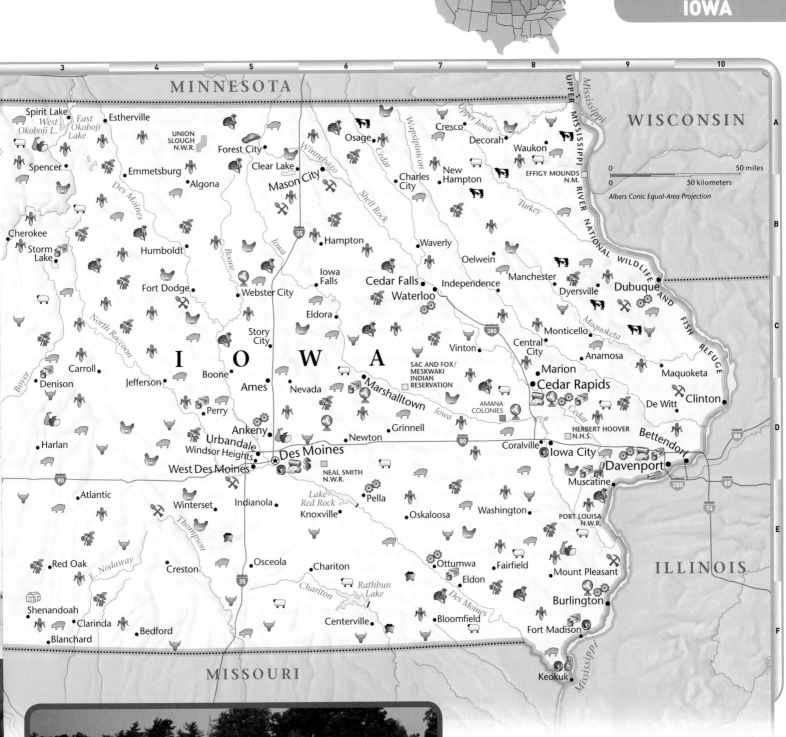

MINNESOTA

WISCONSIN

WISCONSIN

0   50 miles
0   50 kilometers
Albers Conic Equal-Area Projection

Spirit Lake
West Okoboji L.
East Okoboji Lake
Estherville
UNION SLOUGH N.W.R.
Forest City
Clear Lake
Mason City
Spencer
Emmetsburg
Algona
Cherokee
Storm Lake
Humboldt
Fort Dodge
Webster City
Story City

Osage
Cresco
Decorah
Waukon
Charles City
New Hampton
EFFIGY MOUNDS N.M.
Hampton
Waverly
Oelwein
Manchester
Dyersville
Dubuque
Iowa Falls
Cedar Falls
Waterloo
Independence

Carroll
Denison
Jefferson
Boone
Ames
Nevada
Marshalltown
Perry
Ankeny
Urbandale
Windsor Heights
West Des Moines
Des Moines
NEAL SMITH N.W.R.

I O W A

Vinton
Central City
Monticello
Anamosa
Marion
Cedar Rapids
Maquoketa
De Witt
Clinton
SAC AND FOX/ MESKWAKI INDIAN RESERVATION
AMANA COLONIES
Grinnell
Newton
HERBERT HOOVER N.H.S.
Coralville
Iowa City
Bettendorf
Davenport
Muscatine

Harlan
Atlantic
Winterset
Indianola
Knoxville
Pella
Oskaloosa
Washington
PORT LOUISA N.W.R.

Red Oak
Creston
Osceola
Chariton
Lake Red Rock
Rathbun Lake
Ottumwa
Eldon
Fairfield
Mount Pleasant
Burlington
Fort Madison

Shenandoah
Clarinda
Blanchard
Bedford
Centerville
Bloomfield
Keokuk

MISSOURI

ILLINOIS

🚲 **FITNESS RALLY.** Cyclists pass a cluster of farm buildings during the Annual Great Bicycle Ride across Iowa, sponsored by the *Des Moines Register*. Each year 10,000 riders participate in this event.

Economy Symbols

Poultry/eggs	Printing/publishing
Sheep	Stone/gravel/cement
Hogs	Coal
Dairy cows/products	Hydro-electricity
Beef cattle	Machinery
Fruits	Metal manufacturing
Vegetables	Motor vehicles/parts
Nursery stock	Rubber/plastics
Corn	Food processing
Soybeans	Electrical equipment
Furniture	Finance/insurance

THE BASICS

Statehood
January 26, 1837; 26th state

Total area (land and water)
96,714 sq mi (250,487 sq km)

Land area
56,539 sq mi (146,435 sq km)

Population
9,922,576

Capital
Lansing
Population 115,056

Largest city
Detroit
Population 677,116

Racial/ethnic groups
79.7% white; 14.2% African American; 3.0% Asian; 0.7% Native American; 4.9% Hispanic (any race)

Foreign born
6.1%

Urban population
74.6% (2010)

Population density
175.5 per sq mi (67.8 per sq km)

GEO WHIZ

Researchers at the Seney National Wildlife Refuge on the Upper Peninsula have discovered why loons sound different on different lakes: The males change their calls when they move to new territories. Why they do this is still unknown.

The Keweenaw Peninsula offers adventurers a 100-mile (161-km) water trail for canoers, scores of wrecks for divers, 14 miles (23 km) of bike paths, and more than 150 miles (240 km) of hiking trails on nearby Isle Royale National Park.

The Great Lakes contain 20 percent of Earth's freshwater. Industrial dumping, agricultural runoff, and municipal use are some of the threats to the health of Lake Michigan and the other lakes, but the Alliance for the Great Lakes is working to restore their health.

APPLE
BLOSSOM

ROBIN

Michigan

Indians had friendly relations with early French fur traders who came to what is now Michigan, but they waged battles with the British who later assumed control. Completion of New York's Erie Canal in 1825 made it easier for settlers to reach the area, and statehood came in 1837. Michigan consists of two large peninsulas that border four of the five Great Lakes—Erie, Huron, Michigan, and Superior. Most of the population is on the state's Lower Peninsula, while the Upper Peninsula, once a productive mining area, now is popular among vacationing nature lovers. The five-mile (8-km)-long Mackinac Bridge has linked the peninsulas since 1957. In the 20th century Michigan became the center of the American auto industry, and the state's fortunes have risen and fallen with those of the Big Three car companies. Though it remains a big producer of cars and trucks, the state is working to diversify its economy. Michigan's farms grow crops ranging from grains to fruits and vegetables.

◯ **ASSEMBLY LINE.** More than 1,000 robots speed production at Chrysler's Sterling Heights assembly plant near Detroit by making it possible to build different car models on the same assembly line. Motor vehicle production is a major part of the state economy.

DRIVING FORCE

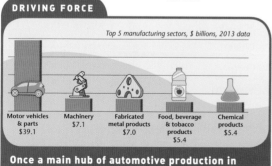

Top 5 manufacturing sectors, $ billions, 2013 data

| Motor vehicles & parts $39.1 | Machinery $7.1 | Fabricated metal products $7.0 | Food, beverage & tobacco products $5.4 | Chemical products $5.4 |

Once a main hub of automotive production in the U.S., Michigan is still among the top auto manufacturing states.

◯ **REFLECTION OF THE PAST.** Victorian-style summer homes, built on Mackinac Island in the late 19th century by wealthy railroad families, now welcome vacationers to the island. To protect the environment, cars are not allowed.

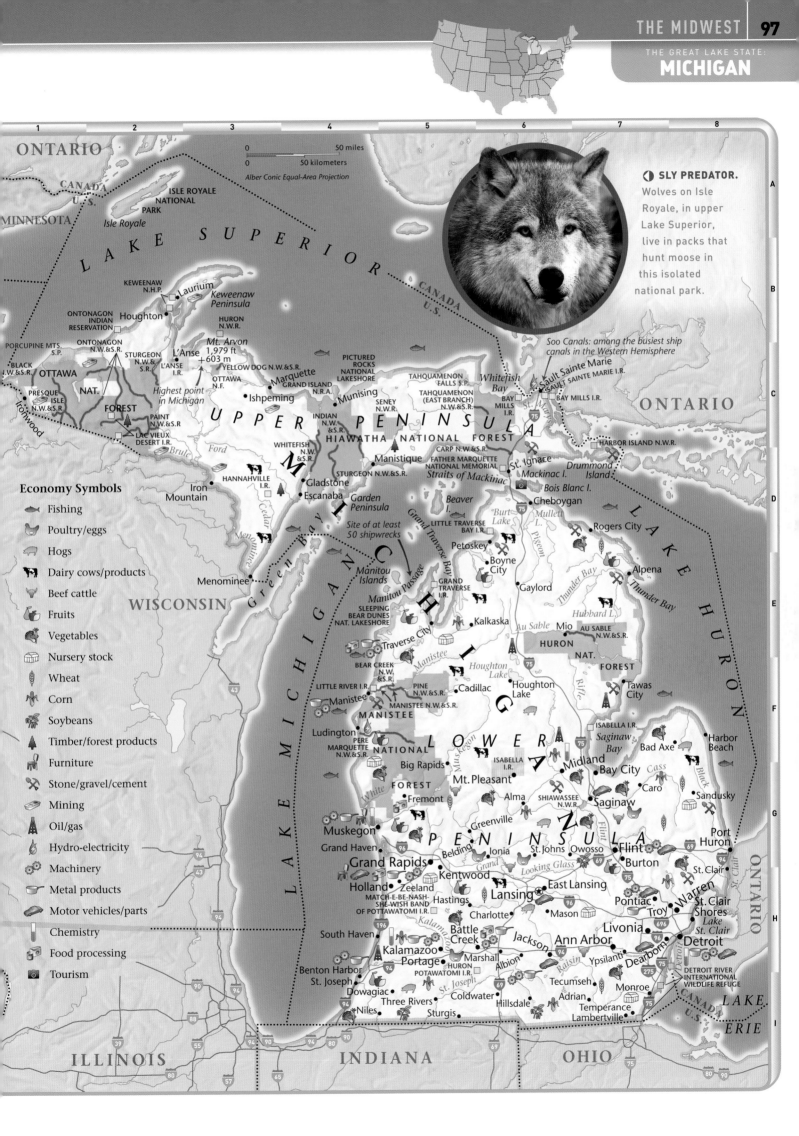

SLY PREDATOR. Wolves on Isle Royale, in upper Lake Superior, live in packs that hunt moose in this isolated national park.

Soo Canals: among the busiest ship canals in the Western Hemisphere

Economy Symbols

- 🐟 Fishing
- 🐔 Poultry/eggs
- 🐷 Hogs
- 🐄 Dairy cows/products
- 🐂 Beef cattle
- 🍒 Fruits
- 🥬 Vegetables
- Nursery stock
- 🌾 Wheat
- 🌽 Corn
- Soybeans
- Timber/forest products
- Furniture
- Stone/gravel/cement
- Mining
- Oil/gas
- Hydro-electricity
- ⚙ Machinery
- Metal products
- Motor vehicles/parts
- Chemistry
- Food processing
- Tourism

Map labels

ONTARIO

CANADA
U.S.

MINNESOTA

ISLE ROYALE NATIONAL PARK

Isle Royale

L A K E   S U P E R I O R

KEWEENAW N.H.P.
Laurium
Keweenaw Peninsula

ONTONAGON INDIAN RESERVATION
Houghton

HURON N.W.R.

CANADA
U.S.

PORCUPINE MTS. S.P.
ONTONAGON N.W.&S.R.
Mt. Arvon 1,979 ft +603 m
L'Anse
L'ANSE I.R.

BLACK J.W.&S.R.
OTTAWA
STURGEON N.W.& S.R.
OTTAWA N.F.
Highest point in Michigan

YELLOW DOG N.W.&S.R.
Marquette
GRAND ISLAND N.R.A.

PICTURED ROCKS NATIONAL LAKESHORE

TAHQUAMENON FALLS S.P.
TAHQUAMENON (EAST BRANCH) N.W.&S.R.

Whitefish Bay

Sault Sainte Marie
SAULT SAINTE MARIE I.R.

PRESQUE ISLE N.W.&S.R.
Ironwood

NAT.
FOREST

PAINT N.W.&S.R.
LAC VIEUX DESERT I.R.

Brule

Ford

Ishpeming
Munising

INDIAN N.W. &S.R.
SENEY N.W.R.

HIAWATHA   NATIONAL   FOREST

BAY MILLS I.R.

St. I.
BAY MILLS I.R.

St. Marys

HARBOR ISLAND N.W.R.

ONTARIO

U P P E R   P E N I N S U L A

WHITEFISH N.W. &S.R.

CARP N.W.&S.R.

HANNAHVILLE I.R.
Iron Mountain
Gladstone
Escanaba

STURGEON N.W.&S.R.
Manistique

FATHER MARQUETTE NATIONAL MEMORIAL
St. Ignace
Straits of Mackinac

Mackinac I.
Drummond Island

Bois Blanc I.

Cheboygan

Menominee

Green Bay

Garden Peninsula

Menominee

Cedar

Site of at least 50 shipwrecks

Manitou Islands

Manitou Passage

Grand Traverse Bay

Beaver I.

Burt Lake
Mullett L.

Pigeon

LITTLE TRAVERSE BAY I.R.
Petoskey
Boyne City
Gaylord

Rogers City
Alpena
Thunder Bay

WISCONSIN

M I C H I G A N

SLEEPING BEAR DUNES NAT. LAKESHORE

GRAND TRAVERSE I.R.

Traverse City

Kalkaska
Mio
AU SABLE N.W.&S.R.

Au Sable
HURON
NAT.
Hubbard L.

L A K E   H U R O N

BEAR CREEK N.W. &S.R.

Manistee

Houghton Lake

FOREST

Tawas City

LITTLE RIVER I.R.
Manistee

PINE N.W.&S.R.
Cadillac
Houghton Lake

Rifle

MANISTEE N.W.&S.R.

MANISTEE

Ludington

PERE MARQUETTE N.W.&S.R.

NATIONAL

ISABELLA I.R.

L O W E R

Saginaw Bay
Bad Axe
Harbor Beach

Big Rapids

ISABELLA I.R.
Mt. Pleasant

Midland
Bay City
Cass
Caro
Sandusky

FOREST

Fremont

Alma
SHIAWASSEE N.W.R.
Saginaw

P E N I N S U L A

White

Greenville

Flint

Port Huron

Muskegon
Grand Haven

Belding
Ionia
St. Johns
Owosso
Flint
Burton
St. Clair

Grand Rapids
Kentwood

Grand

Looking Glass
East Lansing
Pontiac
Troy
Warren

Holland
Zeeland

Hastings

Lansing
Mason

Livonia
St. Clair Shores
Lake St. Clair

MATCH-E-BE-NASH-SHE-WISH BAND OF POTTAWATOMI I.R.

Charlotte

Kalamazoo

South Haven

Battle Creek
Jackson
Ann Arbor
Dearborn
Detroit

Kalamazoo
Portage

Marshall
Albion

Tecumseh
Ypsilanti

DETROIT RIVER INTERNATIONAL WILDLIFE REFUGE

Benton Harbor
St. Joseph

HURON POTAWATOMI I.R.

Raisin
Monroe

CANADA
U.S.

ONTARIO

Dowagiac
Three Rivers
Niles
St. Joseph
Coldwater
Sturgis
Hillsdale
Adrian
Temperance
Lambertville

L A K E   E R I E

ILLINOIS
INDIANA
OHIO

THE BASICS

Statehood
May 11, 1858; 32nd state

Total area (land and water)
86,936 sq mi (225,163 sq km)

Land area
79,627 sq mi (206,232 sq km)

Population
5,489,594

Capital
St. Paul
Population 300,851

Largest city
Minneapolis
Population 410,939

Racial/ethnic groups
85.4% white; 6.0% African American; 4.9% Asian; 1.3% Native American; 5.2% Hispanic (any race)

Foreign born
7.3%

Urban population
73.3% (2010)

Population density
68.9 per sq mi
(26.6 per sq km)

GEO WHIZ

Wild rice is the state grain of Minnesota. Nett Lake, in the Bois Forte Chippewa reservation, has the state's largest continuous beds of wild rice. Native Americans have been harvesting this grain, which they call *manoomin*, for thousands of years.

The Mayo Clinic, a world-famous medical research center founded in 1889 by Dr. William W. Mayo, is in Rochester.

The Boundary Waters Canoe Area Wilderness, along the Minnesota-Ontario border, was the first wilderness area in the U.S. to be set aside for canoeing.

Minnesota

French fur traders began arriving in present-day Minnesota in the mid-17th century. Statehood was established in 1858, and most remaining Indians were forced from the state after a decisive battle in 1862. During the late 1800s large numbers of Germans, Scandinavians, and other immigrants settled a land rich in wildlife, timber, minerals, and fertile soils. Today, farming is concentrated in the south and west. In the northeast, the Mesabi Range's open-pit mines make the state the country's leading source of iron ore. Most of the ore is shipped from Duluth. Both Duluth and nearby Superior in Wisconsin (see page 111) are leading Great Lakes ports. From these ports, ships can reach the Atlantic Ocean via the St. Lawrence Seaway. Scattered across the state's landscape are thousands of lakes—ancient footprints of retreating glaciers—that draw anglers and canoeists. One of those lakes, Lake Itasca, is the source of the mighty Mississippi River, which flows through the Twin Cities of Minneapolis and St. Paul.

COMMON LOON
SHOWY LADY'S SLIPPER

⬤ **SUMMER FUN.** Young girls play on a rope swing near Leech Lake in northern Minnesota. The state's many lakes are remnants of the last ice age, when glaciers gouged depressions that filled with water as the ice sheets retreated.

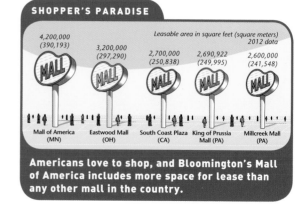

SHOPPER'S PARADISE

4,200,000 (390,193)	3,200,000 (297,290)	2,700,000 (250,838)	2,690,922 (249,995)	2,600,000 (241,548)
Leasable area in square feet (square meters) 2012 data

| Mall of America (MN) | Eastwood Mall (OH) | South Coast Plaza (CA) | King of Prussia Mall (PA) | Millcreek Mall (PA) |

Americans love to shop, and Bloomington's Mall of America includes more space for lease than any other mall in the country.

◖ **INLAND PORT.** Duluth, on the northern shore of Lake Superior, is the westernmost deep-water port on the St. Lawrence Seaway. Barges and container ships move products such as iron ore and grain along the Great Lakes to the Atlantic Ocean and to markets around the world.

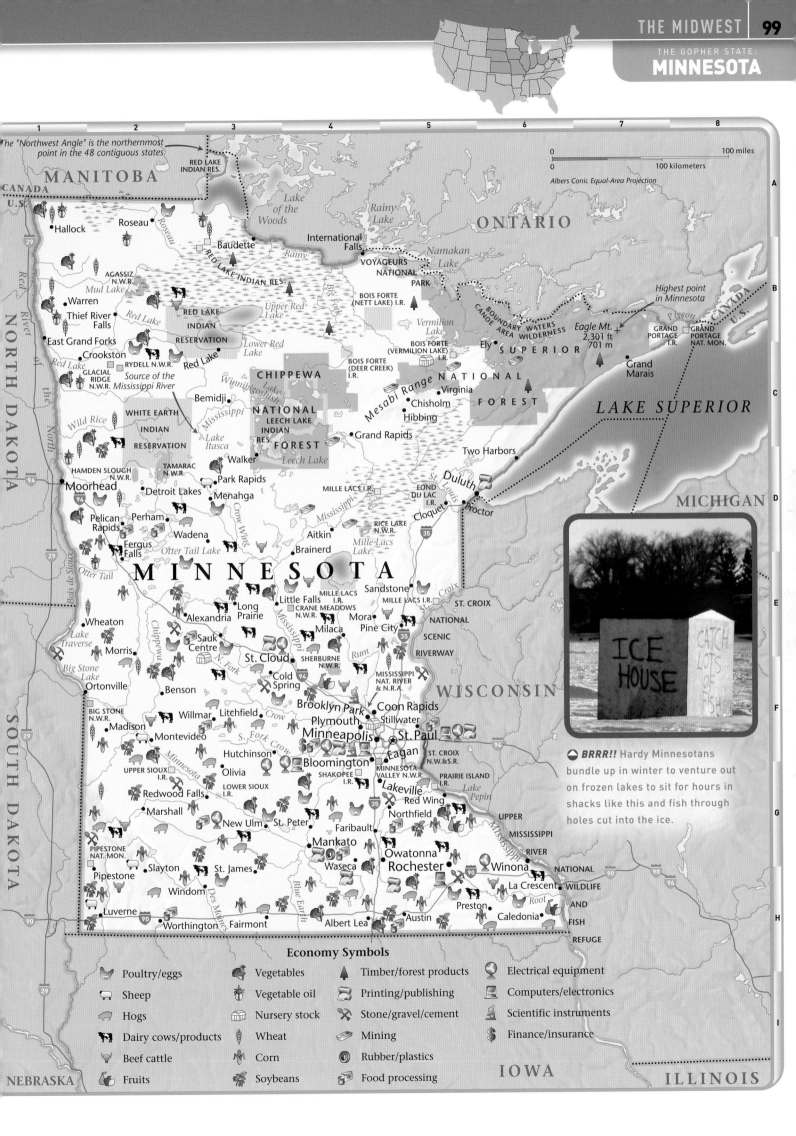

The "Northwest Angle" is the northernmost point in the 48 contiguous states

MANITOBA
CANADA
U.S.

RED LAKE
INDIAN RES.

Lake of the Woods

• Hallock
• Roseau
Roseau
• Baudette
RED LAKE INDIAN RES.

Rainy

International Falls

ONTARIO

Rainy Lake

Namakan Lake

VOYAGEURS NATIONAL PARK

BOUNDARY WATERS CANOE AREA WILDERNESS

Highest point in Minnesota

Eagle Mt. 2,301 ft 701 m

GRAND PORTAGE I.R.

GRAND PORTAGE NAT. MON.

CANADA
U.S.

Pigeon

AGASSIZ N.W.R.
Mud Lake

• Warren
• Thief River Falls
Red Lake
RED LAKE INDIAN RESERVATION

Upper Red Lake

Big Fork

BOIS FORTE (NETT LAKE) I.R.

Vermilion Lake

BOIS FORTE (VERMILION) I.R.

• Ely

SUPERIOR

• Grand Marais

• East Grand Forks
• Crookston
RYDELL N.W.R.
GLACIAL RIDGE N.W.R.
• Red Lake

Lower Red Lake

BOIS FORTE (DEER CREEK) I.R.

Mesabi Range

NATIONAL

FOREST

LAKE SUPERIOR

Source of the Mississippi River

CHIPPEWA

Lake Winnibigoshish

• Virginia
• Chisholm
• Hibbing

NORTH DAKOTA

Red River of the North

WHITE EARTH INDIAN RESERVATION

• Bemidji

Mississippi

Lake Itasca

NATIONAL

LEECH LAKE INDIAN RES.

FOREST

Leech Lake

• Grand Rapids

• Two Harbors

Wild Rice

• Walker

HAMDEN SLOUGH N.W.R.
TAMARAC N.W.R.

• Park Rapids

MILLE LACS I.R.

St. Louis

FOND DU LAC I.R.

• Duluth

• Moorhead
• Detroit Lakes
• Menahga

Mississippi

RICE LAKE N.W.R.

Cloquet • Proctor

MICHIGAN

• Pelican Rapids
• Perham
• Wadena
Crow Wing

• Aitkin

Mille Lacs Lake

I-35

• Pelican Rapids

• Fergus Falls
Otter Tail Lake
• Brainerd

• Wheaton

Otter Tail

MINNESOTA

• Sandstone

Croix

ST. CROIX

Bois de Sioux

• Long Prairie
• Alexandria
CRANE MEADOWS N.W.R.

• Milaca

• Mora

MILLE LACS I.R.

• Pine City

NATIONAL

SCENIC

RIVERWAY

Lake Traverse

• Morris

Chippewa

• Sauk Centre

N. Fork

• St. Cloud

SHERBURNE N.W.R.

Rum

I-94

Big Stone Lake

• Ortonville

• Benson

• Cold Spring

MISSISSIPPI NAT. RIVER & N.R.A.

WISCONSIN

BIG STONE N.W.R.

• Willmar
• Litchfield
Crow

• Brooklyn Park
Coon Rapids •

• Madison

• Plymouth
Stillwater •

ICE HOUSE
CATCH LOTS OF FISH

• Montevideo

S. Fork Crow

Minneapolis
• **St. Paul**

UPPER SIOUX I.R.

Minnesota

• Hutchinson

• Eagan

ST. CROIX N.W.&S.R.

Minnesota

• Olivia

• Bloomington

SHAKOPEE

MINNESOTA VALLEY N.W.R.

PRAIRIE ISLAND I.R.

Lake Pepin

LOWER SIOUX I.R.

• Redwood Falls

• Lakeville

• Red Wing

UPPER

• Marshall

• New Ulm
• St. Peter

I-35

• Northfield

MISSISSIPPI

SOUTH DAKOTA

• Faribault

RIVER

PIPESTONE NAT. MON.

• Mankato

Blue Earth

• Slayton
• St. James

• Waseca

• Owatonna
Rochester

• Winona

NATIONAL

• Pipestone

• Windom

Des Moines

• La Crescent

WILDLIFE

AND

• Luverne

I-90

• Worthington • Fairmont

• Albert Lea

• Austin

• Preston

• Caledonia

Root

FISH

REFUGE

I-90 I-94

NEBRASKA

IOWA

ILLINOIS

▲ BRRR!! Hardy Minnesotans bundle up in winter to venture out on frozen lakes to sit for hours in shacks like this and fish through holes cut into the ice.

Economy Symbols

Poultry/eggs
Sheep
Hogs
Dairy cows/products
Beef cattle
Fruits

Vegetables
Vegetable oil
Nursery stock
Wheat
Corn
Soybeans

Timber/forest products
Printing/publishing
Stone/gravel/cement
Mining
Rubber/plastics
Food processing

Electrical equipment
Computers/electronics
Scientific instruments
Finance/insurance

0   100 miles
0   100 kilometers
Albers Conic Equal-Area Projection

THE SHOW-ME STATE:
MISSOURI

THE BASICS

Statehood
August 10, 1821; 24th state

Total area (land and water)
69,707 sq mi (180,540 sq km)

Land area
68,742 sq mi (178,040 sq km)

Population
6,083,672

Capital
Jefferson City
Population 43,132 (2014)

Largest city
Kansas City
Population 151,306

Racial/ethnic groups
83.3% white; 11.8% African American; 2.0% Asian; 0.6% Native American; 4.1% Hispanic (any race)

Foreign born
3.9%

Urban population
70.4% (2010)

Population density
88.5 per sq mi (34.2 per sq km)

GEO WHIZ

Camp Wood, near St. Louis, was the starting point for Lewis and Clark's Corps of Discovery, commissioned by President Thomas Jefferson to seek a water route to the Pacific. Along the way their encounters included hundreds of new species of plants and animals, nearly 50 Indian tribes, and the Rocky Mountains.

In Ash Grove, near Springfield, Father Moses Berry has turned his family history into a museum for slavery education. His was one of the few families that didn't flee the area after three falsely accused black men were lynched in 1906. The museum is the only one of its kind in the Ozark region.

Missouri

The Osage people were among the largest tribes in present-day Missouri when the French began establishing permanent settlements in the 1700s. The United States obtained the territory as part of the 1803 Louisiana Purchase, and Lewis and Clark began exploring the vast wilderness by paddling up the Missouri River from the St. Louis area. Missouri entered the Union as a slave state in 1821. Though it remained in the Union during the Civil War, sympathies were split between the North and South. For much of the 1800s the state was the staging ground for pioneers traveling to western frontiers on the Santa Fe and Oregon Trails. Today, Missouri leads the country in lead mining. Farmers raise cattle, hogs, poultry, corn, and soybeans. Cotton and rice are grown in the southeastern Bootheel region. Cross-state river-port rivals St. Louis and Kansas City are centers of transportation, manufacturing, and finance. Lakes, caves, scenic views, and Branson's country music shows bring many tourists to the Ozarks.

EASTERN BLUEBIRD
HAWTHORN

⬤ **TALL HATS.** Since its founding in 1865 in St. Joseph, the Stetson Company has been associated with Western hats worn by men and women around the world.

HISTORICAL MONUMENTS

630 feet (192 m)	570 feet (174 m)	555 feet (169 m)	352 feet (107 m)	351 feet (107 m)
Gateway Arch (MO)	San Jacinto Monument (TX)	Washington Monument (DC)	Perry's Victory and International Peace Memorial (OH)	Jefferson Davis Monument (KY)

The tallest of all monuments in the United States is Gateway Arch in St. Louis, which was the departure point for westward-bound pioneers during the 19th century.

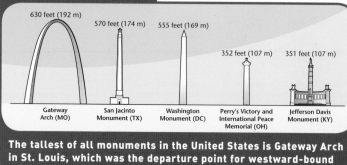

◗ **NATIONAL LANDMARK.** Named a National Historic Landmark in 1987, the steel and concrete Gateway Arch is the tallest arch in the world. Here it frames St. Louis and the Mississippi River.

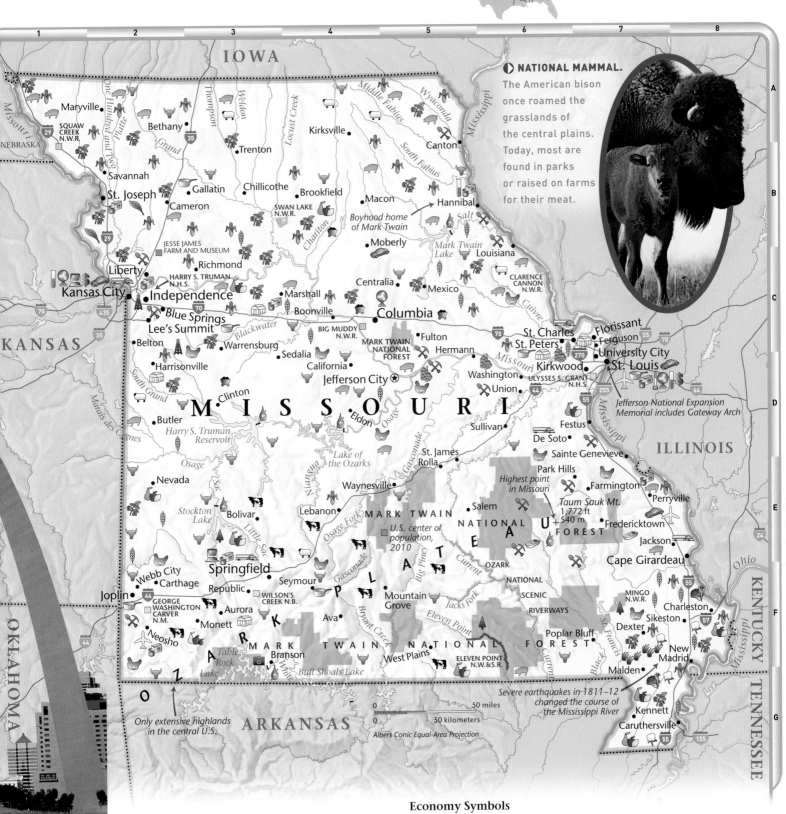

NATIONAL MAMMAL. The American bison once roamed the grasslands of the central plains. Today, most are found in parks or raised on farms for their meat.

IOWA

NEBRASKA

KANSAS

Maryville
SQUAW CREEK N.W.R.
Bethany
Trenton
Kirksville
Canton
Savannah
St. Joseph
Gallatin
Chillicothe
Brookfield
Macon
Hannibal
Cameron
JESSE JAMES FARM AND MUSEUM
Richmond
Boyhood home of Mark Twain
Moberly
Mark Twain Lake
Louisiana
Liberty
HARRY S. TRUMAN N.H.S.
Kansas City
Independence
Marshall
Centralia
Mexico
CLARENCE CANNON N.W.R.
Blue Springs
Lee's Summit
Boonville
Columbia
Belton
Warrensburg
BIG MUDDY N.W.R.
Fulton
St. Charles
Florissant
Ferguson
St. Peters
University City
Harrisonville
Sedalia
MARK TWAIN NATIONAL FOREST
Hermann
Washington
Kirkwood
St. Louis
California
Jefferson City
Union
ULYSSES S. GRANT N.H.S.

MISSOURI

Clinton
Eldon
Sullivan
Festus
De Soto
Jefferson National Expansion Memorial includes Gateway Arch
Butler
Harry S. Truman Reservoir
Lake of the Ozarks
Osage
St. James
Rolla
Sainte Genevieve
ILLINOIS
Nevada
Waynesville
Park Hills
Highest point in Missouri
Farmington
Perryville
Stockton Lake
Bolivar
Lebanon
MARK TWAIN
Salem
NATIONAL
FOREST
Taum Sauk Mt. 1,772 ft +540 m
Fredericktown
Jackson
U.S. center of population, 2010
Cape Girardeau
Webb City
Carthage
Springfield
Seymour
OZARK
NATIONAL
MINGO N.W.R.
Joplin
GEORGE WASHINGTON CARVER N.M.
Republic
WILSON'S CREEK N.B.
Mountain Grove
SCENIC
Charleston
Sikeston
Aurora
Ava
RIVERWAYS
Dexter
Monett
Neosho
MARK TWAIN NATIONAL FOREST
West Plains
Poplar Bluff
New Madrid
Table Rock Lake
Branson
ELEVEN POINT N.W.&S.R.
Malden
Bull Shoals Lake
Severe earthquakes in 1811–12 changed the course of the Mississippi River
Kennett
Only extensive highlands in the central U.S.
Caruthersville

ARKANSAS

OKLAHOMA

KENTUCKY

TENNESSEE

0   50 miles
0   50 kilometers
Albers Conic Equal-Area Projection

Economy Symbols

Poultry/eggs	Wheat	Mining	Food processing
Sheep	Corn	Coal	Electrical equipment
Hogs	Soybeans	Oil/gas	Computers/electronics
Dairy cows/products	Cotton	Hydro-electricity	Aircraft/parts
Beef cattle	Tobacco	Metal products	Aerospace
Fruits	Vineyards	Railroad equipment	Tourism
Vegetables	Timber/forest products	Motor vehicles/parts	Finance/insurance
Nursery stock	Stone/gravel/cement	Chemistry	

THE BASICS

Statehood
March 1, 1867; 37th state

Total area (land and water)
77,348 sq mi (200,330 sq km)

Land area
76,824 sq mi
(198,974 sq km)

Population
1,896,190

Capital
Lincoln
Population 277,348

Largest city
Omaha
Population 443,885

Racial/ethnic groups
89.1% white; 5.0% African
American; 2.3% Asian; 1.4%
Native American; 10.4%
Hispanic (any race)

Foreign born
6.3%

Urban population
73.1% (2010)

Population density
24.7 per sq mi (9.5 per sq km)

GEO WHIZ

Many of Nebraska's early
settlers were called sodbusters
because they cut chunks of the
grassy prairie (sod) to build
their houses. These building
blocks became known as
"Nebraska marble."

Nebraska's state fossil is the
mammoth. The state estimates
that as many as 10 of these prehistoric elephants are buried
beneath an average square mile
of territory.

Boys Town, a village-style
community founded near
Omaha in 1917 as a home
for troubled boys, has provided
a haven for girls, too, since 1979.

Nebraska

For thousands of westbound pioneers on the Oregon and California Trails, Scotts Bluff and Chimney Rock were unforgettable landmarks, towering above the North Platte River. Once reserved for Indians by the government, Nebraska was opened for white settlement in 1854. Following statehood in 1867, ranchers clashed with farmers in an unsuccessful bid to preserve open rangelands. Before white settlers arrived, Indians hunted bison and grew corn, pumpkins, beans, and squash. Today, farms and ranches cover nearly all of the state. Ranchers graze beef cattle on the grass-covered Sand Hills, and farmers grow corn, soybeans, and wheat elsewhere. The vast underground Ogallala Aquifer feeds center-pivot irrigation systems needed to water crops in areas that do not receive enough rain. Processing the state's farm products, especially meatpacking, is a big part of the economy. Omaha, which sits along the Missouri River, is a center of finance, insurance, and agribusiness. Lincoln, the state capital, has the only unicameral, or one-house, legislature in the country.

TAKING FLIGHT.
Migratory Sandhill
cranes pass through
in late winter, stop-
ping in the Platte
River Valley to feed
and rest.

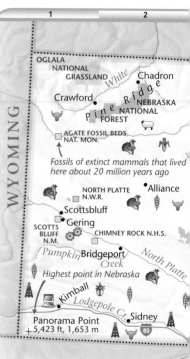

GOLDENROD
WESTERN MEADOWLARK

RIDER DOWN. The Big Rodeo is an annual event in tiny Burwell (population 1,213) in Nebraska's Sand Hills. The town, sometimes called "the place where the Wild West meets the 21st century," has hosted the rodeo for more than 80 years.

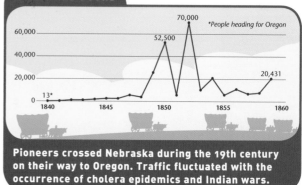

WESTWARD BOUND

*People heading for Oregon

Pioneers crossed Nebraska during the 19th century on their way to Oregon. Traffic fluctuated with the occurrence of cholera epidemics and Indian wars.

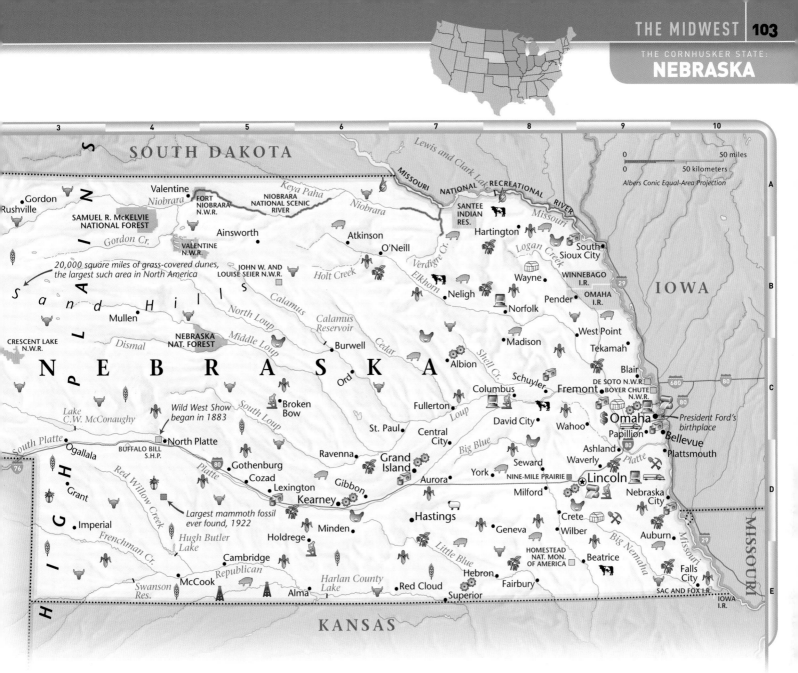

SOUTH DAKOTA

Lewis and Clark Lake

MISSOURI NATIONAL RECREATIONAL RIVER

Missouri

IOWA

Gordon
Rushville
Valentine
Niobrara
FORT NIOBRARA N.W.R.
Keya Paha
NIOBRARA NATIONAL SCENIC RIVER
Niobrara
SANTEE INDIAN RES.
Hartington

SAMUEL R. McKELVIE NATIONAL FOREST
Gordon Cr.
Ainsworth
Atkinson
O'Neill
Holt Creek
Logan Creek
South Sioux City

20,000 square miles of grass-covered dunes, the largest such area in North America
VALENTINE N.W.R.
JOHN W. AND LOUISE SEIER N.W.R.
Verdigre Cr.
Wayne
WINNEBAGO I.R.
Pender
OMAHA I.R.

Mullen
Sand Hills
North Loup
Calamus
Calamus Reservoir
Elkhorn
Neligh
Norfolk
West Point
Tekamah

CRESCENT LAKE N.W.R.
Dismal
NEBRASKA NAT. FOREST
Middle Loup
Burwell
Cedar
Madison
Blair

N E B R A S K A
Ord
Albion
Shell Cr.
Schuyler
Columbus
Fremont
DE SOTO N.W.R.
BOYER CHUTE N.W.R.

Lake C.W. McConaughy
Wild West Show began in 1883
Broken Bow
South Loup
Loup
Fullerton
David City
Omaha
President Ford's birthplace

South Platte
Ogallala
North Platte
BUFFALO BILL S.H.P.
Platte
Gothenburg
Cozad
St. Paul
Central City
Big Blue
Wahoo
Papillion
Bellevue
Plattsmouth

Grant
Red Willow Creek
Lexington
Kearney
Gibbon
Grand Island
Aurora
York
Seward
NINE-MILE PRAIRIE
Waverly
Ashland
Platte
Lincoln
Nebraska City

Imperial
Frenchman Cr.
Largest mammoth fossil ever found, 1922
Minden
Holdrege
Hastings
Geneva
Milford
Crete
Wilber
Auburn

HIGH PLAINS
Hugh Butler Lake
Cambridge
Republican
Swanson Res.
McCook
Alma
Harlan County Lake
Red Cloud
Superior
Fairbury
Hebron
HOMESTEAD NAT. MON. OF AMERICA
Beatrice
Big Nemaha
Falls City
SAC AND FOX I.R.
IOWA I.R.

KANSAS

MISSOURI

Ravenna

0   50 miles
0   50 kilometers
Albers Conic Equal-Area Projection

Economy Symbols

Poultry/eggs		Printing/publishing	
Sheep		Stone/gravel/cement	
Hogs		Oil/gas	
Dairy cows/products		Hydro-electricity	
Beef cattle		Machinery	
Vegetables		Railroad equipment	
Vegetable oil		Food processing	
Nursery stock		Computers/electronics	
Wheat		Scientific instruments	
Corn		Finance/insurance	
Soybeans			

THE WAY WEST. Longhorn cattle and a bison stand knee-deep in grass below Chimney Rock, which rises more than 300 feet (91 m) above western Nebraska's rolling landscape. An important landmark on the Oregon Trail for 19th-century westbound pioneers and now a national historic site, the formation is being worn away by forces of erosion.

THE BASICS

Statehood
November 2, 1889; 39th state

Total area (land and water)
70,698 sq mi (183,108 sq km)

Land area
69,001 sq mi
(178,711 sq km)

Population
756,927

Capital
Bismarck
Population 71,167

Largest city
Fargo
Population 118,523

Racial/ethnic groups
88.6% white; 2.4% African
American; 1.4% Asian; 5.5%
Native American; 3.5%
Hispanic (any race)

Foreign born
2.7%

Urban population
59.9% (2010)

Population density
11.0 per sq mi (4.2 per sq km)

GEO WHIZ

The state's largest reservoir is
named in honor of Sacagawea
(also known as Sakakawea), the
teenage Indian guide who joined
the Lewis and Clark expedition in
the spring of 1805.

Devils Lake has earned the title
Perch Capital of the World for
the large number of walleye—a
kind of perch—caught there.

North Dakota's landscape boasts
some of the world's largest
outdoor animal sculptures,
including Salem Sue, the
world's largest Holstein cow;
a giant grasshopper; and a
snowmobiling turtle.

North Dakota

During the winter of 1804–05 Lewis and Clark camped
at a Mandan village where they met Sacagawea, the young
Shoshone woman who helped guide them
through the Rockies and on to the Pacific Ocean.
White settlement of the vast grassy plains
coincided with the growth of railroads,
and statehood was gained in 1889.
The geographic center of North America
is southwest of Rugby. The state's interior
location helps give it a huge annual
temperature range. A record low temperature of -60°F (-51°C) and record high of
121°F (49°C) were recorded in 1936. Fargo,
located on the northward flowing Red River
of the North, is the state's largest city. Garrison Dam, on the
Missouri River, generates electricity and provides water for
irrigation. The state is a major producer of flaxseed, canola,
sunflowers, and barley, but it is wheat, cattle, and soybeans
that provide the greatest income. Oil and lignite coal are
important in the western part of the state.

🔵 **VIGILANT LOOKOUT.**
A black-tailed prairie
dog watches for signs
of danger. This member
of the squirrel family
lives in burrows in the
Great Plains.

WILD PRAIRIE ROSE
WESTERN
MEADOWLARK

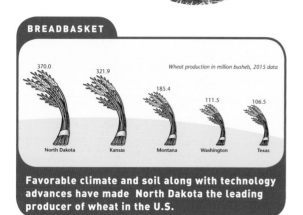

BREADBASKET

Wheat production in million bushels, 2015 data

370.0	321.9	185.4	111.5	106.5
North Dakota	Kansas	Montana	Washington	Texas

Favorable climate and soil along with technology
advances have made North Dakota the leading
producer of wheat in the U.S.

◖ **RUNNING FREE.** A wild horse runs through a landscape
dramatically eroded by the Little Missouri River in Theodore
Roosevelt National Park in North Dakota's Badlands region.

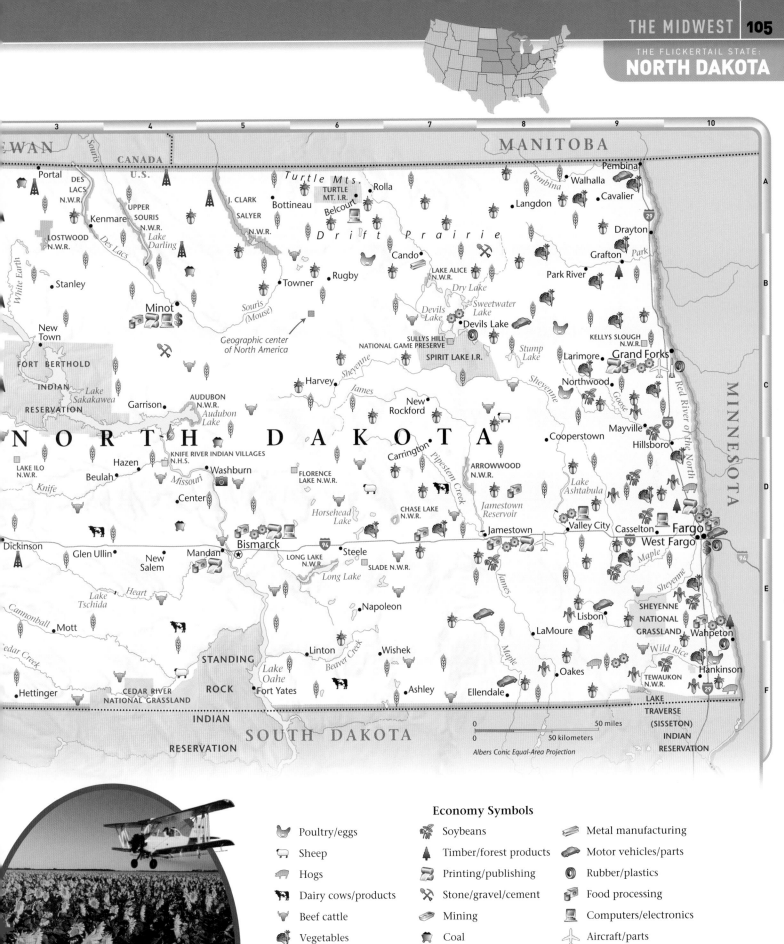

MANITOBA

CANADA
U.S.

SASKATCHEWAN

NORTH DAKOTA

MINNESOTA

SOUTH DAKOTA

Portal
DES LACS N.W.R.
Kenmare
UPPER SOURIS N.W.R.
LOSTWOOD N.W.R.
Des Lacs
Stanley
New Town
FORT BERTHOLD INDIAN RESERVATION
Lake Sakakawea
LAKE ILO N.W.R.
Hazen
Beulah
Knife
Center
Dickinson
Glen Ullin
New Salem
Mandan
Lake Tschida
Heart
Cannonball
Mott
Hettinger
Cedar Creek
CEDAR RIVER NATIONAL GRASSLAND
STANDING ROCK INDIAN RESERVATION
White Earth
Minot
J. CLARK SALYER N.W.R.
Turtle Mts.
Bottineau
TURTLE MT. I.R.
Belcourt
Rolla
Lake Darling
Souris (Mouse)
Towner
Rugby
Cando
Drift Prairie
Geographic center of North America
Harvey
Sheyenne
James
Garrison
AUDUBON N.W.R.
Audubon Lake
KNIFE RIVER INDIAN VILLAGES N.H.S.
Washburn
FLORENCE LAKE N.W.R.
Horsehead Lake
Bismarck
LONG LAKE N.W.R.
Long Lake
Steele
SLADE N.W.R.
Napoleon
Linton
Lake Oahe
Fort Yates
Wishek
Ashley
New Rockford
Carrington
CHASE LAKE N.W.R.
Pipestem Creek
ARROWWOOD N.W.R.
Jamestown Reservoir
Jamestown
LAKE ALICE N.W.R.
Devils Lake
Dry Lake
Devils Lake
SULLYS HILL NATIONAL GAME PRESERVE
SPIRIT LAKE I.R.
Sweetwater Lake
Stump Lake
Cooperstown
Valley City
Lake Ashtabula
LaMoure
Oakes
Ellendale
Pembina
Walhalla
Cavalier
Langdon
Drayton
Grafton
Park River
KELLYS SLOUGH N.W.R.
Larimore
Grand Forks
Northwood
Mayville
Hillsboro
Casselton
Fargo
West Fargo
Maple
Lisbon
SHEYENNE NATIONAL GRASSLAND
Wahpeton
Wild Rice
TEWAUKON N.W.R.
Hankinson
LAKE TRAVERSE (SISSETON) INDIAN RESERVATION
Pembina
Red River of the North
Goose
Sheyenne
James
Maple
Sheyenne

0   50 miles
0   50 kilometers
Albers Conic Equal-Area Projection

Economy Symbols

- Poultry/eggs
- Sheep
- Hogs
- Dairy cows/products
- Beef cattle
- Vegetables
- Vegetable oil
- Wheat
- Corn
- Soybeans
- Timber/forest products
- Printing/publishing
- Stone/gravel/cement
- Mining
- Coal
- Oil/gas
- Hydro-electricity
- Machinery
- Metal manufacturing
- Motor vehicles/parts
- Rubber/plastics
- Food processing
- Computers/electronics
- Aircraft/parts
- Aerospace
- Tourism
- Finance/insurance

GOLDEN HARVEST. A crop duster, spraying for insects, flies low over a field of sunflowers in the Red River Valley in eastern North Dakota. In the fertile soil of the valley, farmers grow sunflowers mainly for the oil in their seeds.

THE BUCKEYE STATE:
OHIO

Ohio

INLAND URBAN CENTER. Cincinnati's skyline sparkles in the red glow of twilight. Founded in 1788, the modern city boasts education and medical centers as well as headquarters for companies such as Procter & Gamble.

Ohio and the rest of the Northwest Territory became part of the United States after the Revolutionary War. The movement of white settlers into the region led to conflicts with the native inhabitants until 1794, when Indian resistance was defeated at Fallen Timbers. Ohio entered the Union nine years later. Lake Erie in the north and the Ohio River in the south, along with canals and railroads, provided transportation links that spurred early immigration and commerce. The state became an industrial giant, producing steel, machinery, rubber, and glass. From 1869 to 1923, seven of twelve U.S. presidents were Ohioans. With 18 electoral votes, the seventh highest number in the country, Ohio is still a big player in presidential elections. Education, government, and finance employ many people in Columbus, the capital and largest city. Manufacturing in Cleveland, Toledo, Cincinnati, and other cities remains a vital segment of the state's economy. Farmers on Ohio's western plains, created by glaciers, grow soybeans and corn, the two largest cash crops.

THE BASICS

Statehood
March 1, 1803; 17th state

Total area (land and water)
44,826 sq mi (116,098 sq km)

Land area
40,861 sq mi (105,829 sq km)

Population
11,613,423

Capital
Columbus
Population 850,106

Largest city
Columbus
Population 850,106

Racial/ethnic groups
82.7% white; 12.7% African American; 2.1% Asian; 0.3% Native American; 3.6% Hispanic (any race)

Foreign born
4.0%

Urban population
77.9% (2010)

Population density
284.2 per sq mi (109.7 per sq km)

GEO WHIZ

Cedar Point Amusement Park, in Sandusky, is known as the Roller Coaster Capital of the World. Top Thrill Dragster, the tallest and fastest roller coaster on Earth when it was built in 2003, has a top speed of 120 miles an hour (193 km/h)!

Ohio's state tree is the buckeye, so-called because the nut it produces resembles the eye of a male deer, or buck.

The state insect is the ladybird beetle, more commonly known as the ladybug. Using these beetles to control plant-eating pests greatly reduces the need for chemical pesticides.

SCARLET CARNATION
CARDINAL

SOUND OF MUSIC. Colorful guitars mark the entrance to the Rock and Roll Hall of Fame in downtown Cleveland. The museum, through its Rockin' the Schools program, attracts thousands of students annually to experience the sounds of rock and roll music and learn about its history.

TRADITIONAL TRAVEL. The horse and buggy is a familiar sight in central Ohio, location of the world's largest Amish population.

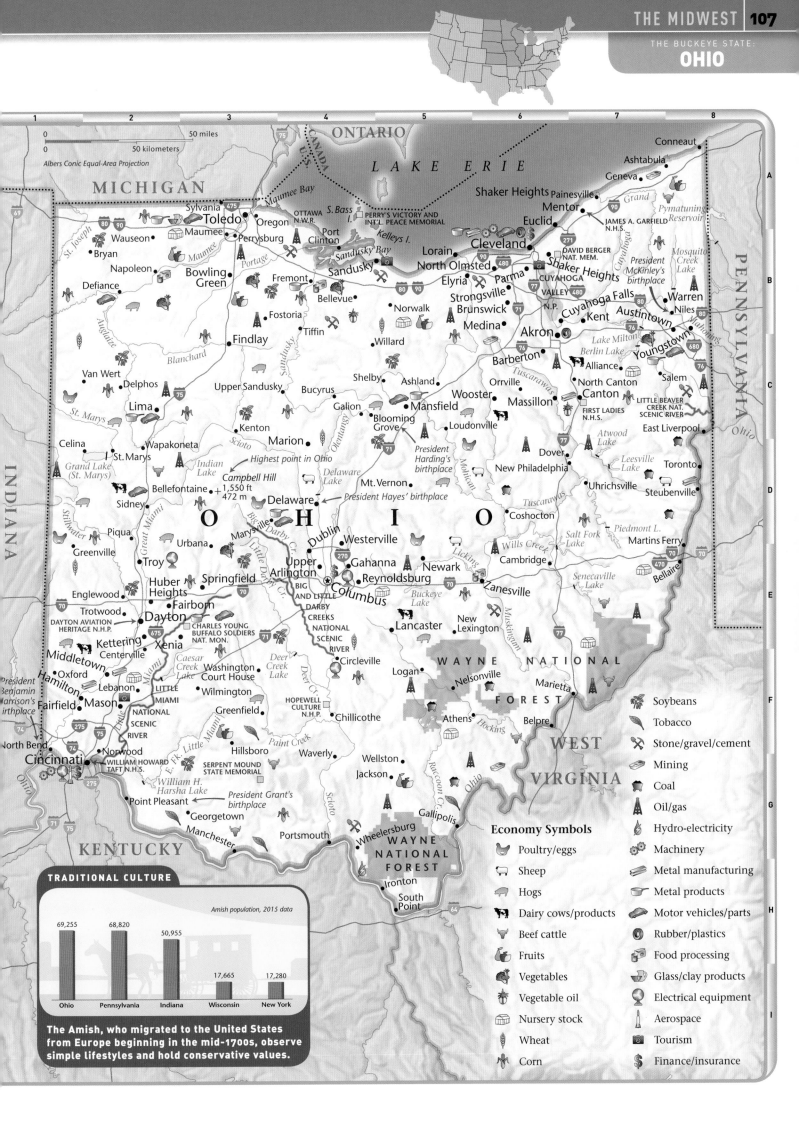

THE BUCKEYE STATE:
OHIO

TRADITIONAL CULTURE

Amish population, 2015 data

Ohio	Pennsylvania	Indiana	Wisconsin	New York
69,255	68,820	50,955	17,665	17,280

The Amish, who migrated to the United States from Europe beginning in the mid-1700s, observe simple lifestyles and hold conservative values.

Economy Symbols

- Poultry/eggs
- Sheep
- Hogs
- Dairy cows/products
- Beef cattle
- Fruits
- Vegetables
- Vegetable oil
- Nursery stock
- Wheat
- Corn
- Soybeans
- Tobacco
- Stone/gravel/cement
- Mining
- Coal
- Oil/gas
- Hydro-electricity
- Machinery
- Metal manufacturing
- Metal products
- Motor vehicles/parts
- Rubber/plastics
- Food processing
- Glass/clay products
- Electrical equipment
- Aerospace
- Tourism
- Finance/insurance

THE BASICS

Statehood
November 2, 1889; 40th state

Total area (land and water)
77,116 sq mi (199,729 sq km)

Land area
75,811 sq mi (196,350 sq km)

Population
858,469

Capital
Pierre
Population 14,054 (2014)

Largest city
Sioux Falls
Population 171,544

Racial/ethnic groups
85.5% white; 1.8% African American; 1.4% Asian; 8.9% Native American; 3.6% Hispanic (any race)

Foreign born
2.8%

Urban population
56.7% (2010)

Population density
11.3 per sq mi (4.4 per sq km)

GEO WHIZ

Thanks to captive breeding programs, the world's largest population of wild black-footed ferrets is thriving in a black-tailed prairie dog colony in south-central South Dakota.

Sometimes known as the Shrine of Democracy, Mount Rushmore National Monument features the faces of four presidents: Washington, Jefferson, Lincoln, and Theodore Roosevelt.

Eight *Tyrannosaurus rex* skeletons, including Sue, Stan, Bucky, and WREX, were all dug up in South Dakota.

PASQUEFLOWER

RING-NECKED PHEASANT

South Dakota

After the discovery of Black Hills gold in 1874, prospectors poured in and established lawless mining towns such as Deadwood. Indians fought this invasion but were defeated, and statehood came in 1889. Today, South Dakota has several reservations, and nearly 9 percent of the state's people are Native Americans. The Missouri River flows through the center of the state, creating two distinct regions: To the east, farmers grow corn and soybeans on the fertile, rolling prairie; to the west, where it is too dry for most crops, farmers grow wheat and graze cattle and sheep on the vast plains. In the southwest the Black Hills, named for the dark coniferous trees blanketing their slopes, are still a rich source of gold. Millions of tourists visit the area to see Mount Rushmore and, nearby, a giant sculpture of Lakota leader Crazy Horse, which has been in the works since 1948. Nearby, the fossil-rich Badlands, a region of eroded buttes and pinnacles, dominate the landscape.

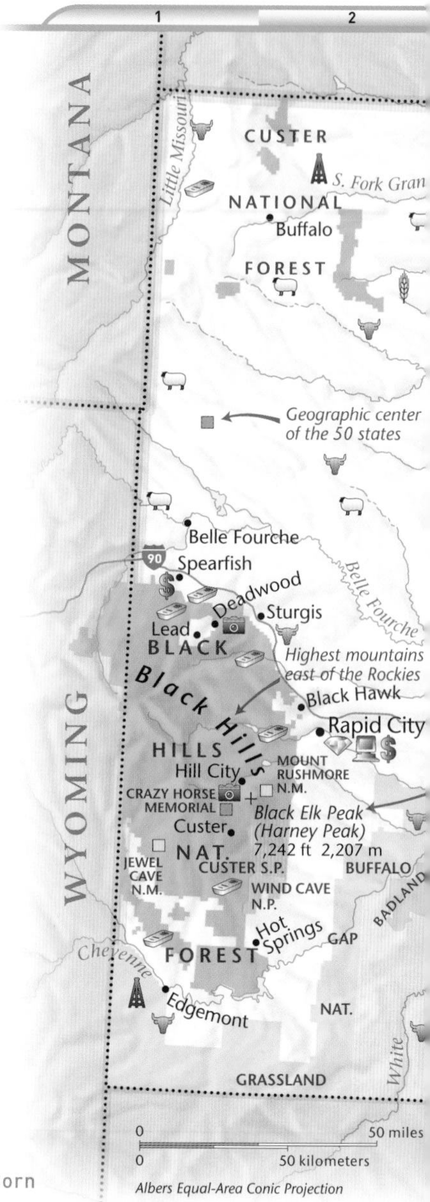

HONORING AGRICULTURE. The face of the Corn Palace in Mitchell is renewed each year using thousands of bushels of grain to create pictures depicting the role of agriculture in the state's history.

OIL FROM SEEDS

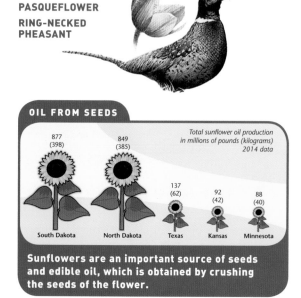

Total sunflower oil production in millions of pounds (kilograms) 2014 data

South Dakota 877 (398)
North Dakota 849 (385)
Texas 137 (62)
Kansas 92 (42)
Minnesota 88 (40)

Sunflowers are an important source of seeds and edible oil, which is obtained by crushing the seeds of the flower.

[Map of South Dakota — Black Hills region]

MONTANA

CUSTER
S. Fork Gran
NATIONAL
Buffalo
FOREST

Geographic center of the 50 states

Belle Fourche
Spearfish
Deadwood
Sturgis
Lead
BLACK
HILLS
Black Hawk
Highest mountains east of the Rockies
Rapid City
Hill City
MOUNT RUSHMORE N.M.
CRAZY HORSE MEMORIAL
Black Elk Peak (Harney Peak) 7,242 ft 2,207 m
Custer
JEWEL CAVE N.M.
NAT.
CUSTER S.P.
WIND CAVE N.P.
BUFFALO
BADLAND
Hot Springs
GAP
FOREST
Cheyenne
Edgemont
NAT.
GRASSLAND
White

WYOMING

0   50 miles
0   50 kilometers

Albers Equal-Area Conic Projection

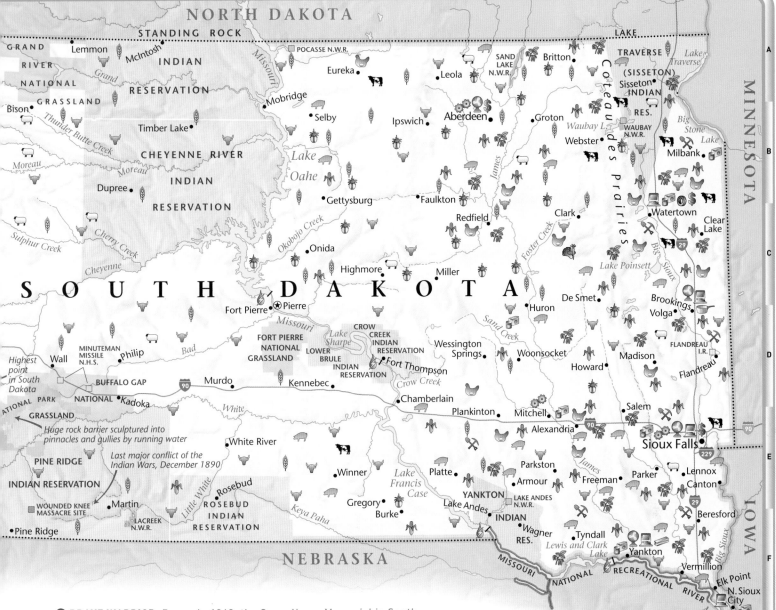

NORTH DAKOTA

MINNESOTA

STANDING ROCK

GRAND
RIVER
NATIONAL
GRASSLAND

Lemmon
McIntosh

INDIAN

RESERVATION

Bison

Timber Lake

CHEYENNE RIVER

INDIAN

RESERVATION

Dupree

POCASSE N.W.R.

Eureka

Mobridge

Selby

Ipswich

SAND
LAKE
N.W.R.

Leola

Aberdeen

Britton

Groton

TRAVERSE
(SISSETON)

Sisseton
INDIAN
RES.

Lake
Traverse

Webster

Waubay L.

WAUBAY
N.W.R.

Big
Stone
Lake

Milbank

Lake
Oahe

Gettysburg

Faulkton

Redfield

Clark

Watertown

Clear
Lake

Onida

Highmore

Miller

Huron

De Smet

Lake Poinsett

Brookings

Volga

S O U T H

D A K O T A

Fort Pierre
Pierre

Missouri

Wessington
Springs

Woonsocket

Madison

Howard

FLANDREAU
I.R.

Flandreau

Bad

FORT PIERRE
NATIONAL
GRASSLAND

LOWER
BRULE
INDIAN
RESERVATION

CROW
CREEK
INDIAN
RESERVATION

Fort Thompson

Lake
Sharpe

Crow Creek

Highest
point
in South
Dakota

Wall

MINUTEMAN
MISSILE
N.H.S.

Philip

Murdo

Kennebec

Chamberlain

Plankinton

Mitchell

Salem

Sioux Falls

BUFFALO GAP

NATIONAL

Kadoka

GRASSLAND

*Huge rock barrier sculptured into
pinnacles and gullies by running water*

White

Alexandria

PINE RIDGE

INDIAN RESERVATION

White River

*Last major conflict of the
Indian Wars, December 1890*

WOUNDED KNEE
MASSACRE SITE

Martin

Pine Ridge

LACREEK
N.W.R.

ROSEBUD
INDIAN
RESERVATION

Rosebud

Winner

Lake
Francis
Case

Platte

Gregory

Burke

YANKTON

Lake Andes

LAKE ANDES
N.W.R.

INDIAN
RES.

Wagner

Parkston

Armour

Freeman

Tyndall

Parker

Lennox

Canton

Beresford

IOWA

Yankton

Vermillion

Elk Point

N. Sioux
City

NEBRASKA

MISSOURI

NATIONAL

RECREATIONAL

RIVER

Lewis and Clark
Lake

BRAVE WARRIOR. Begun in 1948, the Crazy Horse Memorial in South
Dakota's Black Hills honors the culture, tradition, and living heritage of
North American Indians. In the background, sculptors are re-creating the
statue of the Lakota leader and his horse in the mountainside.

Economy Symbols

Poultry/eggs		Hydro-electricity
Sheep		Machinery
Hogs		Metal manufacturing
Dairy cows/products		Metal products
Beef cattle		Rubber/plastics
Vegetable oil		Food processing
Wheat		Jewelry
Corn		Electrical equipment
Soybeans		Computers/electronics
Stone/gravel/cement		Tourism
Mining		Finance/insurance
Oil/gas		

WISCONSIN

WISCONSIN

1848

THE BASICS

Statehood
May 29, 1848; 30th state

Total area (land and water)
65,496 sq mi (169,635 sq km)

Land area
54,158 sq mi (140,268 sq km)

Population
5,771,337

Capital
Madison
Population 248,951

Largest city
Milwaukee
Population 600,155

Racial/ethnic groups
87.6% white; 6.6% African
American; 2.8% Asian; 1.1%
Native American; 6.6%
Hispanic (any race)

Foreign born
4.7%

Urban population
70.2% (2010)

Population density
106.6 per sq mi
(41.1 per sq km)

GEO WHIZ

The Indian Community School in
Milwaukee has courses in native
languages, history, and rituals,
all stressing seven core values:
bravery, love, truth, wisdom,
humility, loyalty, and respect.

Bogs left by retreating ice-age
glaciers provide excellent conditions for raising cranberries.
Wisconsin leads the country in
harvesting this fruit.

Wisconsin's nickname—
Badger State—comes
not from the animal but
from miners who dug
living spaces by burrow-
ing like badgers into the
hillsides during the 1820s.

Wisconsin

Frenchman Jean Nicolet was the first European to reach present-day Wisconsin when he stepped ashore from Green Bay in 1634. After decades of getting along, relations with the region's Indians soured as the number of settlers increased.

The Black Hawk War in 1832 ended the last major Indian resistance, and statehood came in 1848. Many Milwaukee residents are descendants of German immigrants who labored in the city's breweries and meatpacking plants. Even as the economic importance of health care and other services has increased, food processing and the manufacture of machinery and metal products remains significant for the state. More than one million dairy cows graze in America's Dairyland, as the state is often called. Wisconsin leads the country in cheese production and is the second largest producer of milk and butter. Other farmers grow crops ranging from corn and soybeans to potatoes and cranberries. Northern Wisconsin is sparsely populated but heavily forested and is the source of paper and paper products produced by the state.

WOOD VIOLET
ROBIN

⬤ **TASTY GRAZING.**
The largest concentra-
tion of Brown Swiss cows
in the United States is in
Wisconsin. The milk of
this breed is prized by
cheese manufacturers.

⬤ **CITY BY THE LAKE.** Milwaukee, on the shore of Lake Michigan, derives its name from the Algonquian word for "beautiful land." The city, known for brewing and manufacturing, also has a growing service sector.

◖ **RURAL ECONOMY.** The dairy industry is an important part of Wisconsin's rural economy, and dairy farmers control most of the state's farmland.

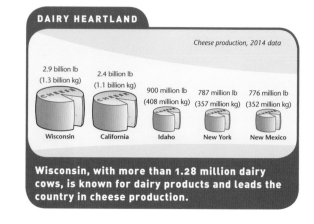

DAIRY HEARTLAND

Cheese production, 2014 data

2.9 billion lb
(1.3 billion kg)
Wisconsin

2.4 billion lb
(1.1 billion kg)
California

900 million lb
(408 million kg)
Idaho

787 million lb
(357 million kg)
New York

776 million lb
(352 million kg)
New Mexico

Wisconsin, with more than 1.28 million dairy cows, is known for dairy products and leads the country in cheese production.

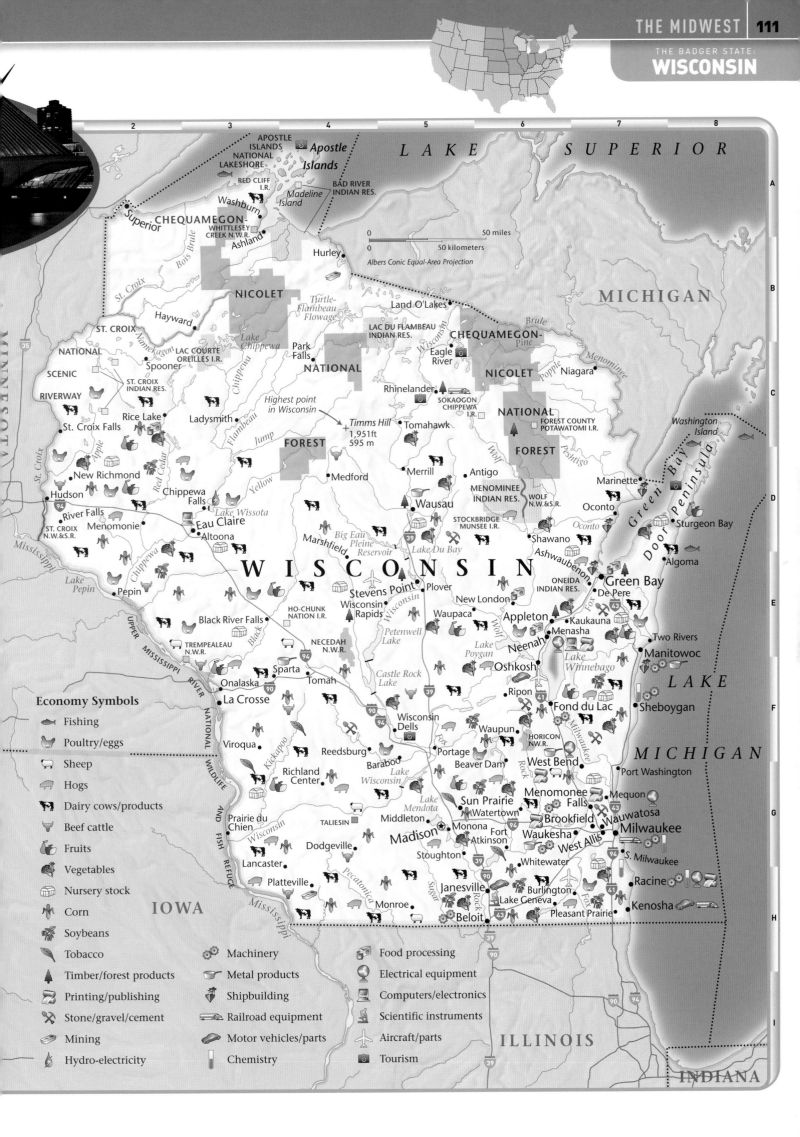

LAKE SUPERIOR

2   3   4   5   6   7   8

A

B

C

D

E

F

G

H

I

MICHIGAN

APOSTLE ISLANDS NATIONAL LAKESHORE
Apostle Islands
RED CLIFF I.R.
Madeline Island
BAD RIVER INDIAN RES.

0   50 miles
0   50 kilometers
Albers Conic Equal-Area Projection

Washburn
Superior
CHEQUAMEGON-WHITTLESEY CREEK N.W.R.
Ashland
Hurley
Bois Brule
St. Croix
NICOLET
Turtle-Flambeau Flowage
Land O'Lakes
Brule
Pine
CHEQUAMEGON-
Hayward
Annekagon
ST. CROIX
NATIONAL
Lake Chippewa
LAC DU FLAMBEAU INDIAN RES.
Eagle River
NICOLET
Popple
Menominee
Niagara

SCENIC
LAC COURTE OREILLES I.R.
Spooner
Park Falls
Wisconsin
Rhinelander
SOKAOGON CHIPPEWA I.R.
NATIONAL

RIVERWAY
ST. CROIX INDIAN RES.
NATIONAL
Chippewa
Flambeau
FOREST COUNTY POTAWATOMI I.R.
Washington Island

Rice Lake
Ladysmith
Highest point in Wisconsin
Timms Hill 1,951ft 595 m
Tomahawk
Wolf
FOREST
Peshtigo

St. Croix Falls
Jump
FOREST
Merrill
Antigo
Marinette

New Richmond
Apple
Chippewa Falls
Medford
Wausau
MENOMINEE INDIAN RES.
WOLF N.W.&S.R.
Oconto
Oconto
Sturgeon Bay

Hudson
Red Cedar
Yellow
Lake Wissota
Eau Claire
STOCKBRIDGE MUNSEE I.R.
Shawano
Ashwaubenon
Green Bay
Door Peninsula

River Falls
St. Croix
ST. CROIX N.W.&S.R.
Menomonie
Altoona
Marshfield
Big Eau Pleine Reservoir
Lake Du Bay
ONEIDA INDIAN RES.
Green Bay
De Pere
Algoma

Mississippi
Chippewa
WISCONSIN

Lake Pepin
Pepin
Stevens Point
Plover
New London
Appleton
Kaukauna
Fox
Two Rivers

Black River Falls
HO-CHUNK NATION I.R.
Wisconsin Rapids
Wisconsin
Waupaca
Menasha
Neenah
Lake Winnebago
Manitowoc

TREMPEALEAU N.W.R.
NECEDAH N.W.R.
Petenwell Lake
Wolf
Lake Poygan
Oshkosh
LAKE

Sparta
Black
Castle Rock Lake
Ripon
Fond du Lac
Sheboygan

Onalaska
Tomah
Wisconsin
Waupun
MICHIGAN

La Crosse
Wisconsin Dells
Fox
HORICON N.W.R.
West Bend
Port Washington

Economy Symbols

Viroqua
Reedsburg
Portage
Beaver Dam
Milwaukee
Mequon

Richland Center
Kickapoo
Baraboo
Lake Wisconsin
Sun Prairie
Watertown
Menomonee Falls
Brookfield
Wauwatosa

Prairie du Chien
TALIESIN
Lake Mendota
Middleton
Madison
Monona
Fort Atkinson
Rock
Waukesha
Milwaukee
West Allis
S. Milwaukee

Dodgeville
Stoughton
Whitewater
Racine

Lancaster
Wisconsin
Kenosha

Platteville
Pecatonica
Janesville
Burlington
Lake Geneva
Pleasant Prairie

IOWA
Monroe
Sugar
Rock
Fox

Beloit

Fishing

Poultry/eggs

Sheep

Hogs

Dairy cows/products

Beef cattle

Fruits

Vegetables

Nursery stock

Corn

Soybeans

Tobacco | Machinery | Food processing

Timber/forest products | Metal products | Electrical equipment

Printing/publishing | Shipbuilding | Computers/electronics

Stone/gravel/cement | Railroad equipment | Scientific instruments

Mining | Motor vehicles/parts | Aircraft/parts

Hydro-electricity | Chemistry | Tourism

MINNESOTA

UPPER MISSISSIPPI RIVER NATIONAL WILDLIFE AND FISH REFUGE

ILLINOIS

INDIANA

THE REGION

PHYSICAL

Total area (land and water) 574,075 sq mi (1,486,850 sq km)	**Lowest point** Sea level, shores of the Gulf of Mexico	**Vegetation** Mixed, broadleaf, and needleleaf forest; grassland; desert
Highest point Wheeler Peak, NM 13,161 ft (4,011 m)	**Longest rivers** Rio Grande, Arkansas, Colorado	**Climate** Humid subtropical, semiarid and arid, with warm to hot summers and cool winters
	Largest lakes Toledo Bend, Sam Rayburn, Eufaula (all reservoirs)	

POLITICAL

Total population 40,293,626	**Smallest state** Oklahoma: 69,899 sq mi (181,037 sq km)
States (4): Arizona, New Mexico, Oklahoma, Texas	**Most populous state** Texas: 27,469,114
	Least populous state New Mexico: 2,085,109
Largest state Texas: 268,596 sq mi (695,662 sq km)	**Largest city proper** Houston, 2,296,224

The Southwest

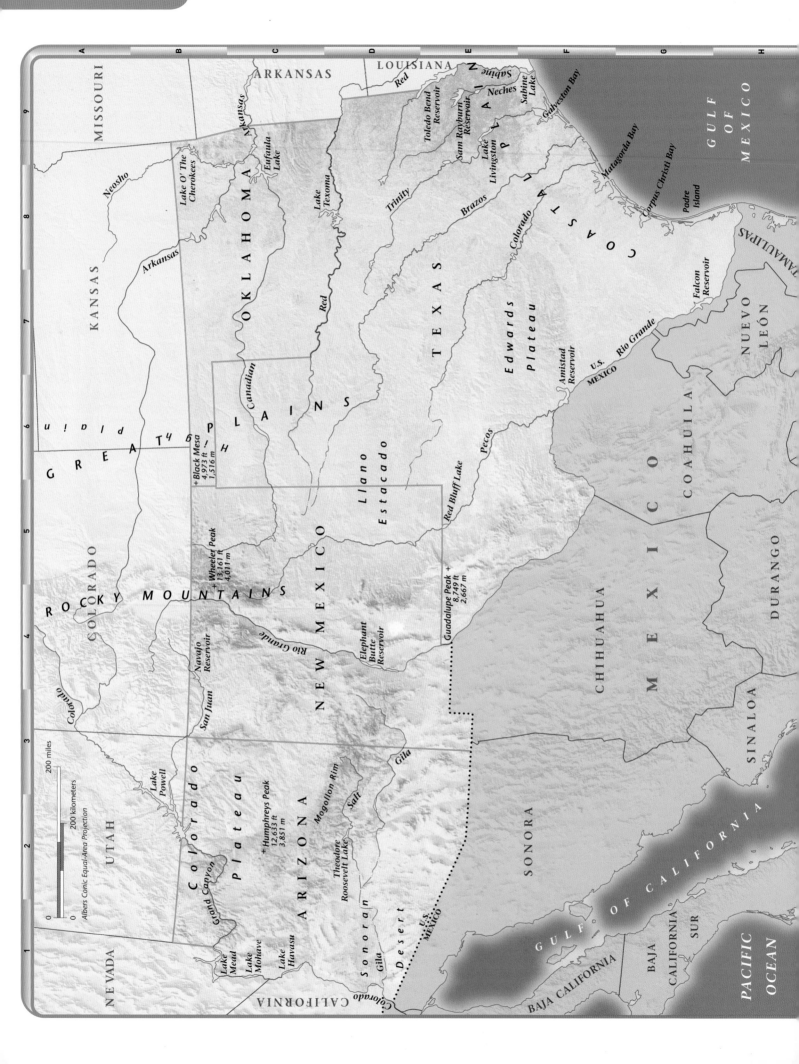

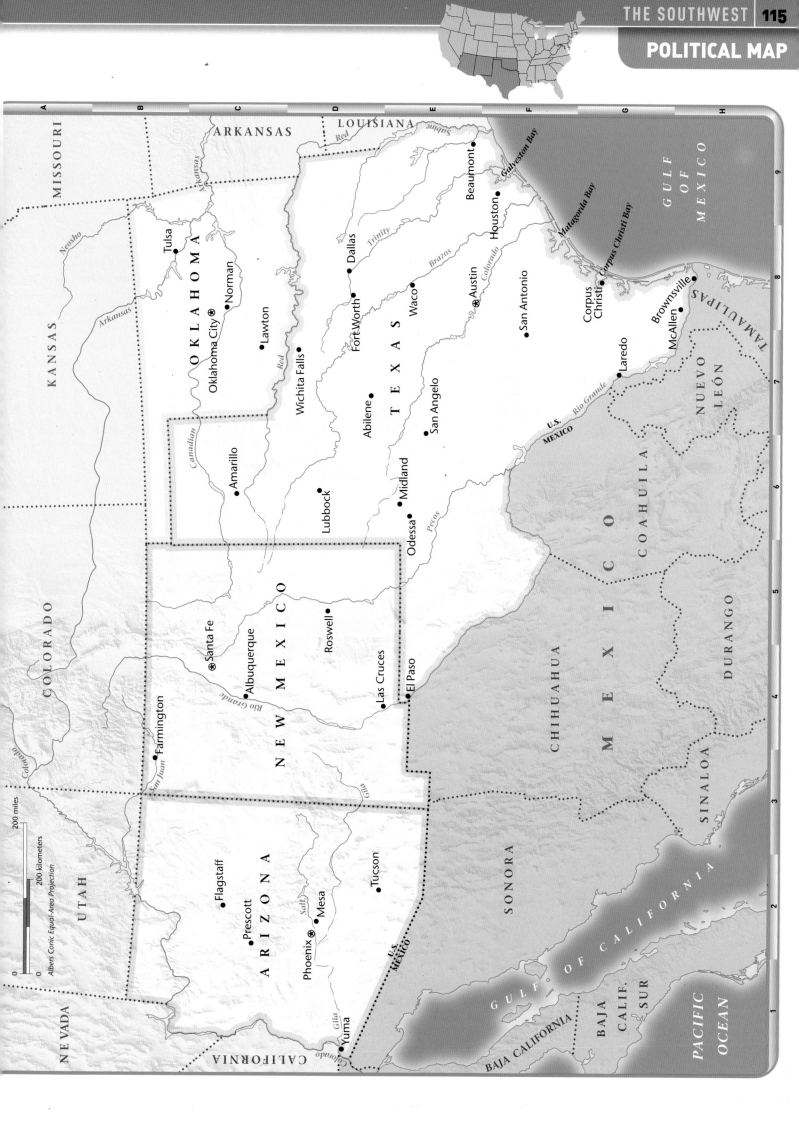

NEVADA

MISSOURI

ARKANSAS

LOUISIANA

Red

Sabine

GULF OF MEXICO

KANSAS

OKLAHOMA

Tulsa

Norman

Oklahoma City⊛

Lawton

Wichita Falls

Arkansas

Neosho

Canadian

Amarillo

Red

COLORADO

Santa Fe⊛

Albuquerque

Farmington

San Juan

Rio Grande

Colorado

NEW MEXICO

Roswell

Las Cruces

El Paso

Gila

UTAH

ARIZONA

Flagstaff

Prescott

Phoenix⊛

Mesa

Tucson

Salt

Gila

Yuma

Colorado

CALIFORNIA

Lubbock

Odessa

Midland

Pecos

Abilene

San Angelo

Waco

Fort Worth

Dallas

Trinity

Brazos

T E X A S

Austin⊛

San Antonio

Houston

Beaumont

Galveston Bay

Matagorda Bay

Corpus Christi

Corpus Christi Bay

Laredo

McAllen

Brownsville

Colorado

U.S.
MEXICO

Rio Grande

U.S.
MEXICO

BAJA CALIFORNIA

BAJA
CALIF.
SUR

GULF OF CALIFORNIA

SONORA

CHIHUAHUA

M E X I C O

COAHUILA

DURANGO

SINALOA

NUEVO
LEÓN

TAMAULIPAS

GULF OF MEXICO

PACIFIC OCEAN

200 miles

200 kilometers

Albers Conic Equal-Area Projection

A B C D E F G H

9 8 7 6 5 4 3 2 1

◗ SKY STONE. According to Indian legend, turquoise stole its color from the sky. This Zuni woman is wearing turquoise jewelry for a festival in Phoenix. Zuni Indians, whose reservation is in western New Mexico, have made jewelry for more than one thousand years.

The Southwest
FROM CANYONS TO GRASSLANDS

Legendary cities of gold lured Spanish conquistadors to the Southwest in the 1500s. Today, the promise of economic opportunities brings people from other states as well as immigrants, both legal and illegal, from countries south of the border. This part of the Sunbelt region boasts future-oriented cities while preserving Wild West tales and Native American traditions. Its climate ranges from humid subtropical along the Gulf Coast to arid in Arizona's deserts, and the landscape ranges from sprawling plains in the east to plateaus cut by dramatic canyons in the west. Water is a major concern in the Southwest, one of the country's fastest-growing regions.

⬣ HIGH SOCIETY. Dressed in an elegant ball gown, a young woman participates in the Society of Martha Washington Pageant in Laredo, Texas. This event presents daughters of wealthy and long-established Hispanic families to the local community.

◔ MODERN METROPOLIS. Towering skyscrapers tell a story of success and wealth. Although incorporated as a town in 1856, it was not until 1930 that Dallas, Texas, experienced explosive growth and prosperity due to the discovery of oil. Today, the city is a center of the U.S. oil industry and a leader in technology-based industries.

◖ DEADLY VIPER. Shaking the rattles on the tip of its tail, this diamondback rattlesnake—coiled for attack—warns intruders to stay away. Common throughout the arid Southwest, the snake eats mainly small rodents.

◖ STANDING TALL.
The saguaro cactus, which often rises more than 30 feet (9 m) above the shrubs of the Sonoran Desert, frequently has several branches and produces creamy-white flowers that bloom at night. The Sonoran, the hottest desert in North America, is located in the borderlands of southern Arizona and California and extends into northern Mexico.

WHERE THE PICTURES ARE

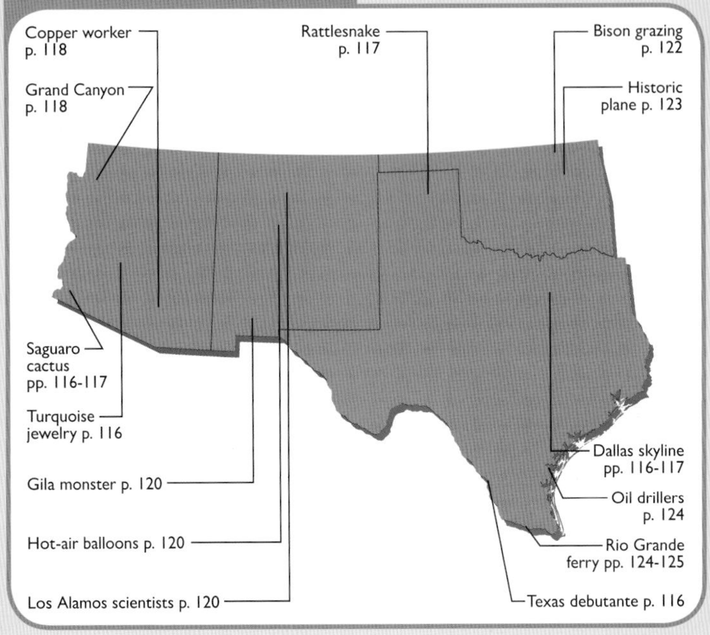

Copper worker p. 118
Grand Canyon p. 118
Rattlesnake p. 117
Bison grazing p. 122
Historic plane p. 123
Saguaro cactus pp. 116-117
Turquoise jewelry p. 116
Gila monster p. 120
Hot-air balloons p. 120
Los Alamos scientists p. 120
Dallas skyline pp. 116-117
Oil drillers p. 124
Rio Grande ferry pp. 124-125
Texas debutante p. 116

THE BASICS

Statehood
February 14, 1912; 48th state

Total area (land and water)
113,990 sq mi (295,234 sq km)

Land area
113,594 sq mi (294,207 sq km)

Population
6,828,065

Capital
Phoenix
Population 1,563,025

Largest city
Phoenix
Population 1,563,025

Racial/ethnic groups
83.5% white; 4.8% African American; 3.4% Asian; 5.3% Native American; 30.7% Hispanic (any race)

Foreign born
13.4%

Urban population
89.8% (2010)

Population density
60.1 per sq mi (23.2 per sq km)

GEO WHIZ

The California condor, once common throughout the Southwest, nearly became extinct in 1987. Through captive breeding and other conservation measures, the species has been reintroduced to the wild in areas such as the Grand Canyon.

People have been carving pictures called petroglyphs into rock cliffs in Verde Valley near Flagstaff for thousands of years. The meanings of most are a mystery, but some reveal plants and animals of bygone eras.

Introduced as wild game for sportspeople, bullfrogs have made Arizona their new home on the range. With no natural predators and plenty to eat, bullfrogs are taking over.

Arizona

⬤ **HOT WORK.** A man in protective clothing works near a furnace that melts and refines copper ore at Magma Copper Company near Tucson. Arizona is one of the largest copper-producing regions in the world.

The first Europeans to visit what is now Arizona were the Spanish in the 1500s. The territory passed from Spain to Mexico and then to the United States over the next three centuries. In the 1800s settlers clashed with the Apache warriors Cochise and Geronimo—and with one another in lawless towns like Tombstone. Youngest of the 48 contiguous states, Arizona achieved statehood in 1912. Arizona's economy was long based on the Five C's: copper, cattle, cotton, citrus, and climate—but manufacturing and service industries have gained prominence. A fast-growing population, sprawling cities, and agricultural irrigation strain limited water supplies in this dry state, which depends on water from the Colorado River and underground aquifers. Tourists flock to the Colorado Plateau in the north to see stunning vistas of the Grand Canyon, Painted Desert, and Monument Valley. To the south, the Sonoran Desert's unique ecosystem includes the giant saguaro cactus. Indian reservations scattered around the state offer visitors the chance to learn about tribal history and culture.

CACTUS WREN

SAGUARO

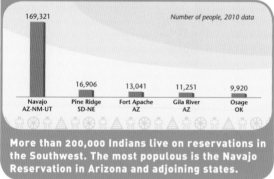

INDIAN RESERVATIONS

Number of people, 2010 data

Navajo AZ-NM-UT	Pine Ridge SD-NE	Fort Apache AZ	Gila River AZ	Osage OK
169,321	16,906	13,041	11,251	9,920

More than 200,000 Indians live on reservations in the Southwest. The most populous is the Navajo Reservation in Arizona and adjoining states.

⬤ **NATURAL WONDER.** Carved by the rushing waters of the Colorado River, the Grand Canyon's geologic features and fossil record reveal almost two billion years of Earth's history. Archaeological evidence indicates human habitation dating back 12,000 years.

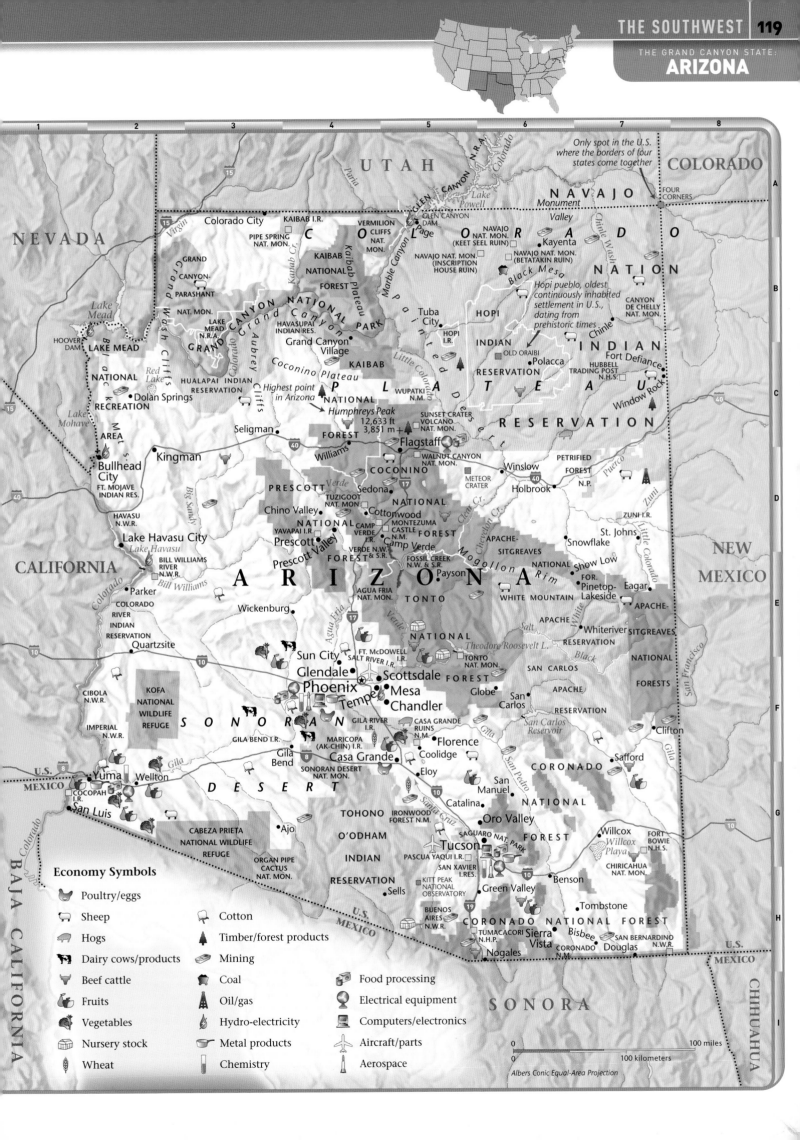

UTAH

COLORADO

NEVADA

NAVAJO

Only spot in the U.S. where the borders of four states come together

FOUR CORNERS

N.R.A.

GLEN CANYON

Colorado City

KAIBAB I.R.

VERMILION CLIFFS NAT. MON.

Page

Lake Powell

Monument Valley

NAVAJO NAT. MON. (KEET SEEL RUIN)

Kayenta

PIPE SPRING NAT. MON.

GLEN CANYON DAM

NAVAJO NAT. MON. (INSCRIPTION HOUSE RUIN)

NAVAJO NAT. MON. (BETATAKIN RUIN)

KAIBAB

Marble Canyon

Black Mesa

CANYON DE CHELLY NAT. MON.

GRAND CANYON-PARASHANT NAT. MON.

NATIONAL

FOREST

Kaibab Plateau

Tuba City

Hopi pueblo, oldest continuously inhabited settlement in U.S., dating from prehistoric times

Chinle

NATION

Lake Mead

Havasupai Indian Res.

Grand Canyon Village

HOPI

HOPI I.R.

OLD ORAIBI

INDIAN

Polacca

Fort Defiance

Window Rock

HUBBELL TRADING POST N.H.S.

Hoover Dam

LAKE MEAD N.R.A.

GRAND CANYON NATIONAL PARK

KAIBAB

INDIAN

INDIAN

LAKE MEAD

NATIONAL

Red Lake

Coconino Plateau

RESERVATION

Little Colorado

WUPATKI N.M.

RESERVATION

PLATEAU

Dolan Springs

HUALAPAI INDIAN RESERVATION

Cliffs

Highest point in Arizona

NATIONAL

Humphreys Peak 12,633 ft 3,851 m

SUNSET CRATER VOLCANO NAT. MON.

Lake Mohave

RECREATION

FOREST

Seligman

Williams

Flagstaff

WALNUT CANYON NAT. MON.

Winslow

PETRIFIED FOREST N.P.

AREA

Kingman

COCONINO

Holbrook

METEOR CRATER

Puerco

Bullhead City

PRESCOTT

Verde

Sedona

Zuni

FT. MOJAVE INDIAN RES.

TUZIGOOT NAT. MON.

NATIONAL

ZUNI I.R.

HAVASU N.W.R.

Big Sandy

Chino Valley

Cottonwood

St. Johns

Snowflake

Lake Havasu City

NATIONAL

MONTEZUMA CASTLE N.M.

FOREST

APACHE-SITGREAVES

Show Low

Lake Havasu

YAVAPAI I.R.

CAMP VERDE I.R.

NATIONAL

BILL WILLIAMS RIVER N.W.R.

Prescott

VERDE N.W. & S.R.

Camp Verde

FOR.

Pinetop-Lakeside

Eagar

CALIFORNIA

Bill Williams

Prescott Valley

FOSSIL CREEK N.W. & S.R.

Mogollon

Rim

NEW

MEXICO

Colorado

FOREST

Payson

WHITE MOUNTAIN

APACHE-SITGREAVES

Parker

ARIZONA

TONTO

APACHE

Whiteriver

COLORADO RIVER INDIAN RESERVATION

Wickenburg

AGUA FRIA NAT. MON.

NATIONAL

Salt

White

San Francisco

Quartzsite

NATIONAL

Theodore Roosevelt L.

RESERVATION

FORESTS

FT. McDOWELL I.R.

Black

Sun City

SALT RIVER I.R.

TONTO NAT. MON.

SAN CARLOS

CIBOLA N.W.R.

KOFA NATIONAL WILDLIFE REFUGE

Glendale

Scottsdale

San Carlos Reservoir

Phoenix

Mesa

Globe

APACHE

IMPERIAL N.W.R.

SONORAN

Tempe

Chandler

San Carlos

RESERVATION

Gila

Clifton

Casa Grande Ruins N.M.

CASA GRANDE RUINS N.M.

CORONADO

GILA RIVER I.R.

GILA BEND I.R.

Florence

Safford

U.S.

Gila

MARICOPA (AK-CHIN) I.R.

Casa Grande

Coolidge

NATIONAL

MEXICO

COCOPAH I.R.

Yuma

Wellton

Gila Bend

SONORAN DESERT NAT. MON.

Eloy

San Manuel

San Pedro

FOREST

DESERT

San Luis

Catalina

Santa Cruz

TOHONO

IRONWOOD FOREST N.M.

Oro Valley

Willcox

FORT BOWIE N.H.S.

CABEZA PRIETA NATIONAL WILDLIFE REFUGE

Ajo

Willcox Playa

O'ODHAM

SAGUARO NAT. PARK

Tucson

ORGAN PIPE CACTUS NAT. MON.

INDIAN

PASCUA YAQUI I.R.

CHIRICAHUA NAT. MON.

SAN XAVIER I.R.

Benson

RESERVATION

KITT PEAK NATIONAL OBSERVATORY

Green Valley

Sells

CORONADO

NATIONAL FOREST

Tombstone

BUENOS AIRES N.W.R.

TUMACACORI N.H.P.

Sierra Vista

Bisbee

SAN BERNARDINO N.W.R.

Nogales

CORONADO N.M.

Douglas

U.S. MEXICO

BAJA CALIFORNIA

SONORA

CHIHUAHUA

Economy Symbols

- 🐔 Poultry/eggs
- 🐑 Sheep
- 🐖 Hogs
- 🐄 Dairy cows/products
- 🐂 Beef cattle
- 🍓 Fruits
- 🥬 Vegetables
- Nursery stock
- 🌾 Wheat
- Cotton
- 🌲 Timber/forest products
- Mining
- Coal
- Oil/gas
- Hydro-electricity
- Metal products
- Chemistry
- Food processing
- Electrical equipment
- Computers/electronics
- ✈ Aircraft/parts
- Aerospace

0   100 miles

0   100 kilometers

Albers Conic Equal-Area Projection

THE LAND OF ENCHANTMENT STATE:
NEW MEXICO

THE BASICS

Statehood
January 6, 1912; 47th state

Total area (land and water)
121,590 sq mi (314,917 sq km)

Land area
121,298 sq mi (314,161 sq km)

Population
2,085,109

Capital
Santa Fe
Population 84,099

Largest city
Albuquerque
Population 559,121

Racial/ethnic groups
82.5% white; 2.6% African
American; 1.7% Asian; 10.5%
Native American; 48.0% Hispanic
(any race)

Foreign born
9.8%

Urban population
77.4% (2010)

Population density
17.2 per sq mi (6.6 per sq km)

GEO WHIZ

Carlsbad Caverns National Park
has more than a hundred caves,
including the deepest limestone
cavern in the U.S. From May
through October visitors can
watch hundreds of thousands of
Mexican free-tailed bats emerge
from the caverns on their nightly
search for food.

Taos Pueblo, in north-central
New Mexico, has been continuously inhabited by Pueblo people
for more than 1,000 years. When
Spanish explorers reached it
in 1540, they thought they had
found one of the fabled golden
cities of Cibola.

In 2011 Spaceport America offi-
cially opened in the high desert
near Truth or Consequences.
Private companies hope to offer
sub-orbital space flights from
this port in the near future.

New Mexico

New Mexico is among the youngest states—statehood was established in 1912—but its capital city is the country's oldest. The Spanish founded Santa Fe in 1610, a decade before the *Mayflower* reached America. Beginning in the 1820s, the Santa Fe Trail brought trade and settlers, and the United States acquired the territory from Mexico by 1853. Most large cities are in the center of the state, along the Rio Grande. The Rocky Mountains divide the plains in the east from eroded mesas and canyons in the west. Cattle and sheep ranching on the plains is the chief agricultural activity, but hay, onions, and chili peppers are also important. Copper, potash, and natural gas produce mineral wealth. Cultural richness created by the historic interaction of Indian, Hispanic, and Anglo peoples abounds. Visitors experience this unique culture in the state's spicy cuisine, the famous art galleries of Taos, and the crafts made by Indians on the state's many reservations.

● PAINFUL BITE.
The most poisonous lizard native to the United States is the strikingly patterned gila monster, which lives in desert areas of the Southwest.

● FLYING HIGH. Brightly colored balloons rise into a brilliant blue October sky during Albuquerque's annual International Balloon Fiesta, the largest such event in the world. During the nine-day festival more than 500 hot-air balloons drift on variable air currents created by surrounding mountains.

ROADRUNNER
YUCCA

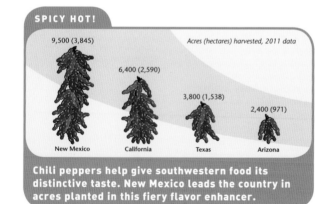

SPICY HOT!

Acres (hectares) harvested, 2011 data

9,500 (3,845) New Mexico
6,400 (2,590) California
3,800 (1,538) Texas
2,400 (971) Arizona

Chili peppers help give southwestern food its distinctive taste. New Mexico leads the country in acres planted in this fiery flavor enhancer.

◐ NUCLEAR MYSTERIES. Scientists at Los Alamos National Laboratory, a leading scientific and engineering research institution, use 3-D simulations to study nuclear explosions.

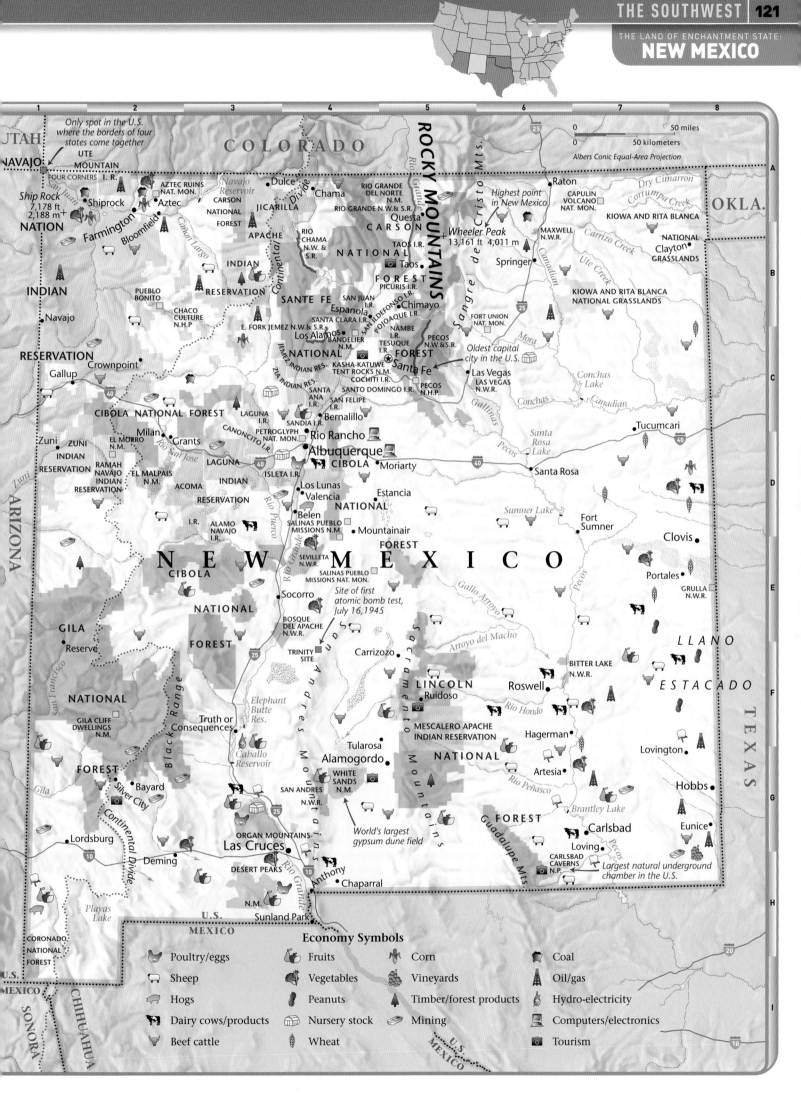

Only spot in the U.S. where the borders of four states come together

UTAH

NAVAJO

COLORADO

ROCKY MOUNTAINS

Highest point in New Mexico

Wheeler Peak
13,161 ft 4,011 m

OKLA.

FOUR CORNERS I. R.

UTE MOUNTAIN

Ship Rock
7,178 ft
2,188 m

Shiprock

NATION

Farmington

Bloomfield

Aztec

AZTEC RUINS NAT. MON.

CARSON NATIONAL FOREST

JICARILLA

APACHE

INDIAN

RESERVATION

Navajo Reservoir

Dulce

Chama

RIO GRANDE DEL NORTE N.M.

RIO GRANDE N.W. & S.R.

Questa

CARSON

NATIONAL

FOREST

PICURIS I.R.

Raton

CAPULIN VOLCANO NAT. MON.

Dry Cimarron

Corrumpa Creek

KIOWA AND RITA BLANCA

MAXWELL N.W.R.

Springer

Carrizo Creek

Ute Creek

Canadian

KIOWA AND RITA BLANCA NATIONAL GRASSLANDS

NATIONAL Clayton GRASSLANDS

INDIAN

Navajo

RESERVATION

Gallup

Crownpoint

PUEBLO BONITO

CHACO CULTURE N.H.P

Continental Divide

RIO CHAMA N.W. & S.R.

SANTE FE

Espanola

SAN JUAN I.R.

SANTA CLARA I.R.

E. FORK JEMEZ N.W. & S.R.

Los Alamos

BANDELIER N.M.

JEMEZ INDIAN RES.

KASHA-KATUWE TENT ROCKS N.M.

COCHITI I.R.

TAOS I.R.

Taos

SAN ILDEFONSO I.R.

POJOAQUE I.R.

NAMBE I.R.

TESUQUE I.R.

Chimayo

PECOS N.W. & S.R.

Santa Fe

FORT UNION NAT. MON.

Mora

Las Vegas

LAS VEGAS N.W.R.

Oldest capital city in the U.S.

PECOS N.H.P.

Conchas Lake

Canadian

Conchas

Sangre de Cristo Mts.

Tucumcari

Gallinas

Santa Rosa Lake

Pecos

Zuni

ZUNI INDIAN RESERVATION

EL MORRO N.M.

RAMAH NAVAJO INDIAN RESERVATION

CIBOLA NATIONAL FOREST

Milan

Grants

EL MALPAIS N.M.

ACOMA

LAGUNA

CANONCITO I.R.

PETROGLYPH NAT. MON.

SANTA ANA I.R.

SAN FELIPE I.R.

ZIA INDIAN RES.

SANTO DOMINGO I.R.

SANDIA I.R.

Bernalillo

Rio Rancho

Albuquerque

CIBOLA

Moriarty

Santa Rosa

ARIZONA

Zuni

Rio San Jose

LAGUNA I.R.

ISLETA I.R.

Los Lunas

Valencia

Belen

Rio Puerco

SALINAS PUEBLO MISSIONS N.M.

INDIAN RESERVATION

I.R.

ALAMO NAVAJO I.R.

Estancia

NATIONAL

Mountainair

FOREST

Sumner Lake

Fort Sumner

Clovis

Portales

GRULLA N.W.R.

N E W   M E X I C O

CIBOLA

SEVILLETA N.W.R.

Socorro

SALINAS PUEBLO MISSIONS NAT. MON.

Rio Grande

NATIONAL

BOSQUE DEL APACHE N.W.R.

FOREST

TRINITY SITE

Site of first atomic bomb test, July 16, 1945

Carrizozo

LLANO

ESTACADO

GILA

Reserve

San Francisco

NATIONAL

GILA CLIFF DWELLINGS N.M.

FOREST

Gila

Silver City

Bayard

Continental Divide

Lordsburg

Deming

Black Range

Truth or Consequences

Elephant Butte Res.

Caballo Reservoir

SAN ANDRES N.W.R.

San Andres Mountains

ORGAN MOUNTAINS

Las Cruces

DESERT PEAKS N.M.

Anthony

Chaparral

Tularosa

Alamogordo

WHITE SANDS N.M.

World's largest gypsum dune field

Arroyo del Macho

Gallo Arroyo

Sacramento Mountains

LINCOLN

Ruidoso

MESCALERO APACHE INDIAN RESERVATION

NATIONAL

FOREST

Guadalupe Mts.

Rio Hondo

BITTER LAKE N.W.R.

Roswell

Hagerman

Artesia

Rio Penasco

Brantley Lake

CARLSBAD CAVERNS N.P.

Largest natural underground chamber in the U.S.

Carlsbad

Loving

Eunice

Lovington

Hobbs

TEXAS

Pecos

Playas Lake

CORONADO NATIONAL FOREST

Sunland Park

U.S.

MEXICO

U.S.

MEXICO

SONORA

CHIHUAHUA

Economy Symbols

Poultry/eggs	Fruits	Corn	Coal
Sheep	Vegetables	Vineyards	Oil/gas
Hogs	Peanuts	Timber/forest products	Hydro-electricity
Dairy cows/products	Nursery stock	Mining	Computers/electronics
Beef cattle	Wheat		Tourism

50 miles
50 kilometers
Albers Conic Equal-Area Projection

OKLAHOMA

THE BASICS

Statehood
November 16, 1907; 46th state

Total area (land and water)
69,899 sq mi (181,037 sq km)

Land area
68,595 sq mi (177,660 sq km)

Population
3,911,338

Capital
Oklahoma City
Population 631,346

Largest city
Oklahoma City
Population 631,346

Racial/ethnic groups
74.8% white; 7.8% African American; 2.2% Asian; 9.1% Native American; 10.1% Hispanic (any race)

Foreign born
5.5%

Urban population
66.2% (2010)

Population density
57.0 per sq mi (22.0 per sq km)

GEO WHIZ

An area of Oklahoma City has earned the nickname Little Saigon. In the 1960s the city opened its doors to tens of thousands of refugees from Vietnam. Today, the area is a thriving business district that includes people of many Asian nationalities.

"Hillbilly Speed Bump" is one of several nicknames for the armadillo. Native to South America, large populations of this armor-plated mammal are found as far north as Oklahoma.

Before it became a state in 1907, Oklahoma was known as Indian Territory. Today 39 tribes, including Cherokee, Osage, Creek, and Choctaw, have their headquarters in the state.

Oklahoma

The U.S. government declared most of present-day Oklahoma as an Indian Territory in 1834. To reach this new homeland, southeastern Indians were forced to travel the Trail of Tears, named for its brutal conditions. By 1889 areas were opened for white homesteaders who staked claims in frenzied land runs. White and Indian lands were combined to form the state of Oklahoma in 1907. During the 1930s many Oklahoma natives fled drought and dust storms that smothered everything in sight. Some traveled as far as California in search of work. Better farming methods and the return of rain helped agriculture recover, and today cattle and wheat are among the chief products. Oil and natural gas wells are found throughout the state. The Red River, colored by the region's iron-rich soils, marks the state's southern boundary. Along the eastern border, the Ozark Plateau and Ouachita Mountains form rugged bluffs and valleys. To the west, rolling plains rise toward the High Plains in the state's panhandle.

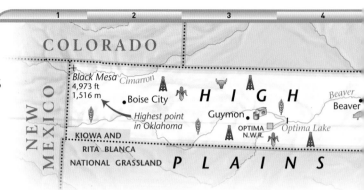

MISTLETOE
SCISSOR-TAILED FLYCATCHER

FOOD SUPPLIER

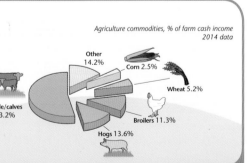

Agriculture commodities, % of farm cash income
2014 data

Other 14.2%
Corn 2.5%
Wheat 5.2%
Broilers 11.3%
Hogs 13.6%
Cattle/calves 53.2%

With more than 80,000 farms, agriculture is important in Oklahoma, contributing almost $8 billion to the state's economy.

⬤ **NATURAL LANDSCAPE.** A bison herd grazes in the Tallgrass Prairie Preserve, near Pawhuska. In years when rain is abundant, the grasses can grow as tall as 8 feet (2.5 m). Tallgrass prairie once covered 140 million acres (57 million ha), extending from Minnesota to Texas, but today less than 10 percent remains because of urban sprawl and cropland expansion.

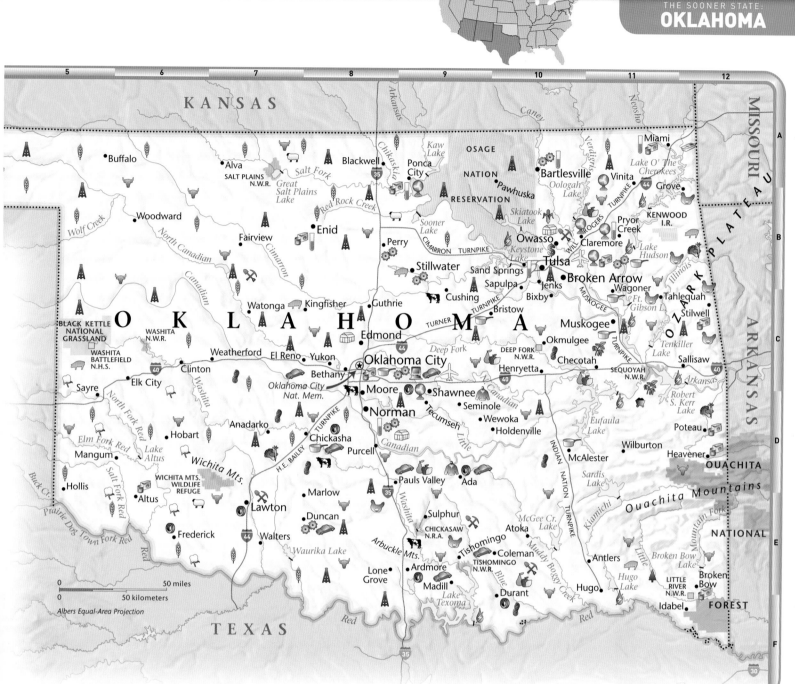

KANSAS

5 6 7 8 9 10 11 12

A B C D E F

Buffalo
Alva
SALT PLAINS N.W.R.
Salt Fork
Great Salt Plains Lake
Blackwell
Chikaskia
Kaw Lake
Ponca City
OSAGE NATION
Pawhuska
RESERVATION
Miami
Lake O' The Cherokees
Vinita
Grove
Bartlesville
Oologah Lake
Woodward
Red Rock Creek
Wolf Creek
Skiatook Lake
Pryor Creek
KENWOOD I.R.
Fairview
Enid
North Canadian
Cimarron
Sooner Lake
Perry
Keystone Lake
Owasso
Claremore
Lake Hudson
Watonga
Kingfisher
Canadian
Stillwater
Sand Springs
Sapulpa
Tulsa
Jenks
Bixby
Broken Arrow
Wagoner
Ft. Gibson L.
Tahlequah
Guthrie
Cushing
Bristow
TURNER TURNPIKE
Muskogee
Stilwell
OKLAHOMA
Edmond
Deep Fork
DEEP FORK N.W.R.
Okmulgee
Tenkiller Lake
Sallisaw
Weatherford
El Reno
Yukon
Oklahoma City
Checotah
SEQUOYAH N.W.R.
Arkansas
BLACK KETTLE NATIONAL GRASSLAND
WASHITA N.W.R.
WASHITA BATTLEFIELD N.H.S.
Clinton
Bethany
Henryetta
Robert S. Kerr Lake
Poteau
Sayre
Elk City
Oklahoma City Nat. Mem.
Moore
Shawnee
Canadian
Eufaula Lake
Anadarko
Norman
Seminole
Tecumseh
Wewoka
Holdenville
McAlester
Wilburton
Heavener
OUACHITA
Hobart
Chickasha
Purcell
Canadian
Little
Mangum
Lake Altus
Wichita Mts.
H.E. BAILEY
Pauls Valley
Ada
Sardis Lake
Ouachita Mountains
Hollis
WICHITA MTS. WILDLIFE REFUGE
Altus
Marlow
Indian Nation Turnpike
NATIONAL
Lawton
Duncan
Sulphur
McGee Cr. Lake
Atoka
Kiamichi
Frederick
Walters
CHICKASAW N.R.A.
Tishomingo
Coleman
Antlers
Broken Bow Lake
Broken Bow
FOREST
Waurika Lake
Arbuckle Mts.
TISHOMINGO N.W.R.
Muddy Boggy Creek
Hugo Lake
LITTLE RIVER N.W.R.
Lone Grove
Ardmore
Madill
Blue
Durant
Hugo
Idabel
Lake Texoma
Red

0 50 miles
0 50 kilometers
Albers Equal-Area Projection

TEXAS

MISSOURI — **PLATEAU** — **ARKANSAS** — **OZARK**

Economy Symbols

- Poultry/eggs
- Sheep
- Hogs
- Dairy cows/products
- Beef cattle
- Fruits
- Vegetables
- Peanuts
- Nursery stock
- Wheat
- Corn
- Soybeans
- Cotton
- Stone/gravel/cement
- Mining

- Coal
- Oil/gas
- Hydro-electricity
- Machinery
- Metal products
- Motor vehicles/parts
- Rubber/plastics
- Chemistry
- Food processing
- Clothing/textiles
- Electrical equipment
- Computers/electronics
- Aircraft/parts
- Finance/insurance

HISTORY IN THE AIR. Tulsa's mayor pilots one of the Spirit of Tulsa Squadron's vintage PT-17 airplanes above the city. In 1990 the squadron became part of the Commemorative Air Force, a national organization committed to preserving aviation history by restoring and flying World War II aircraft.

THE LONE STAR STATE:
TEXAS

THE BASICS

Statehood
December 29, 1845; 28th state

Total area (land and water)
268,596 sq mi (695,662 sq km)

Land area
261,232 sq mi (676,587 sq km)

Population
27,469,114

Capital
Austin
Population 931,830

Largest city
Houston
Population 2,296,224

Racial/ethnic groups
79.7% white; 12.5% African
American; 4.7% Asian; 1.0%
Native American; 38.8% Hispanic
(any race)

Foreign born
16.3%

Urban population
84.7% (2010)

Population density
105.2 per sq mi (40.6 per sq km)

GEO WHIZ

The Fossil Rim Wildlife Research
Center in the Texas Hill Country
is breeding black rhinos and
other endangered African
animals. The center's goal is to
reintroduce offspring into the
wild in their native environment.
Meanwhile, visitors get a chance
to see a bit of Africa in Texas.

Six national flags have flown
over Texas during the course
of its history—Spanish, French,
Mexican, Texan, Confederate,
and American.

Texas has a long history of
Bigfoot sightings. The ape-man
creature was part of local Indian
lore, and white settlers told
stories about a wild woman
along the Navidad River.
Most sightings have been in
the eastern part of the state
near rivers or lakes.

Texas

Huge size, geographic diversity, and rich natural resources make Texas seem like its own country. In fact, it was an independent republic after throwing off Mexican rule in 1836. A famous battle in the fight for independence produced the Texan battle cry "Remember the Alamo!" In 1845 Texas was annexed by the U.S. Texas is the second largest state (behind Alaska) and the second most populous (behind California). It is a top producer of many agricultural products, including cattle, sheep, cotton, citrus fruits, vegetables, rice, and pecans. It also has huge oil and natural gas fields and is a manufacturing powerhouse. Pine forests cover East Texas, the wettest region. The Gulf Coast has swamps and extensive barrier islands. Grassy plains stretch across the northern panhandle, and the rolling Hill Country is famous for beautiful wildflowers. Mountains, valleys, and sandy plains sprawl across dry West Texas. The Rio Grande, sometimes barely a trickle, separates Texas and Mexico.

MOCKINGBIRD
BLUEBONNET

◉ **BLACK GOLD.** Workers plug an oil well. Discovery of oil early in the 20th century transformed life in Texas. Today, the state leads the U.S. in oil and natural gas production.

WHIRLING DANGER

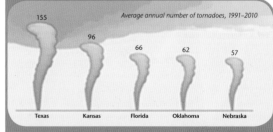

Average annual number of tornadoes, 1991–2010

155	96	66	62	57
Texas	Kansas	Florida	Oklahoma	Nebraska

Every state in the U.S. has experienced a tornado, but Texas has more than any other. These violent storms occur when cold air collides with warm, moist air.

◖ **BORDERLAND RELIC.** Los Ebanos Ferry, which takes its name from a grove of ebony trees growing nearby, is the last remaining government-licensed, hand-pulled ferry on any U.S. border. The privately owned ferry near Mission, Texas, can carry three cars at a time across the Rio Grande.

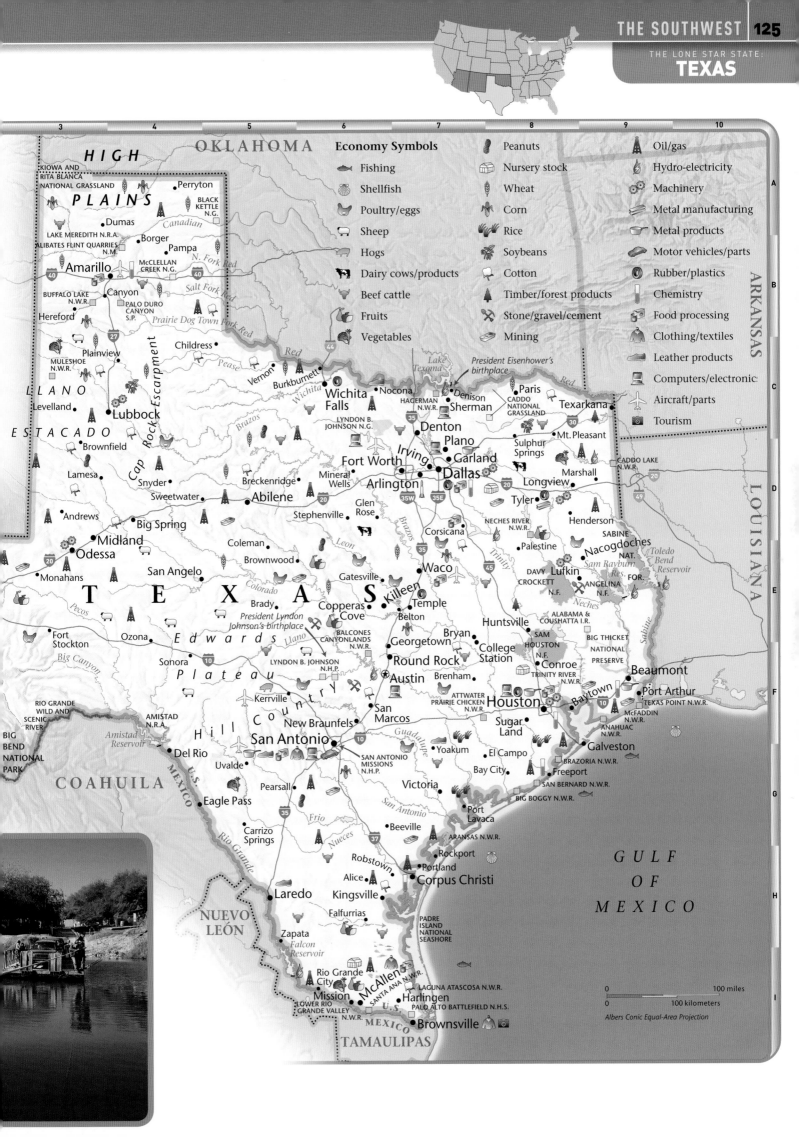

Economy Symbols

- Fishing
- Shellfish
- Poultry/eggs
- Sheep
- Hogs
- Dairy cows/products
- Beef cattle
- Fruits
- Vegetables
- Peanuts
- Nursery stock
- Wheat
- Corn
- Rice
- Soybeans
- Cotton
- Timber/forest products
- Stone/gravel/cement
- Mining
- Oil/gas
- Hydro-electricity
- Machinery
- Metal manufacturing
- Metal products
- Motor vehicles/parts
- Rubber/plastics
- Chemistry
- Food processing
- Clothing/textiles
- Leather products
- Computers/electronic
- Aircraft/parts
- Tourism

OKLAHOMA

HIGH PLAINS

KIOWA AND RITA BLANCA NATIONAL GRASSLAND
Perryton
BLACK KETTLE N.G.
Dumas
Canadian
Borger
Pampa
LAKE MEREDITH N.R.A.
ALIBATES FLINT QUARRIES N.M.
McCLELLAN CREEK N.G.
N. Fork Red
Amarillo
Canyon
BUFFALO LAKE N.W.R.
PALO DURO CANYON S.P.
Hereford
Salt Fork Red
Prairie Dog Town Fork Red
Childress
Pease
Plainview
MULESHOE N.W.R.
Red
Vernon
Burkburnett
Wichita
Nocona
Paris
Denison
HAGERMAN N.W.R.
Sherman
CADDO NATIONAL GRASSLAND
Texarkana
LLANO
Levelland
Lubbock
LYNDON B. JOHNSON N.G.
Wichita Falls
Denton
Sulphur Springs
Mt. Pleasant
ESTACADO
Brownfield
Brazos
Plano
CADDO LAKE N.W.R.
Marshall
Cap Rock Escarpment
Lamesa
Snyder
Breckenridge
Mineral Wells
Fort Worth
Irving
Garland
Dallas
Longview
Sweetwater
Abilene
Arlington
Tyler
Andrews
Stephenville
Glen Rose
Henderson
Big Spring
Coleman
Corsicana
NECHES RIVER N.W.R.
Palestine
SABINE NAT.
Nacogdoches
Toledo Bend Reservoir
Midland
Brownwood
Leon
Waco
DAVY CROCKETT N.F.
Lufkin
Sam Rayburn Res.
ANGELINA N.F.
Odessa
Gatesville
Killeen
FOR.
Neches
Monahans
San Angelo
Brady
Copperas Cove
Temple
Belton
Pecos
Colorado
President Lyndon Johnson's birthplace
BALCONES CANYONLANDS N.W.R.
Bryan
ALABAMA & COUSHATTA I.R.
BIG THICKET NATIONAL PRESERVE
Fort Stockton
Ozona
Edwards
Llano
Georgetown
College Station
SAM HOUSTON N.F.
Sonora
LYNDON B. JOHNSON N.H.P.
Round Rock
Conroe
TRINITY RIVER N.W.R.
Beaumont
Big Canyon
Plateau
Austin
Brenham
Trinity
Baytown
Port Arthur
RIO GRANDE WILD AND SCENIC RIVER
AMISTAD N.R.A.
Kerrville
Hill
ATTWATER PRAIRIE CHICKEN N.W.R.
Houston
TEXAS POINT N.W.R.
McFADDIN N.W.R.
BIG BEND NATIONAL PARK
Amistad Reservoir
Del Rio
Country
New Braunfels
San Marcos
Sugar Land
ANAHUAC N.W.R.
Galveston
San Antonio
Guadalupe
Yoakum
El Campo
BRAZORIA N.W.R.
COAHUILA
MEXICO
Uvalde
SAN ANTONIO MISSIONS N.H.P.
Bay City
Freeport
SAN BERNARD N.W.R.
Eagle Pass
Pearsall
San Antonio
Victoria
BIG BOGGY N.W.R.
Frio
Port Lavaca
Carrizo Springs
Nueces
Beeville
ARANSAS N.W.R.
Rockport
Robstown
Portland
GULF OF MEXICO
Alice
Corpus Christi
Laredo
Kingsville
PADRE ISLAND NATIONAL SEASHORE
NUEVO LEÓN
Falfurrias
Zapata
Falcon Reservoir
Rio Grande City
McAllen
SANTA ANA N.W.R.
LAGUNA ATASCOSA N.W.R.
Mission
Harlingen
LOWER RIO GRANDE VALLEY N.W.R.
PALO ALTO BATTLEFIELD N.H.S.
MEXICO
Brownsville
TAMAULIPAS

President Eisenhower's birthplace
Lake Texoma

ARKANSAS

LOUISIANA

Rio Grande

0   100 miles
0   100 kilometers
Albers Conic Equal-Area Projection

The West

PHYSICAL

Total area (land and water)
1,637,673 sq mi
(4,241,549 sq km)

Highest point
Denali (Mount McKinley), AK:
20,320 ft (6,194 m)

Lowest point
Death Valley, CA:
-282 ft (-86 m)

Longest rivers
Missouri, Yukon,
Rio Grande, Colorado

Largest lakes
Great Salt, Iliamna,
Becharof

Vegetation
Needleleaf, broadleaf, and mixed
forest; grassland; desert; tundra
(Alaska); tropical (Hawai'i)

Climate
Mild along the coast, with warm
summers and mild winters; semiarid
to arid inland; polar in parts of
Alaska; tropical in Hawai'i

POLITICAL

Total population
67,131,505

States (11):
Alaska, California, Colorado, Hawai'i,
Idaho, Montana, Nevada, Oregon, Utah,
Washington, Wyoming

Largest state
Alaska: 665,384 sq mi
(1,723,337 sq km)

Smallest state
Hawai'i: 10,932 sq mi (28,311 sq km)

Most populous state
California: 39,144,818

Least populous state
Wyoming: 586,107

Largest city proper
Los Angeles, CA: 3,971,883

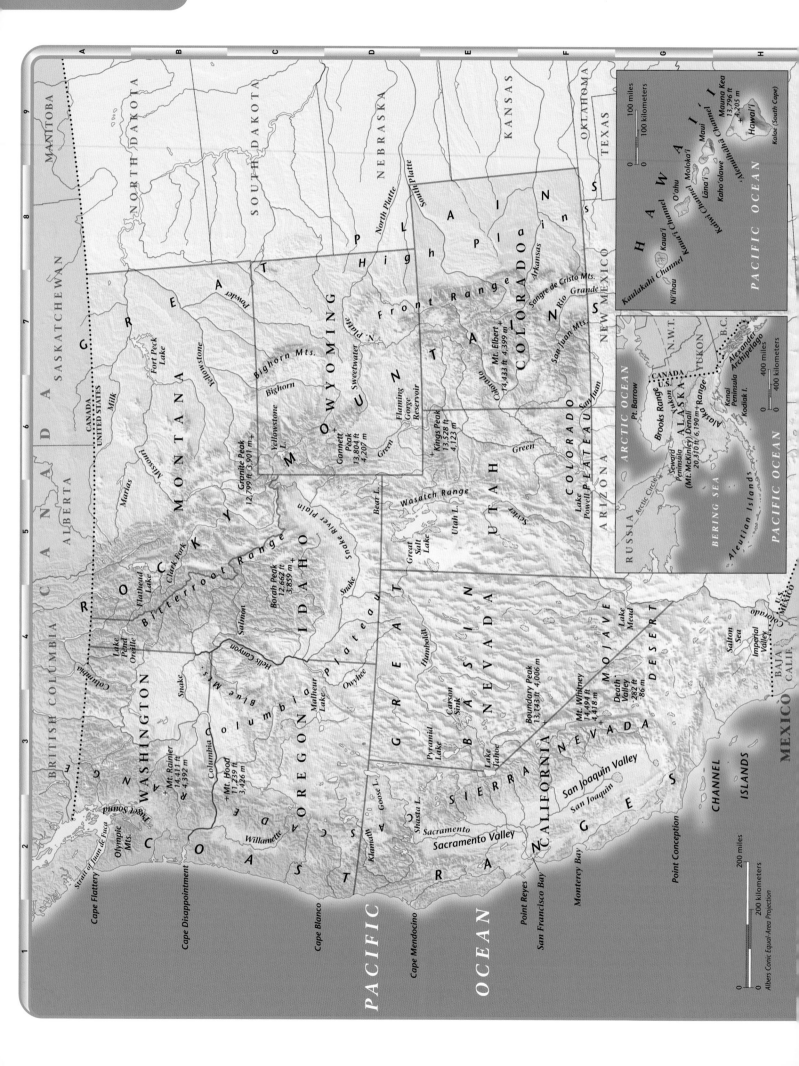

POLITICAL MAP

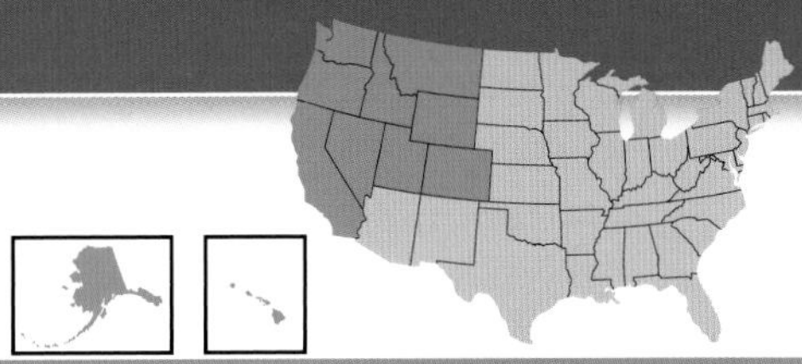

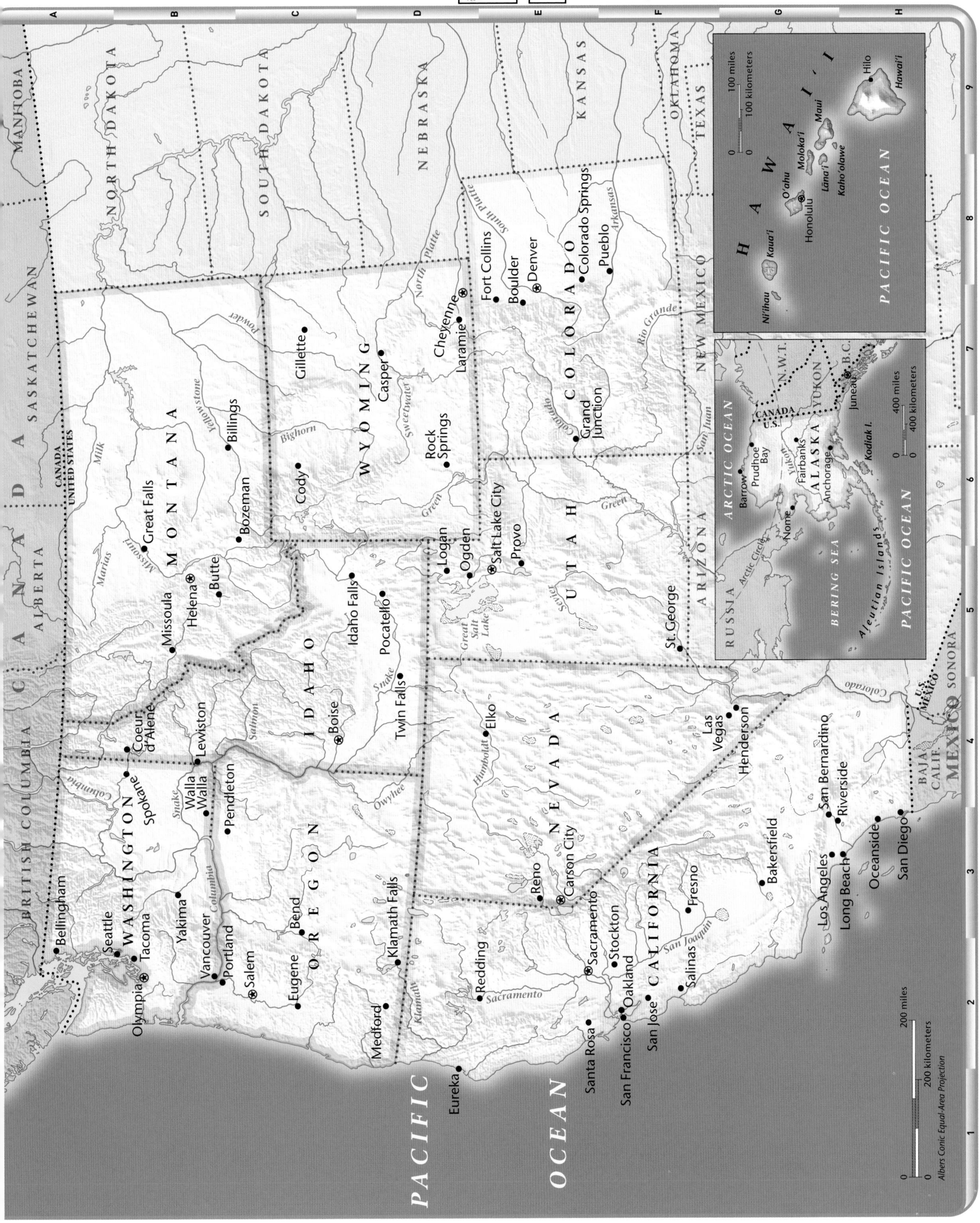
CANADA
UNITED STATES
BRITISH COLUMBIA
ALBERTA
SASKATCHEWAN
MANITOBA
NORTH DAKOTA
SOUTH DAKOTA
NEBRASKA
KANSAS
OKLAHOMA
TEXAS
NEW MEXICO
ARIZONA
SONORA
BAJA CALIF.
MEXICO
U.S.
WASHINGTON
OREGON
IDAHO
MONTANA
WYOMING
UTAH
COLORADO
NEVADA
CALIFORNIA
PACIFIC OCEAN
Bellingham
Seattle
Tacoma
Olympia
Yakima
Spokane
Walla Walla
Vancouver
Portland
Salem
Eugene
Bend
Medford
Klamath Falls
Pendleton
Lewiston
Coeur d'Alene
Boise
Twin Falls
Pocatello
Idaho Falls
Missoula
Helena
Butte
Great Falls
Bozeman
Billings
Cody
Gillette
Casper
Rock Springs
Laramie
Cheyenne
Fort Collins
Boulder
Denver
Colorado Springs
Pueblo
Grand Junction
Logan
Ogden
Salt Lake City
Provo
St. George
Great Salt Lake
Elko
Reno
Carson City
Las Vegas
Henderson
Eureka
Redding
Santa Rosa
Sacramento
Stockton
San Francisco
Oakland
San Jose
Salinas
Fresno
Bakersfield
Los Angeles
Long Beach
San Bernardino
Riverside
Oceanside
San Diego
Columbia
Snake
Salmon
Owyhee
Missouri
Marias
Milk
Yellowstone
Powder
Bighorn
Sweetwater
Green
North Platte
South Platte
Arkansas
Rio Grande
Colorado
San Juan
Sevier
Humboldt
Klamath
Sacramento
San Joaquin
HAWAI'I
Ni'ihau
Kaua'i
O'ahu
Honolulu
Moloka'i
Lāna'i
Maui
Kaho'olawe
Hawai'i
Hilo
PACIFIC OCEAN
0 100 miles
0 100 kilometers
RUSSIA
ARCTIC OCEAN
Arctic Circle
BERING SEA
Aleutian Islands
PACIFIC OCEAN
Barrow
Prudhoe Bay
Yukon
Nome
Fairbanks
ALASKA
Anchorage
Kodiak I.
Juneau
CANADA
U.S.
N.W.T.
YUKON
B.C.
0 400 miles
0 400 kilometers
0 200 miles
0 200 kilometers
Albers Conic Equal-Area Projection

◑ **OLD AND NEW.** A cable car carries passengers in San Francisco. In the background, modern buildings, including the Transamerica Pyramid, rise above older neighborhoods in this earthquake-prone city.

The West

THE HIGH FRONTIER

T he western states, which make up almost half of the country's land area, have diverse landscapes and climates, ranging from the frozen heights of Denali, in Alaska, to the desolation of Death Valley, in California, and the lush, tropical islands of Hawai'i. More than half the region's population lives in California, and the Los Angeles metropolitan area is second in population only to that of New York City. Yet many parts of the region are sparsely populated, and much of the land is set aside as parkland and military bases. The region also faces many natural hazards—earthquakes, landslides, wildfires, and even volcanic eruptions.

◑ **NORTHERN GIANT.**
Denali, a name meaning "High One" in the Athabascan language, rises more than 20,000 feet (6,100 m) in the Alaska Range. Also known as Mount McKinley, it is North America's highest peak. The same tectonic forces that trigger earthquakes in Alaska are slowly pushing this huge block of granite ever higher.

ELUSIVE PREDATOR. Known by many names, including cougar and mountain lion, these big cats are found mainly in remote mountainous areas of the West, where they hunt deer and smaller animals.

STEAMY BATH. Colorful, mineral-rich hot springs are just one geothermal feature of Yellowstone National Park. Runoff from rain and snowmelt seeps into cracks in the ground, sinking to a depth of 10,000 feet (3,050 m), where it is heated by molten rock before rising back to the surface.

BALANCING ACT. For many years rivers have been used to move logs from forest to market, taking advantage of the buoyancy of logs and the power of moving water. A logger stands on a floating log raft in Coos Bay, Oregon.

TRADITIONAL SAILING CRAFT. A Hawaiian outrigger canoe on Waikiki Beach promises fun in the surf for visitors to the 50th state. An important part of Polynesian culture, the canoes were once used to travel from island to island.

Alaska

Alaska—from Alyeska, an Aleut word meaning "great land"—was purchased by the U.S. from Russia in 1867 for just two cents an acre. Many people thought it was a bad investment, but it soon paid off when gold was discovered, and again when major petroleum deposits were discovered in 1968. Today, an 800-mile (1,287-km)-long pipeline links North Slope oil fields to the ice-free port at Valdez, but critics worry about the long-term environmental impact. Everything is big in Alaska. It is the largest state, with one-sixth of the country's land area; it has the highest peak in the United States, Denali (Mount McKinley); and the largest earthquake ever recorded in the United States—a 9.2 magnitude—occurred there in 1964. It is first in forestland, a leading source of seafood, and a major oil producer. Alaska's population has a higher percentage of native people than that of any other state.

THE BASICS

Statehood
January 3, 1959; 49th state

Total area (land and water)
665,384 sq mi
(1,723,337 sq km)

Land area
570,641 sq mi
(1,477,953 sq km)

Population
738,432

Capital
Juneau
Population 32,406 (2014)

Largest city
Anchorage
Population 110,229

Racial/ethnic groups
66.5% white; 3.9% African American; 6.3% Asian; 14.8% Native American; 7.0% Hispanic (any race)

Foreign born
7.0%

Urban population
66.0% (2010)

Population density
1.3 per sq mi (0.5 per sq km)

GEO WHIZ

During the summer, migrating humpback whales work together in Alaskan waters to catch fish. While swimming in circles, the whales blow bubbles that form a net around schools of herring. Each whale can eat hundreds of fish in one gulp.

Climate change and population growth are changing the route of the famous Iditarod sled-dog race. Since 2002, lack of snow in Wasilla has forced the starting point for the competition first to Willow and then as far north as Fairbanks.

The Tongass National Forest is the largest national forest in the United States.

⊖ **TIME FOR LUNCH.**
A grizzly bear wades into the rushing waters of Brooks Falls, in Katmai National Park, to catch a leaping salmon.

FORGET-ME-NOT
WILLOW PTARMIGAN

◖ **NORTHERN METROPOLIS.** Anchorage, established in 1915 as a construction port for the Alaska Railroad, sits in the shadow of the snow-covered Chugach Mountains.

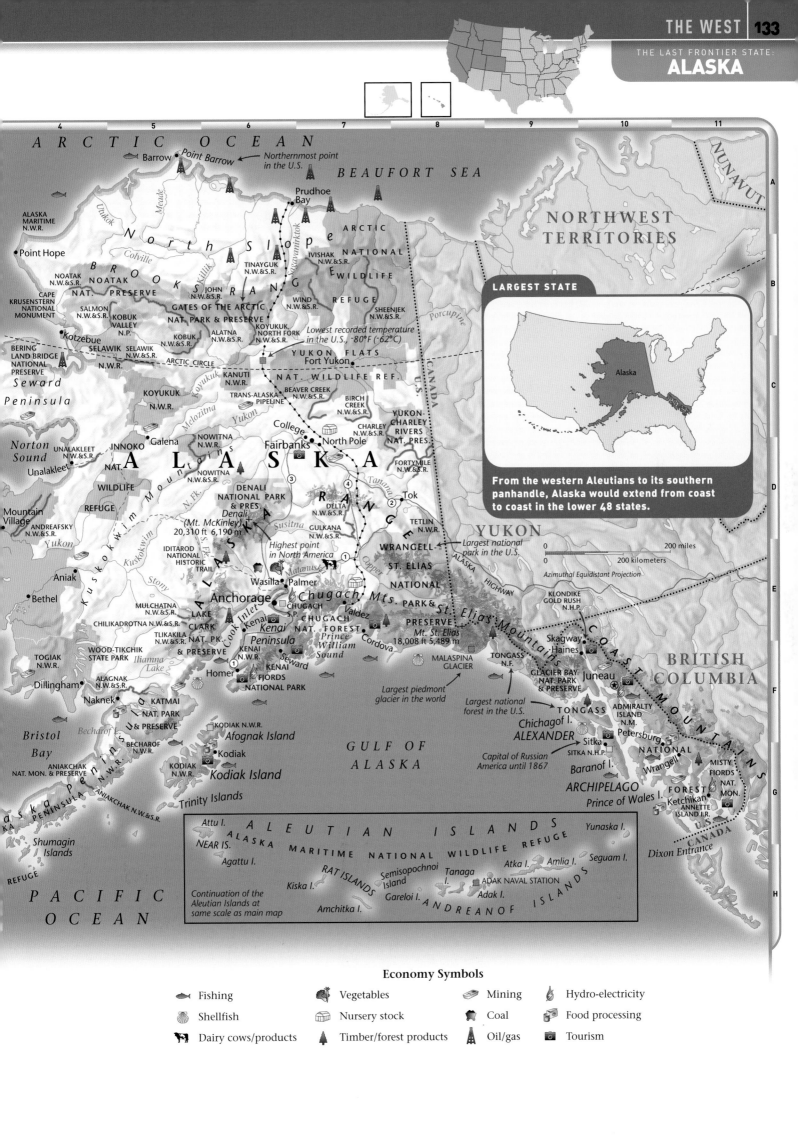

ARCTIC OCEAN

Barrow • Point Barrow ← Northernmost point in the U.S.

BEAUFORT SEA

NUNAVUT

Prudhoe Bay

• Point Hope

ALASKA MARITIME N.W.R.

ARCTIC NATIONAL

North Slope

BROOKS RANGE

NOATAK N.A.T. PRESERVE

NOATAK N.W.&S.R.

CAPE KRUSENSTERN NATIONAL MONUMENT

SALMON N.W.&S.R.

KOBUK VALLEY N.P.

• Kotzebue

SELAWIK N.W.&S.R.

SELAWIK

BERING LAND BRIDGE NATIONAL PRESERVE N.W.R.

TINAYGUK N.W.&S.R.

JOHN N.W.&S.R.

GATES OF THE ARCTIC NAT. PARK & PRESERVE

KOBUK N.W.&S.R.

ALATNA N.W.&S.R.

KOYUKUK, NORTH FORK N.W.&S.R.

IVISHAK N.W.&S.R.

WIND N.W.&S.R.

WILDLIFE REFUGE

SHEENJEK N.W.&S.R.

Porcupine

CANADA U.S.

Lowest recorded temperature in the U.S., -80°F (-62°C)

ARCTIC CIRCLE

YUKON FLATS

Fort Yukon

NORTHWEST TERRITORIES

LARGEST STATE

Seward Peninsula

KANUTI N.W.R.

NAT. WILDLIFE REF.

KOYUKUK N.W.R.

TRANS-ALASKA PIPELINE

BEAVER CREEK N.W.&S.R.

BIRCH CREEK N.W.&S.R.

YUKON-CHARLEY RIVERS NAT. PRES.

CHARLEY N.W.&S.R.

Alaska

Norton Sound

INNOKO N.W.R.

Galena

College

North Pole

Fairbanks

FORTYMILE N.W.&S.R.

Unalakleet

UNALAKLEET N.W.&S.R.

NOWITNA N.W.R.

ALASKA

NOWITNA N.W.&S.R.

Mountains

Tanana

Tok

Azimuthal Equidistant Projection

From the western Aleutians to its southern panhandle, Alaska would extend from coast to coast in the lower 48 states.

Mountain Village

ANDREAFSKY N.W.&S.R.

WILDLIFE REFUGE

DENALI NATIONAL PARK & PRES.

N. Fk.

RANGE

DELTA N.W.&S.R.

TETLIN N.W.R.

Aniak

Kuskokwim

Denali (Mt. McKinley) 20,310 ft 6,190 m

Susitna

GULKANA N.W.&S.R.

WRANGELL- ST. ELIAS

Largest national park in the U.S.

YUKON

• Bethel

Stony

IDITAROD NATIONAL HISTORIC TRAIL

Highest point in North America

Mt. St. Elias 18,008 ft 5,489 m

0   200 miles
0   200 kilometers

MULCHATNA N.W.&S.R.

LAKE CLARK

Wasilla • Palmer

Matanuska

Valdez

NATIONAL PARK & PRESERVE

St. Elias Mountains

KLONDIKE GOLD RUSH N.H.P.

CHILIKADROTNA N.W.&S.R.

NAT. PK. & PRESERVE

Anchorage

CHUGACH S.P.

Kenai

CHUGACH NAT. FOREST

Prince William Sound

Cordova

ALASKA HIGHWAY

Skagway • Haines

COAST MOUNTAINS

BRITISH COLUMBIA

TLIKAKILA N.W.&S.R.

Cook Inlet

Kenai Peninsula

MALASPINA GLACIER

TONGASS N.F.

GLACIER BAY NAT. PARK & PRESERVE

Juneau

WOOD-TIKCHIK STATE PARK

Iliamna Lake

KENAI N.W.R.

Seward

KENAI FJORDS NATIONAL PARK

Largest piedmont glacier in the world

Largest national forest in the U.S.

TONGASS

ADMIRALTY ISLAND N.M.

TOGIAK N.W.R.

ALAGNAK N.W.&S.R.

Homer

Chichagof I.

ALEXANDER

NATIONAL

Dillingham

Naknek

KATMAI NAT. PARK & PRESERVE

Capital of Russian America until 1867

Sitka

SITKA N.H.P.

Baranof I.

Petersburg

Bristol Bay

ANIAKCHAK NAT. MON. & PRESERVE

Becharof L.

BECHAROF N.W.R.

KODIAK N.W.R.

Afognak Island

ARCHIPELAGO

Prince of Wales I.

Wrangell

MISTY FIORDS NAT. MON.

FOREST

KODIAK N.W.R.

• Kodiak

GULF OF ALASKA

Ketchikan

ANNETTE ISLAND I.R.

Alaska Peninsula

ANIAKCHAK N.W.&S.R.

Kodiak Island

Trinity Islands

CANADA U.S.

Shumagin Islands

Dixon Entrance

REFUGE

Attu I.

NEAR IS.

ALEUTIAN ISLANDS

ALASKA MARITIME NATIONAL WILDLIFE REFUGE

Yunaska I.

PACIFIC OCEAN

Agattu I.

RAT ISLANDS

Kiska I.

Semisopochnoi Island

Tanaga I.

Atka I.

Amlia I.

Seguam I.

ADAK NAVAL STATION

Garoloi I.

Adak I.

ANDREANOF ISLANDS

Continuation of the Aleutian Islands at same scale as main map

Amchitka I.

Economy Symbols

- Fishing
- Vegetables
- Mining
- Hydro-electricity
- Shellfish
- Nursery stock
- Coal
- Food processing
- Dairy cows/products
- Timber/forest products
- Oil/gas
- Tourism

CALIFORNIA REPUBLIC

THE BASICS

Statehood
September 9, 1850; 31st state

Total area (land and water)
163,695 sq mi (423,967 sq km)

Land area
155,779 sq mi (403,466 sq km)

Population
39,144,818

Capital
Sacramento
Population 490,712

Largest city
Los Angeles
Population 3,971,883

Racial/ethnic groups
72.9% white; 6.5% African American; 14.7% Asian; 1.7% Native American; 38.8% Hispanic (any race)

Foreign born
27.0%

Urban population
95.0% (2010)

Population density
251.3 per sq mi (97.0 per sq km)

GEO WHIZ

Every December, one of the largest gatherings of northern elephant seals in the world converges on the beaches of Año Nuevo State Reserve, south of San Francisco, to rest, mate, and give birth.

The Monterey Bay Aquarium has been working to save endangered sea otters for more than 20 years. Rescued animals that cannot be rehabilitated for re-release into the wild find a permanent home here.

Castroville, known as the Artichoke Capital of the World, crowned future movie legend Marilyn Monroe its first ever artichoke queen in 1947.

California

The coast of what is now California was visited by Spanish and English explorers in the mid-1500s, but colonization did not begin until 1769 when the first of 21 Spanish missions was established in San Diego. The missions, built to bring Christianity to the many native people living in the area, eventually extended up the coast as far as Sonoma along a road known as El Camino Real. The United States gained control of California in 1847, following a war with Mexico. The next year, gold was discovered near Sutter's Mill, triggering a gold rush and migration from the eastern United States and around the world. Today, California is the most populous state, and its economy ranks above that of most of the world's countries. It is a major source of fruits, nuts, and vegetables, accounting for more than half of the U.S. output. The state is an industrial leader, producing jet aircraft, ships, and high-tech equipment. It is also a center for the entertainment industry.

⬤ **ENGINEERING WONDER.** Stretching more than a mile (1.6 km) across the entrance to San Francisco Bay, the Golden Gate Bridge opened to traffic in 1937. The bridge is painted vermilion orange, a color chosen in part because it is visible in fog.

CALIFORNIA QUAIL
GOLDEN POPPY

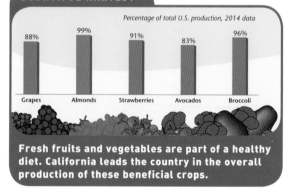

BOUNTIFUL HARVEST

Percentage of total U.S. production, 2014 data

88%	99%	91%	83%	96%
Grapes	Almonds	Strawberries	Avocados	Broccoli

Fresh fruits and vegetables are part of a healthy diet. California leads the country in the overall production of these beneficial crops.

◖ **FOREST GIANT.** Sequoias in Yosemite National Park's Mariposa Grove exceed 200 feet (61 m), making them the world's tallest trees. The trees, some of which are 3,000 years old, grow in isolated groves on the western slopes of the Sierra Nevada.

THE GOLDEN STATE:
CALIFORNIA

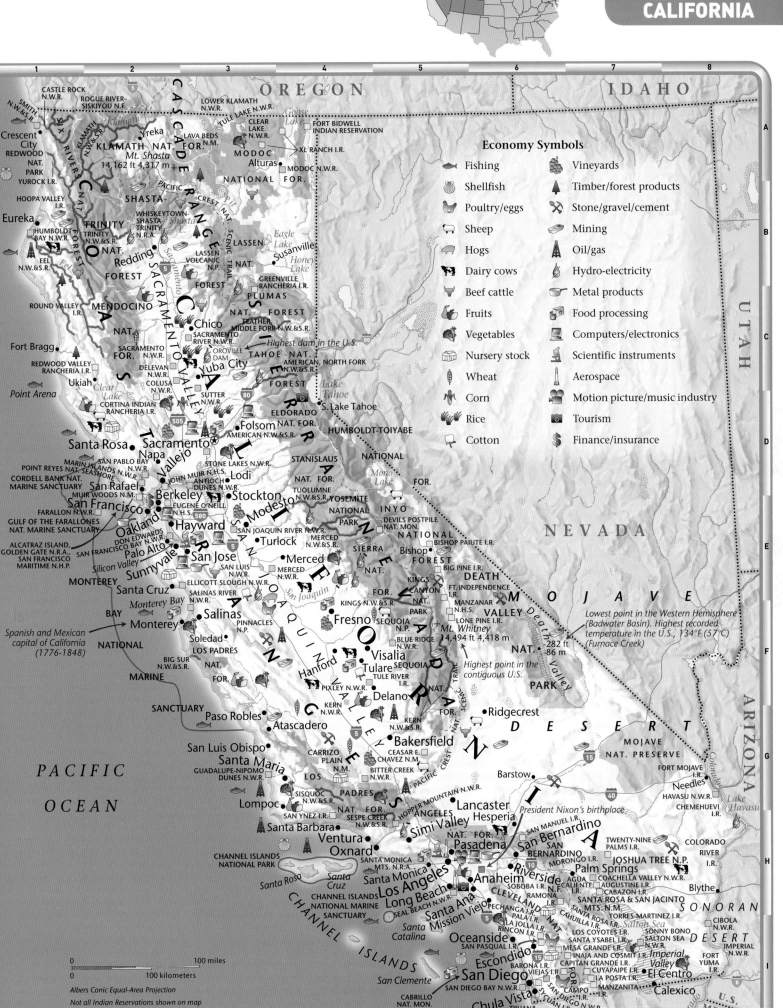

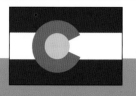

THE BASICS

Statehood
August 1, 1876; 38th state

Total area (land and water)
104,094 sq mi (269,601 sq km)

Land area
103,642 sq mi (268,431 sq km)

Population
5,456,574

Capital
Denver
Population 682,545

Largest city
Denver
Population 682,545

Racial/ethnic groups
87.5% white; 4.5% African
American; 3.2% Asian; 1.6%
Native American; 21.3% Hispanic
(any race)

Foreign born
9.7%

Urban population
86.2% (2010)

Population density
52.7 per sq mi (20.3 per sq km)

GEO WHIZ

The Black Canyon of the
Gunnison is one of the newest
national parks in the Rockies. As
it flows through the canyon, the
Gunnison River drops an average
of 95 feet (29 m) per mile—one
of the steepest descents in North
America. The craggy rock walls
are a mecca for rock climbers.

Colorado's lynx population is
making a comeback, thanks to
a program that releases wild
cats captured in Canada into
Colorado's southern Rockies.
Since 1999 when the program
began, more than 200 cats
have been released, and at
least 141 lynx kittens have
been born.

Colorado

Indians were the earliest inhabitants of present-day Colorado. Some were cliff dwellers; others were plains dwellers. Spanish explorers arrived in Colorado in 1541. In 1803 eastern Colorado became U.S. territory as part of the Louisiana Purchase. Gold was discovered in 1858, and thousands were attracted by the prospect of quick wealth. The sudden jump in population led to conflict with native Cheyenne and Arapaho over control of the land, but the settlers prevailed. Completion of the transcontinental railroad in 1869 helped link Colorado to the eastern states and opened its doors for growth. Cattle ranching and farming developed on the High Plains of eastern Colorado, while mining was the focus in the mountainous western part of the state. Mining is still important in Colorado, but the focus has shifted to energy resources—oil, natural gas, and coal. Agriculture is also a major source of income, with cattle accounting for half of farm income. And Colorado's majestic mountains attract thousands of tourists each year.

COLUMBINE
LARK BUNTING

🌊 **THRILLING SPORT.**
Colorado's snow-covered mountains attract winter sports enthusiasts from near and far. In the past, skis were used by gold prospectors. Today, skiing and snowboarding are big moneymakers in the state's recreation and tourism industry.

◖ **ANCIENT CULTURE.** Ancestral Puebloans lived from about A.D. 600 to A.D. 1300 in the canyons that today are a part of Mesa Verde National Park. More than 600 stone structures were built on protected cliffs of the canyon walls; others were located on mesas. These dwellings hold many clues to a past way of life.

BROWNS PARK N.W.R.
Vermillion Cr.
Green R.
DINOSAUR NATIONAL MONUMENT
White R.
Rangely
Cathedral Bluffs
Roan Plateau
UTAH
Colorado R.
Grand Valley
70
COLORADO NAT. MON.
Grand Junction
GRAND MESA N.F.
Dolores R.
Uncompahgre
San Miguel R.
MANTI-LA SAL N.F.
UNC
CANYONS OF THE ANCIENTS N.M.
S A
HOVENWEEP N.M.
Cortez
MESA VERDE N.P.
YUCCA HOUSE N.M.
UTE MOUNTAIN I.R.
FOUR CORNERS
San Juan R.
ARIZONA
Only spot in the U.S. where the borders of 4 states come together

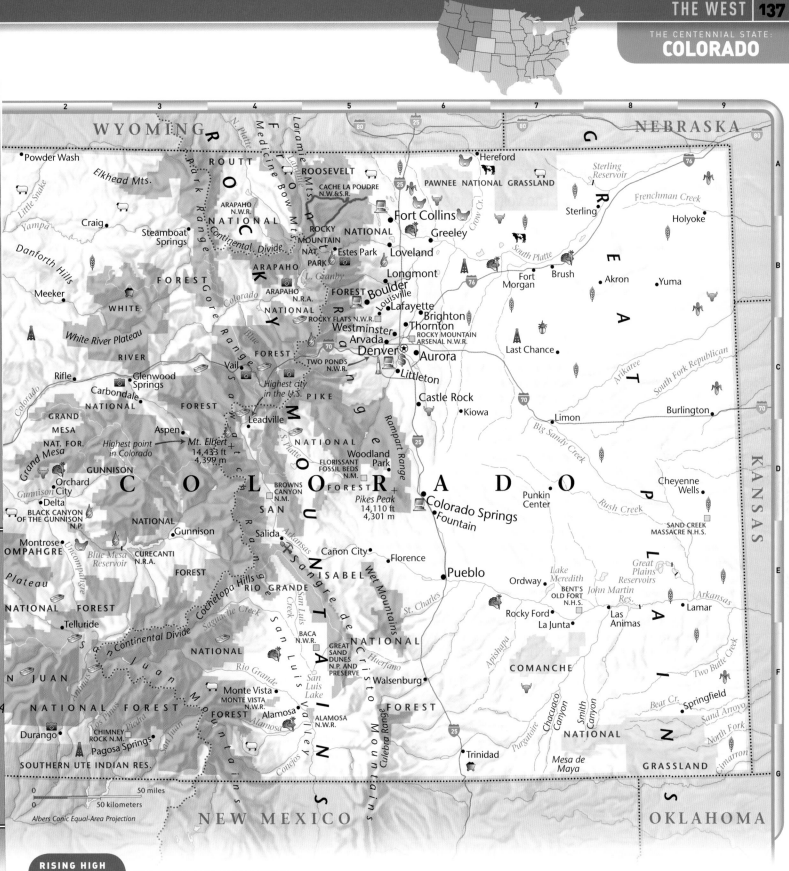

WYOMING

NEBRASKA

• Powder Wash

Little Snake

Elkhead Mts.

Yampa

Danforth Hills

• Craig

Steamboat Springs

• Meeker

ROUTT

ROOSEVELT

• Hereford

PAWNEE NATIONAL GRASSLAND

Sterling Reservoir

CACHE LA POUDRE N.W.&S.R.

ROCKY MOUNTAIN NATIONAL

Fort Collins

Greeley

• Sterling

Frenchman Creek

• Holyoke

ARAPAHO N.W.R.

Continental Divide

ROCKY MOUNTAIN NAT. PARK

Estes Park

Loveland

Longmont

Crow Cr.

South Platte

• Brush

• Akron

• Yuma

WHITE

White River Plateau

RIVER

NATIONAL

FOREST

L. Granby

ARAPAHO N.R.A.

ARAPAHO NATIONAL FOREST

Boulder

Louisville

Lafayette

Brighton

Thornton

ROCKY FLATS N.W.R.

Westminster

Arvada

Denver

Aurora

Littleton

ROCKY MOUNTAIN ARSENAL N.W.R.

TWO PONDS N.W.R.

I-76

Fort Morgan

• Last Chance

Arikaree

South Fork Republican

G R E A T

• Rifle

Colorado

Glenwood Springs

Carbondale

GRAND MESA

NAT. FOR.

Grand Mesa

Gunnison

Orchard City

• Delta

Vail

Highest city in the U.S.

Leadville

Highest point in Colorado

Mt. Elbert 14,433 ft 4,399 m

GORE RANGE

Blue R.

Gore Range

S. Platte

PIKE

NATIONAL

Castle Rock

• Kiowa

Limon

Big Sandy Creek

Burlington

I-70

Cheyenne Wells

P L A I N S

BLACK CANYON OF THE GUNNISON N.P.

GUNNISON

NATIONAL

FOREST

• Gunnison

BROWNS CANYON N.M.

SAN

Salida

FLORISSANT FOSSIL BEDS N.M.

Woodland Park

FOREST

Pikes Peak 14,110 ft 4,301 m

Colorado Springs

Fountain

Punkin Center

Rush Creek

SAND CREEK MASSACRE N.H.S.

• Lamar

Gunnison River

Montrose

OMPAHGRE

Blue Mesa Reservoir

CURECANTI N.R.A.

Uncompahgre

Plateau

NATIONAL FOREST

• Telluride

Cochetopa Hills

Saguache Creek

RIO GRANDE

San Luis Creek

Arkansas

Cañon City

ISABEL

Wet Mountains

• Florence

Pueblo

St. Charles

Ordway

Lake Meredith

Great Plains Reservoirs

BENT'S OLD FORT N.H.S.

Rocky Ford

La Junta

John Martin Res.

Las Animas

Arkansas

Continental Divide

S A N

J U A N

NATIONAL FOREST

• Durango

CHIMNEY ROCK N.M.

Pagosa Springs

Rio Grande

Rio Grande

San Luis Valley

BACA N.W.R.

GREAT SAND DUNES N.P. AND PRESERVE

San Luis Lake

Monte Vista

MONTE VISTA N.W.R.

Alamosa

ALAMOSA N.W.R.

Conejos

Sangre de Cristo Mountains

NATIONAL

Walsenburg

Huerfano

FOREST

Culebra Range

I-25

Trinidad

COMANCHE

Apishapa

Purgatoire

Chacuaco Canyon

Smith Canyon

Mesa de Maya

NATIONAL

GRASSLAND

Bear Cr.

• Springfield

Sand Arroyo

North Fork

Cimarron

SOUTHERN UTE INDIAN RES.

C O L O R A D O

M O U N T A I N S

KANSAS

NEW MEXICO

OKLAHOMA

0 ___ 50 miles
0 ___ 50 kilometers
Albers Conic Equal-Area Projection

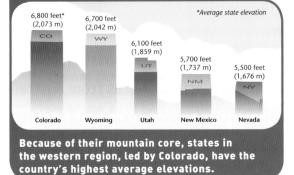

RISING HIGH

RISING HIGH

*Average state elevation

6,800 feet* (2,073 m) CO	6,700 feet (2,042 m) WY	6,100 feet (1,859 m) UT	5,700 feet (1,737 m) NM	5,500 feet (1,676 m) NV
Colorado	Wyoming	Utah	New Mexico	Nevada

Because of their mountain core, states in the western region, led by Colorado, have the country's highest average elevations.

Economy Symbols

Poultry/eggs	Vegetable oil	Oil/gas
Sheep	Wheat	Hydro-electricity
Dairy cows/products	Corn	Computers/electronics
Beef cattle	Stone/gravel/cement	Aerospace
Fruits	Mining	Tourism
Vegetables	Coal	Finance/insurance

THE BASICS

Statehood
November 8, 1889; 41st state

Total area (land and water)
147,040 sq mi (380,831 sq km)

Land area
145,546 sq mi (376,962 sq km)

Population
1,032,949

Capital
Helena
Population 29,943 (2014)

Largest city
Billings
Population 110,263

Racial/ethnic groups
89.2% white; 0.6% African American; 0.8% Asian; 6.6% Native American; 3.6% Hispanic (any race)

Foreign born
2.0%

Urban population
55.9% (2010)

Population density
7.1 per sq mi (2.7 per sq km)

GEO WHIZ

The fossil of a turkey-size dinosaur is being called the missing link between Asian and North American horned dinosaurs. Paleontologist Paul Horner discovered the fossil while sitting on it during a lunch break at a dig near Choteau.

Montana is the only state with river systems that empty into the Gulf of Mexico, Hudson Bay, and the Pacific Ocean.

Grasshopper Glacier is littered with frozen locusts (which look like grasshoppers) that became trapped in the ice. Scientists believe this species became extinct about 200 years ago.

Montana

Long before the arrival of Europeans, numerous native groups lived and hunted in the plains and mountains of present-day Montana. Although contact between European explorers and Native Americans was often peaceful, Montana was the site of the historic 1876 Battle of the Little Bighorn, in which Lakota (Sioux) and Cheyenne warriors defeated George Armstrong Custer's troops. In the mid-19th century the discovery of gold and silver attracted many prospectors, and later cattle ranching became big business, adding to tensions with the Indians. Montana became the 41st state in 1889. Today, Indians still make up more than 6 percent of the state's population—only four other states have a larger percentage. Agriculture is important to the economy, producing wheat, hay, and barley as well as beef cattle. Mining and timber industries have seen a decline, but service industries and tourism are growing. Montana's natural environment, including Glacier and Yellowstone National Parks, remains one of its greatest resources.

WESTERN MEADOWLARK
BITTERROOT

⬤ **STEP BACK IN TIME.** Just like in the past, Montana ranchers move their cattle herds from low winter pastures to higher elevations for summer grazing. Some ranches allow adventurous tourists to participate in the drives.

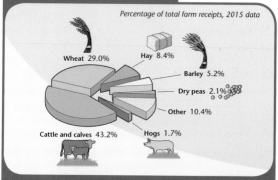

ECONOMIC CORNERSTONE

Percentage of total farm receipts, 2015 data

Wheat 29.0%
Hay 8.4%
Barley 5.2%
Dry peas 2.1%
Other 10.4%
Cattle and calves 43.2%
Hogs 1.7%

Agriculture, especially cattle and grain, is important in Montana's economy, adding more than $4 billion to the state income each year.

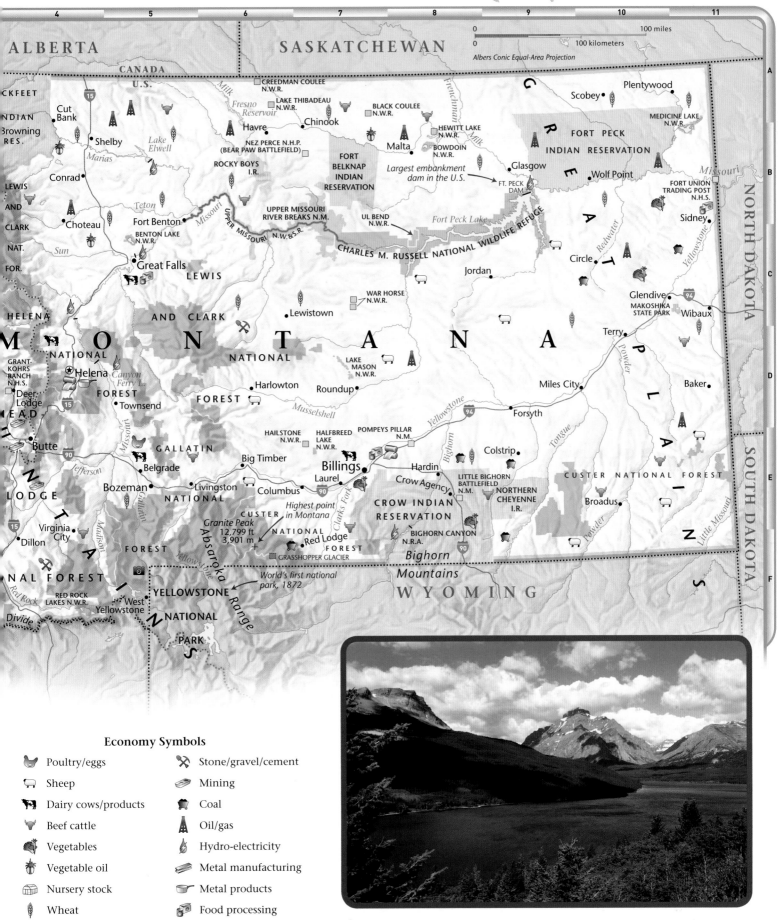

4 5 6 7 8 9 10 11

ALBERTA | SASKATCHEWAN

0 100 miles
0 100 kilometers
Albers Conic Equal-Area Projection

CANADA
U.S.

CKFEET | Cut Bank | Milk | CREEDMAN COULEE N.W.R. | Scobey | Plentywood
INDIAN | Fresno Reservoir | LAKE THIBADEAU N.W.R. | BLACK COULEE N.W.R. | Frenchman | MEDICINE LAKE N.W.R.
Browning RES. | Shelby | Havre | Chinook | Malta | HEWITT LAKE N.W.R. | FORT PECK INDIAN RESERVATION | GREAT
Lake Elwell | NEZ PERCE N.H.P. (BEAR PAW BATTLEFIELD) | BOWDOIN N.W.R. | Glasgow | Wolf Point | Missouri
Conrad | Marias | ROCKY BOYS I.R. | FORT BELKNAP INDIAN RESERVATION | Largest embankment dam in the U.S. | FT. PECK DAM | FORT UNION TRADING POST N.H.S.
LEWIS | Teton | Fort Benton | UPPER MISSOURI RIVER BREAKS N.M. | UL BEND N.W.R. | Fort Peck Lake | Circle | Redwater | Sidney
AND | Choteau | UPPER MISSOURI N.W.&S.R. | CHARLES M. RUSSELL NATIONAL WILDLIFE REFUGE
CLARK | BENTON LAKE N.W.R. | Sun | Great Falls | LEWIS
NAT. | FOR. | AND CLARK | Jordan | Glendive | I-94
HELENA | NATIONAL | WAR HORSE N.W.R. | Lewistown | MAKOSHIKA STATE PARK | Wibaux
M | O | N | T | A | N | A | Terry
GRANT-KOHRS RANCH N.H.S. | NATIONAL | Powder | Baker
Helena | Canyon Ferry L. | FOREST | LAKE MASON N.W.R.
Deer Lodge | Townsend | Harlowton | Roundup | Miles City
HEAD | FOREST | Musselshell | Yellowstone | I-94 | Forsyth
Butte | GALLATIN | HAILSTONE N.W.R. | HALFBREED LAKE N.W.R. | POMPEYS PILLAR N.M. | Bighorn | Colstrip | Tongue
LODGE | Belgrade | Big Timber | Billings | Hardin | CUSTER NATIONAL FOREST
Virginia City | NATIONAL | Livingston | Columbus | Laurel | Crow Agency | LITTLE BIGHORN BATTLEFIELD N.M. | NORTHERN CHEYENNE I.R. | Broadus
Dillon | Bozeman | CUSTER | Highest point in Montana | CROW INDIAN RESERVATION | Little Missouri
NAL FOREST | Madison | Granite Peak 12,799 ft 3,901 m | NATIONAL | BIGHORN CANYON N.R.A. | I-90 | Powder
Red Rock | RED ROCK LAKES N.W.R. | Gallatin | Red Lodge | FOREST | Bighorn
Divide | West Yellowstone | GRASSHOPPER GLACIER | Mountains
YELLOWSTONE | World's first national park, 1872 | Absaroka Range | WYOMING
NATIONAL PARK

NORTH DAKOTA
SOUTH DAKOTA
PLAINS

Economy Symbols

Poultry/eggs	Stone/gravel/cement
Sheep	Mining
Dairy cows/products	Coal
Beef cattle	Oil/gas
Vegetables	Hydro-electricity
Vegetable oil	Metal manufacturing
Nursery stock	Metal products
Wheat	Food processing
Timber/forest products	Tourism
Printing/publishing	

NATURAL BEAUTY. The rugged mountains and glacier-fed rivers of Montana offer many opportunities to outdoor lovers, including hiking and backpacking as well as fishing in summer, skiing in winter, and year-round wildlife viewing.

THE SILVER STATE:
NEVADA

THE BASICS

Statehood
October 31, 1864; 36th state

Total area (land and water)
110,572 sq mi (286,380 sq km)

Land area
109,781 sq mi (284,332 sq km)

Population
2,890,845

Capital
Carson City
Population 54,521

Largest city
Las Vegas
Population 623,747

Racial/ethnic groups
75.7% white; 9.3% African American; 8.5% Asian; 1.6% Native American; 28.1% Hispanic (any race)

Foreign born
19.1%

Urban population
94.2% (2010)

Population density
26.3 per sq mi (10.2 per sq km)

GEO WHIZ

The Applegate Trail, named for two brothers who first traveled it in 1846, offered a shorter alternative to the Oregon Trail. The Applegate Trail headed south from Idaho, across Nevada's Black Rock Desert into northern California, and then north into Oregon.

So many people claim to have seen extraterrestrials along a 98-mile (158-km) stretch of Nevada Highway 375 that the state transportation board named it Extraterrestrial Highway in 1996.

Nevada

Nevada's earliest settlers were native people about whom little is known. Around 2,000 years ago, they began establishing permanent dwellings of clay and stone perched atop rocky ledges in what today is the state of Nevada. This was what Spanish explorers saw when they arrived in 1776. In years following, many expeditions passing through the area faced challenges of a difficult environment and native groups protecting their land. In the mid-1800s gold and silver were discovered. In 1861 the Nevada Territory was created, and three years later statehood was granted. Today, the Nevada landscape is dotted with ghost towns—places once prosperous but now abandoned except for curious tourists. Mining is now overshadowed by other economic activities. Casinos, modern hotels, and lavish entertainment attract thousands of visitors each year. Hoover Dam, on the Colorado River, supplies water and power to much of Nevada as well as two adjoining states. But limited water promises to be a challenge to Nevada's future growth.

TURNING BACK TIME. The Luxor, re-creating a scene from ancient Egypt, is one of the many hotel-casinos that attract thousands of tourists to the four-mile (6-km) section of Las Vegas known as the Strip.

MOUNTAIN BLUEBIRD
SAGEBRUSH

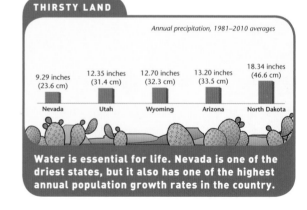

THIRSTY LAND

Annual precipitation, 1981–2010 averages

9.29 inches (23.6 cm)	12.35 inches (31.4 cm)	12.70 inches (32.3 cm)	13.20 inches (33.5 cm)	18.34 inches (46.6 cm)
Nevada	Utah	Wyoming	Arizona	North Dakota

Water is essential for life. Nevada is one of the driest states, but it also has one of the highest annual population growth rates in the country.

DESERT BEAUTY. A beavertail cactus thrives in the dry environment of Valley of Fire State Park. The park, Nevada's oldest, gets its name from red sandstone formations visible in the distance.

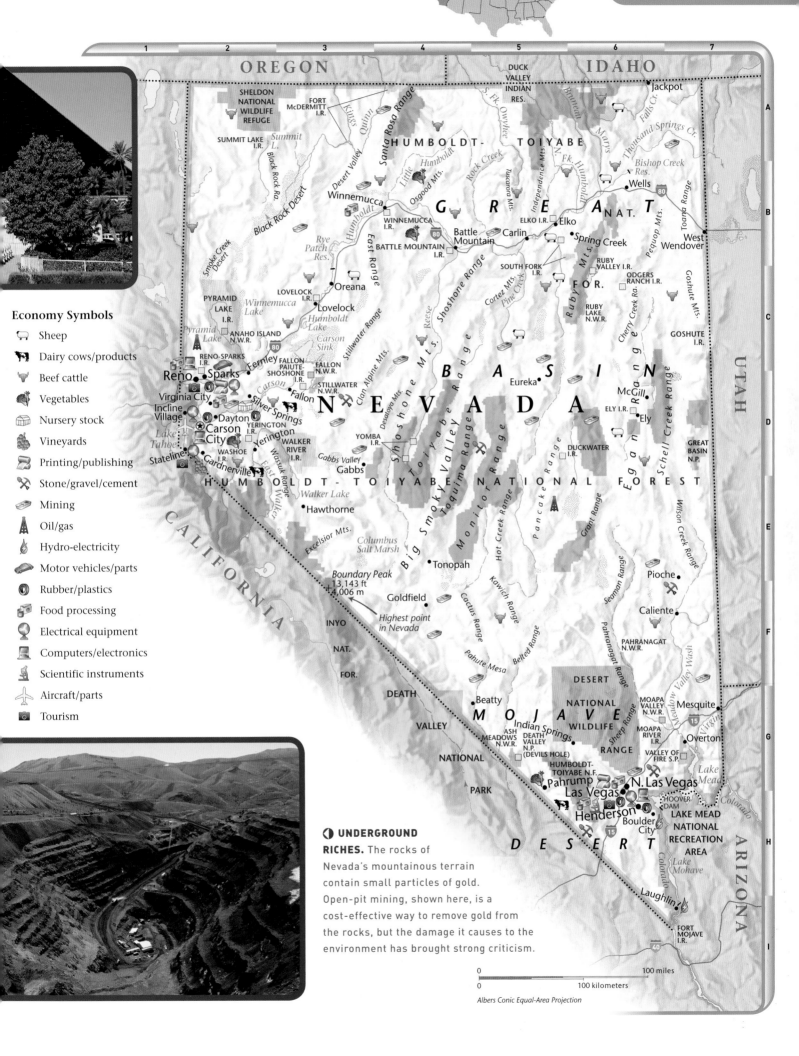

Economy Symbols

- 🐑 Sheep
- 🐄 Dairy cows/products
- 🐂 Beef cattle
- 🥬 Vegetables
- 🌱 Nursery stock
- 🍇 Vineyards
- 🖨 Printing/publishing
- ⚒ Stone/gravel/cement
- ▭ Mining
- ⛽ Oil/gas
- 💧 Hydro-electricity
- 🚗 Motor vehicles/parts
- ◎ Rubber/plastics
- 📦 Food processing
- 🌐 Electrical equipment
- 💻 Computers/electronics
- 🔬 Scientific instruments
- ✈ Aircraft/parts
- 📷 Tourism

OREGON   IDAHO

DUCK VALLEY INDIAN RES.

Jackpot

SHELDON NATIONAL WILDLIFE REFUGE

FORT McDERMITT I.R.

Kings

SUMMIT LAKE I.R.

Summit L.

Santa Rosa Range

Quinn

S. Fk. Owyhee

Bruneau

Falls Cr.

Thousand Springs Cr.

HUMBOLDT- TOIYABE

Black Rock Ra.

Desert Valley

Little Humboldt

Osgood Mts.

Rock Creek

Tuscarora Mts.

Independence Mts.

N. Fk. Humboldt

Marys

Wells

Bishop Creek Res.

Smoke Creek Desert

Black Rock Desert

Rye Patch Res.

Winnemucca

Humboldt

WINNEMUCCA I.R.

G   R   E   A   T

Battle Mountain

Carlin

ELKO I.R.

Elko

Spring Creek

N. A   T.

Pequop Mts.

Toano Range

West Wendover

East Range

BATTLE MOUNTAIN I.R.

Shoshone Range

SOUTH FORK I.R.

Ruby Mts.

RUBY VALLEY I.R.

ODGERS RANCH I.R.

Goshute Mts.

FOR.

Oreana

Reese River

Cortez Mts.

Pine Creek

RUBY LAKE N.W.R.

Cherry Creek Ra.

GOSHUTE I.R.

LOVELOCK I.R.

PYRAMID LAKE I.R.

Winnemucca Lake

Lovelock

Humboldt Lake

Stillwater Range

B   A   S   I   N

Egan Range

ANAHO ISLAND N.W.R.

Pyramid Lake

Carson Sink

Clan Alpine Mts.

N   E   V   A   D   A

Eureka

McGill

ELY I.R.

Ely

Schell Creek Range

RENO-SPARKS I.R.

Reno   Sparks

Fernley

FALLON PAIUTE-SHOSHONE I.R.

FALLON N.W.R.

STILLWATER N.W.R.

Shoshone Mts.

Toiyabe Range

Smoky Valley Range

DUCKWATER I.R.

Virginia City

Carson

Fallon

YOMBA I.R.

Big Smoky Valley

Toquima Range

Monitor Range

Pancake Range

Grant Range

Incline Village

Silver Springs

Dayton

YERINGTON I.R.

Gabbs Valley

Gabbs

H   U   M   B   O   L   D   T   -   T   O   I   Y   A   B   E   N   A   T   I   O   N   A   L   F   O   R   E   S   T

Lake Tahoe

★ Carson City

Yerington

WALKER RIVER I.R.

Hot Creek Range

DUCKWATER I.R.

Stateline

WASHOE

Gardnerville

Wassuk Range

East Walker

Walker Lake

Hawthorne

Excelsior Mts.

Columbus Salt Marsh

Tonopah

Kawich Range

Wilson Creek Range

Pioche

Caliente

Boundary Peak 13,143 ft 4,006 m

Cactus Range

Goldfield

Belted Range

Seaman Range

CALIFORNIA

INYO

NAT.

FOR.

Highest point in Nevada

Pahute Mesa

PAHRANAGAT N.W.R.

Pahranagat Range

DESERT

Meadow Valley Wash

DEATH VALLEY

Beatty

NATIONAL

WILDLIFE

MOAPA VALLEY N.W.R.

Mesquite

ASH MEADOWS N.W.R.

Indian Springs

Sheep Range

MOAPA RIVER I.R.

Overton

Virgin

NATIONAL

DEATH VALLEY N.P. (DEVILS HOLE)

M   O   J   A   V   E

RANGE

VALLEY OF FIRE S.P.

Lake Mead

PARK

HUMBOLDT-TOIYABE N.F.

Pahrump

Las Vegas

N. Las Vegas

HOOVER DAM

LAKE MEAD

D   E   S   E   R   T

Henderson

Boulder City

NATIONAL

RECREATION AREA

Lake Mohave

Colorado

Laughlin

ARIZONA

FORT MOJAVE I.R.

UTAH

◖ **UNDERGROUND
RICHES.** The rocks of
Nevada's mountainous terrain
contain small particles of gold.
Open-pit mining, shown here, is a
cost-effective way to remove gold from
the rocks, but the damage it causes to the
environment has brought strong criticism.

0 ——————— 100 miles
0 ——————— 100 kilometers

Albers Conic Equal-Area Projection

STATE OF OREGON
1859

THE BASICS

Statehood
February 14, 1859; 33rd state

Total area (land and water)
98,379 sq mi (254,799 sq km)

Land area
95,988 sq mi (248,608 sq km)

Population
4,028,977

Capital
Salem
Population 164,549

Largest city
Portland
Population 632,309

Racial/ethnic groups
87.6% white; 2.1% African American; 4.4% Asian; 1.8% Native American; 12.7% Hispanic (any race)

Foreign born
9.8%

Urban population
81.0% (2010)

Population density
42.0 per sq mi (16.2 per sq km)

GEO WHIZ

To recover wetlands and save two endangered fish species, 100 tons (90 t) of explosives were used to blast through levees so that water from the Williamson River could again flow into Upper Klamath Lake.

Crater Lake, at 1,932 feet (589 m), is the deepest in the United States. It fills a depression created when an eruption caused the top of a mountain to collapse. Wizard Island, at the center of the 6-mile (10-km)-wide lake is the top of the volcano.

Mount Hood, a dormant volcano near Portland, is Oregon's highest peak, rising 11,239 feet (3,426 m). Its last major eruption was in the 1790s, a few years before the Lewis and Clark expedition reached the region.

Oregon

Long before the Oregon Trail brought settlers from the eastern United States, Indians fished and hunted in Oregon's coastal waters and forested valleys. Spanish explorers sailed along Oregon's coast in 1543, and in the 18th century fur traders from Europe set up forts in the region. In the mid-1800s settlers began farming the rich soil of the Willamette Valley. Oregon achieved statehood in 1859, and by 1883 railroads linked Oregon to the East, and Portland had become an important shipping center. Today, forestry, fishing, and agriculture make up an important part of the state economy, but Oregon is making an effort to diversify into manufacturing and high-tech industries. Dams on the Columbia River generate inexpensive electricity to support energy-hungry industries, such as aluminum production. Computers, electronics, and research-based industries are expanding. The state's natural beauty—snowcapped volcanoes, old-growth forests, and a rocky coastline—makes tourism an important growth industry.

OREGON GRAPE
WESTERN MEADOWLARK

◗ TOWER OF HISTORY.
The 125-foot (38-m) Astoria Column, built in 1926 near the mouth of the Columbia River, is decorated with historic scenes of exploration and settlement along the Pacific Northwest coast.

◖ CHANGING LANDSCAPE.
Oregon's Pacific coast is a lesson on erosion and deposition. Rocky outcrops called sea stacks are leftovers of a former coastline that has been eroded by waves. The sandy beach is a result of eroded material being deposited along the shore.

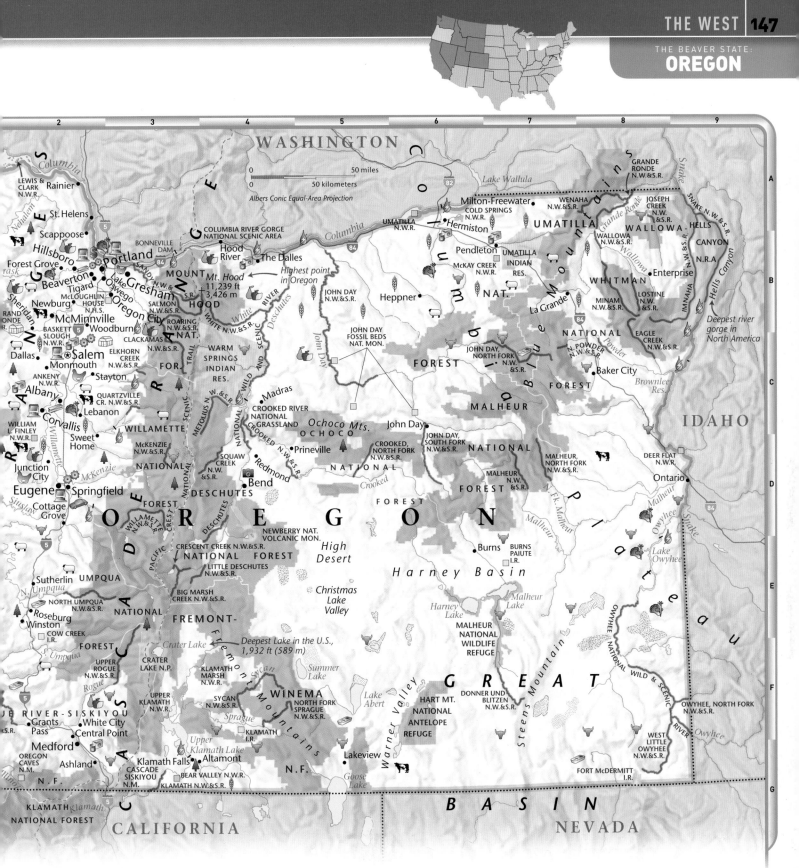

WASHINGTON

50 miles

50 kilometers

Albers Conic Equal-Area Projection

Highest point in Oregon
Mt. Hood
11,239 ft
3,426 m

Deepest river gorge in North America

Deepest Lake in the U.S.,
1,932 ft (589 m)

IDAHO

O R E G O N

CASCADE RANGE

COLUMBIA

Blue Mountains

Owyhee Plateau

G R E A T   B A S I N

CALIFORNIA

NEVADA

Christmas trees harvested, 2012 data

6.5 million	4.3 million	1.7 million	1.0 million	0.6 million
Oregon	North Carolina	Michigan	Pennsylvania	Wisconsin

Oregon's marine west coast climate provides an ideal environment for growing firs and spruce for the lucrative Christmas tree market.

Economy Symbols

- Fishing
- Shellfish
- Poultry/eggs
- Sheep
- Dairy cows/products
- Beef cattle
- Fruits
- Vegetables
- Nursery stock
- Wheat
- Timber/forest products
- Mining
- Hydro-electricity
- Machinery
- Metal manufacturing
- Motor vehicles/parts
- Food processing
- Computers/electronics
- Tourism
- Finance/insurance

THE BASICS

Statehood
January 4, 1896; 45th state

Total area (land and water)
84,897 sq mi (219,882 sq km)

Land area
82,170 sq mi (212,818 sq km)

Population
2,995,919

Capital
Salt Lake City
Population 192,672

Largest city
Salt Lake City
Population 192,672

Racial/ethnic groups
91.2% white; 1.3% African American; 2.5% Asian; 1.5% Native American; 13.7% Hispanic (any race)

Foreign born
8.2%

Urban population
90.6% (2010)

Population density
36.5 per sq mi (14.1 per sq km)

GEO WHIZ

A giant duck-billed dinosaur is among the many kinds of dinosaur fossils that have been found in the Grand Staircase–Escalante National Monument. Scientists think the plant eater was at least 30 feet (9 m) long and had a mouthful of 300 teeth.

Drought and water withdrawals have caused the level of Lake Powell to drop to only 42 percent of its capacity, revealing the walls of Glen Canyon, which was submerged in 1983 when a dam created the lake.

Great Salt Lake is the largest natural lake west of the Mississippi River. The lake, which has a high level of evaporation, contains about 4.5 billion tons (4 billion t) of salt.

Utah

For thousands of years present-day Utah was populated by Native Americans living in small hunter-gatherer groups, including the Ute for whom the state is named. Spanish explorers passed through Utah in 1776, and in the early 19th century trappers came from the East searching for beavers. In 1847 the arrival of Mormons seeking freedom to practice their religion marked the beginning of widespread settlement of the territory. They established farms and introduced irrigation. Discovery of precious metals in the 1860s brought miners to the territory. Today, almost 65 percent of Utah's land is set aside by the federal government for use by the military and defense industries and as national parks, which attract large numbers of tourists annually. As a result, government is a leading employer in the state. Another important force in Utah is the Church of Latter-day Saints (Mormons), which has influenced culture and politics in the state for more than a century. Salt Lake City is the world headquarters of the church.

NATURE'S HANDIWORK. Arches National Park includes more than 2,000 arches carved by forces of water and ice, extreme temperatures, and the shifting of underground salt beds over a period of 100 million years. Delicate Arch stands on the edge of a canyon, with the snowcapped La Sal Mountains in the distance.

SEGO LILY
CALIFORNIA GULL

SPREADING THE FAITH

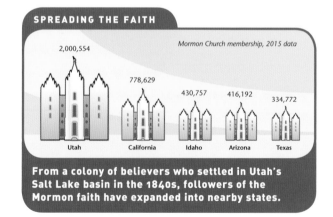

Mormon Church membership, 2015 data

2,000,554	778,629	430,757	416,192	334,772
Utah	California	Idaho	Arizona	Texas

From a colony of believers who settled in Utah's Salt Lake basin in the 1840s, followers of the Mormon faith have expanded into nearby states.

MONUMENT TO FAITH. Completed in 1893, the Salt Lake Temple is where Mormons gather to worship and participate in religious ceremonies. Church members regard temples as the most sacred places on Earth.

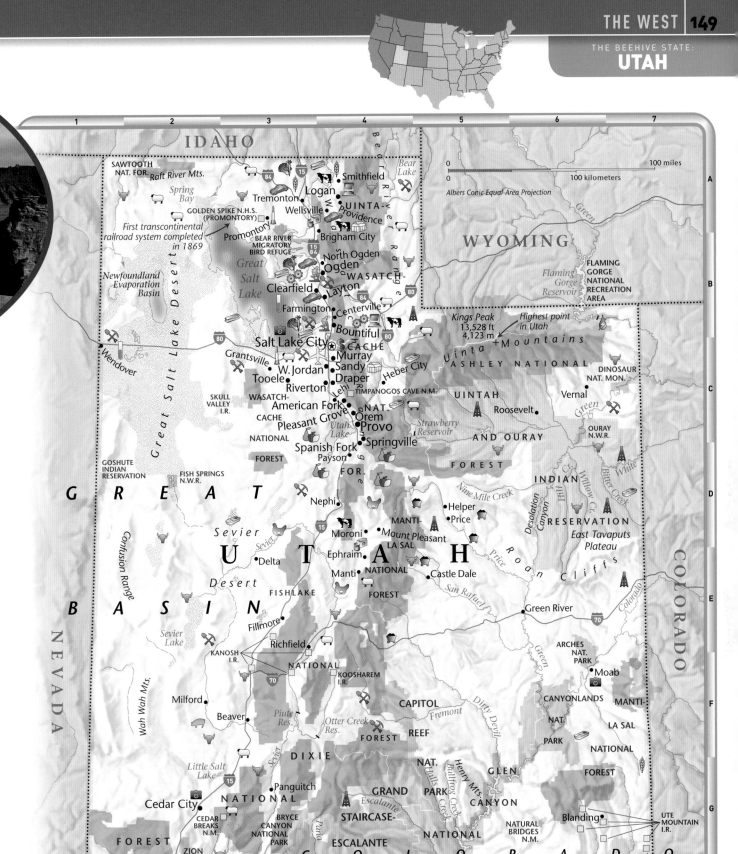

IDAHO

WYOMING

SAWTOOTH NAT. FOR. Raft River Mts.

Spring Bay

Smithfield

Bear Lake

Tremonton
Logan
Wellsville
Providence

GOLDEN SPIKE N.H.S. (PROMONTORY)

First transcontinental railroad system completed in 1869

Promontory

Brigham City

FLAMING GORGE NATIONAL RECREATION AREA

Newfoundland Evaporation Basin

Great Salt Lake Desert

BEAR RIVER MIGRATORY BIRD REFUGE

Great Salt Lake

North Ogden
Ogden
WASATCH

Flaming Gorge Reservoir

Clearfield
Layton
Farmington
Centerville
Bountiful

Kings Peak 13,528 ft 4,123 m Highest point in Utah

+Mountains

Uinta

Salt Lake City
Murray

CACHE

ASHLEY NATIONAL

DINOSAUR NAT. MON.

Wendover

Grantsville
W. Jordan
Tooele
Riverton
Draper
Lehi

Sandy
Heber City

UINTAH

Vernal

Roosevelt

Green

SKULL VALLEY I.R.

American Fork
Pleasant Grove

WASATCH-
CACHE

Utah Lake

Orem
Provo
Springville

NAT.

Strawberry Reservoir

AND OURAY

OURAY N.W.R.

GOSHUTE INDIAN RESERVATION

NATIONAL

Spanish Fork
Payson

FOR.

FOREST

INDIAN

Willow Cr.

Bitter Creek

White

FISH SPRINGS N.W.R.

FOREST

Nine Mile Creek

RESERVATION

Nephi

Helper
Price

East Tavaputs Plateau

Confusion Range

Sevier

Sevier

UTAH

Moroni
Ephraim
Manti

MANTI-
LA SAL

Mount Pleasant

NATIONAL

Desolation Canyon

Roan

Cliffs

G R E A T

Delta

Castle Dale

Price

San Rafael

B A S I N

Desert

FISHLAKE

FOREST

Green River

Colorado

Fillmore

Sevier Lake

Richfield

KANOSH I.R.

NATIONAL

KOOSHAREM I.R.

ARCHES NAT. PARK

Moab

CANYONLANDS NAT. PARK

MANTI-
LA SAL

N E V A D A

Wah Wah Mts.

Milford

Beaver

Piute Res.

Otter Creek Res.

CAPITOL REEF

Dirty Devil

Fremont

NATIONAL

FOREST

C O L O R A D O

Little Salt Lake

FOREST

DIXIE

NAT.

Halls Creek

Henry Mts.

Bullfrog Creek

GLEN

CANYON

NATIONAL BRIDGES N.M.

Blanding

UTE MOUNTAIN I.R.

Panguitch

NATIONAL

GRAND

Escalante

STAIRCASE-

PARK

CEDAR BREAKS N.M.

Cedar City

BRYCE CANYON NATIONAL PARK

ESCALANTE

Paria

NATIONAL

RECREATION

Lake Powell

Colorado

San Juan

HOVENWEEP NAT. MON.

PAIUTE I.R.

ZION NAT. PARK

Virgin

Kanab Cr.

MONUMENT

RAINBOW BRIDGE N.M.

AREA

Monument

Only spot in the U.S. where the borders of four states come together

FOUR CORNERS

Santa Clara
St. George
Hurricane
Kanab

A R I Z O N A

P L A T E A U

NAVAJO

Valley

N A T I O N

N.M.

INDIAN

RESERVATION

0   100 miles
0   100 kilometers
Albers Conic Equal-Area Projection

Economy Symbols

Poultry/eggs	Fruits	Mining	Motor vehicles/parts	Aircraft/parts
Sheep	Vegetables	Coal	Chemistry	Aerospace
Hogs	Nursery stock	Oil/gas	Food processing	Tourism
Dairy cows/products	Wheat	Hydro-electricity	Computers/electronics	Finance/insurance
Beef cattle	Stone/gravel/cement	Metal manufacturing	Scientific instruments	

THE BASICS

Statehood
November 11, 1889; 42nd state

Total area (land and water)
71,298 sq mi (184,661 sq km)

Land area
66,456 sq mi (172,119 sq km)

Population
7,170,351

Capital
Olympia
Population 49,218 (2014)

Largest city
Seattle
Population 684,451

Racial/ethnic groups
80.3% white; 4.1% African
American; 8.4% Asian; 1.9%
Native American; 12.4% Hispanic
(any race)

Foreign born
13.2%

Urban population
84.1% (2010)

Population density
107.9 per sq mi (41.7 per sq km)

GEO WHIZ

The Olympic Peninsula is among
the world's rainiest places, and its
Hoh Rain Forest is one of Earth's
few temperate rain forests.

Mount St. Helens, the most active
volcano in the lower 48 states, is
close to both Seattle and Portland,
Oregon. The eruption in May 1980
reduced its elevation by 1,314 feet
(401 m) and triggered the largest
landslide in recorded history.

Orcas, also known as killer
whales, are the world's largest
dolphins. The 90 or so that call the
waters of Puget Sound home have
been placed on the government's
Endangered Species List.

Washington

Long before Europeans explored the coast of the Pacific Northwest, Native Americans inhabited the area, living mainly off abundant seafood found in coastal waters and rivers. In the late 18th century Spanish sailors and then British explorers, including Captain James Cook, visited the region. Under treaties with Spain (1819) and Britain (1846), the United States gained control of the land, and in 1853 the Washington Territory was formally separated from the Oregon Territory. Settlers soon based their livelihood on fishing, farming, and lumbering. Washington became the 42nd state in 1889. The 20th century was a time of growth and development for the state. Seattle became a major Pacific seaport. The Grand Coulee Dam, completed in 1941, provided the region with inexpensive electricity. Today, industry, led by Boeing and Microsoft, is a mainstay of the economy. Washington leads the country in production of apples and sweet cherries, and the state is home to the headquarters of the popular Starbucks chain of coffee shops.

AMERICAN GOLDFINCH
COAST RHODODENDRON

⬣ **HARVEST TIME.** Once a semiarid grassland, the Palouse Hills north of the Snake River in eastern Washington is now a major wheat-producing area.

⬤ **PACIFIC GATEWAY.** The city of Seattle, easily recognizable by its distinctive Space Needle tower, is a major West Coast port and home to the North Pacific fishing fleet.

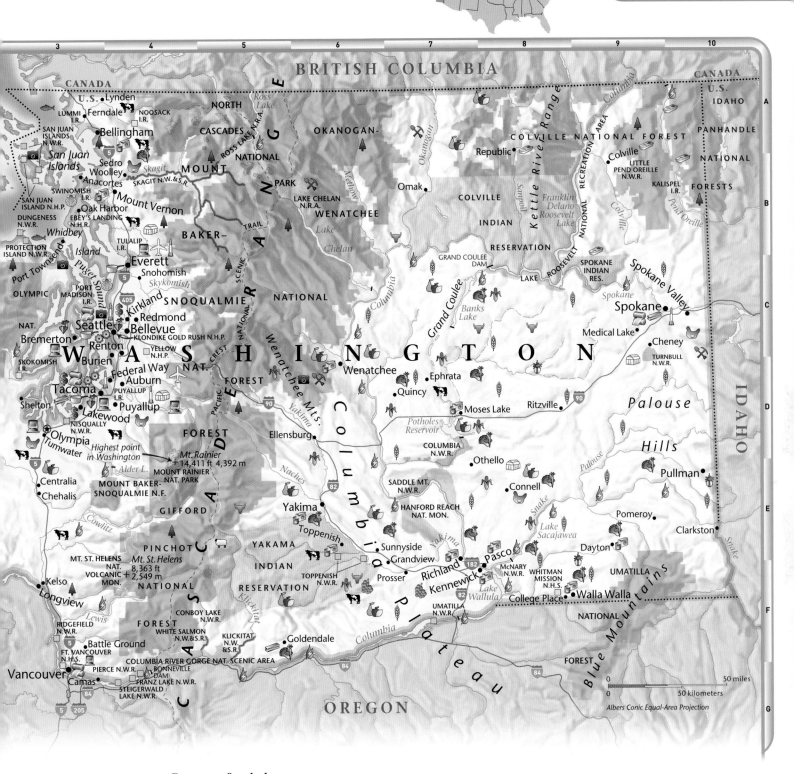

CANADA
U.S. • Lynden
LUMMI • Ferndale NOOSACK
I.R.   I.R.
Bellingham
SAN JUAN
ISLANDS
N.W.R.
San Juan
Islands
Sedro
Woolley Skagit
Anacortes
SKAGIT N.W.&S.R.
SWINOMISH
I.R.
SAN JUAN
ISLAND N.H.P. Oak Harbor
DUNGENESS EBEY'S LANDING
N.W.R. N.H.R.
Whidbey
PROTECTION Island
ISLAND N.W.R. Port Townsend
Port Madison Everett
OLYMPIC I.R. Snohomish
PORT Skykomish
MADISON
I.R.
NAT. Kirkland SNOQUALMIE
WASHINGTON Redmond
Seattle Bellevue
Bremerton KLONDIKE GOLD RUSH N.H.P.
Renton YELLOW
SKOKOMISH Burien N.H.P.
I.R. Federal Way NAT.
Tacoma Auburn
PUYALLUP
I.R. PUYALLUP
Shelton Lakewood Puyallup
NISQUALLY
N.W.R.
Olympia Highest point
Tumwater in Washington
Mt. Rainier
+ 14,411 ft 4,392 m
MOUNT RAINIER
Centralia Alder L. NAT. PARK
Chehalis MOUNT BAKER-
SNOQUALMIE N.F.
GIFFORD
MT. ST. HELENS
NAT. Mt. St. Helens
Kelso VOLCANIC 8,363 ft
Longview MON. + 2,549 m
NATIONAL
Lewis
RIDGEFIELD FOREST
N.W.R. PINCHOT
Battle Ground CONBOY LAKE
FT. VANCOUVER N.W.R.
N.H.S. WHITE SALMON
N.W.&S.R. KLICKITAT
Vancouver PIERCE N.W.R. N.W.
Camas BONNEVILLE &S.R.
STEIGERWALD DAM
LAKE N.W.R. FRANZ LAKE N.W.R.
COLUMBIA RIVER GORGE NAT. SCENIC AREA

BRITISH COLUMBIA
CANADA
U.S.
IDAHO
PANHANDLE

NORTH
CASCADES
NATIONAL
PARK
ROSS LAKE N.R.A.
Ross
Lake
MOUNT
BAKER-
RANGE
SCENIC
TRAIL
Skagit
Mount Vernon
WENATCHEE

OKANOGAN-
Okanogan
Republic
Methow
Omak
LAKE CHELAN
N.R.A.
Lake
Chelan

COLVILLE NATIONAL FOREST
Colville
LITTLE
PEND OREILLE
N.W.R.
KALISPEL
I.R.
NATIONAL
FORESTS
Kettle River Range
Columbia
Sanpoil
Franklin
Delano
Roosevelt
Lake
Colville
Pend Oreille

COLVILLE
INDIAN
RESERVATION
LAKE ROOSEVELT
GRAND COULEE DAM
GRAND COULEE
Grand Coulee
Banks
Lake
Columbia
SPOKANE
INDIAN
RES.
Spokane Valley
Spokane
Spokane

NATIONAL
FOREST
WENATCHEE Mts.
PACIFIC CREST NATIONAL SCENIC
Wenatchee
Wenatchee
Ephrata
Quincy
Moses Lake
Ritzville
Medical Lake
Cheney
TURNBULL
N.W.R.
Palouse

CASCADE RANGE
Yakima
Ellensburg
Naches
82
90
Columbia Plateau
Othello
COLUMBIA
N.W.R.
Potholes
Reservoir
SADDLE MT.
N.W.R.
HANFORD REACH
NAT. MON.
Connell
Palouse
Hills
Pullman
90
Palouse
Snake
Lake
Sacajawea
Pomeroy
Dayton
Clarkston

Yakima
Toppenish
YAKAMA
INDIAN
RESERVATION
TOPPENISH
N.W.R.
Klickitat
Sunnyside
Grandview
Prosser
Yakima
McNARY
N.W.R.
Richland
Kennewick
College Place
UMATILLA
N.W.R.
Pasco
182
Lake
Wallula
WHITMAN
MISSION
N.H.S.
Walla Walla
UMATILLA
NATIONAL
Blue Mountains
FOREST

Goldendale
KLICKITAT
N.W.
Columbia
84
82
84
50 miles
50 kilometers
Albers Conic Equal-Area Projection

OREGON
IDAHO

Economy Symbols

- Fishing
- Shellfish
- Poultry/eggs
- Sheep
- Dairy cows/products
- Beef cattle
- Fruits
- Vegetables
- Vegetable oil
- Nursery stock

- Wheat
- Corn
- Vineyards
- Timber/forest products
- Printing/publishing
- Stone/gravel/cement
- Mining
- Hydro-electricity
- Machinery
- Metal manufacturing

- Metal products
- Shipbuilding
- Food processing
- Computers/electronics
- Aircraft/parts
- Aerospace
- Tourism
- Finance/insurance

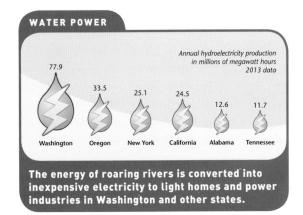

WATER POWER

Annual hydroelectricity production in millions of megawatt hours 2013 data

Washington	Oregon	New York	California	Alabama	Tennessee
77.9	33.5	25.1	24.5	12.6	11.7

The energy of roaring rivers is converted into inexpensive electricity to light homes and power industries in Washington and other states.

THE BASICS

Statehood
July 10, 1890; 44th state

Total area (land and water)
97,813 sq mi (253,335 sq km)

Land area
97,093 sq mi (251,470 sq km)

Population
586,107

Capital
Cheyenne
Population 63,335

Largest city
Cheyenne
Population 63,335

Racial/ethnic groups
92.7% white; 1.4% African American; 1.0% Asian; 2.7% Native American; 9.9% Hispanic (any race)

Foreign born
3.3%

Urban population
64.8% (2010)

Population density
6.0 per sq mi (2.3 per sq km)

GEO WHIZ

The successful reintroduction of wolves into Yellowstone National Park has become a worldwide model for saving endangered carnivores. At the end of 2014 there were at least 1,657 wolves in 282 packs living in Wyoming's northern Rockies.

The National Elk Refuge, in Jackson Hole, provides a winter home for more than 6,000 elk. The herd's migration from the refuge to their summer home in Yellowstone National Park is the longest elk herd migration in the lower 48 states.

Devils Tower, the country's first national monument, was featured in the science-fiction classic *Close Encounters of the Third Kind.*

Wyoming

When Europeans arrived in the 18th century in what would become Wyoming, various native groups were already there, living as nomads following herds of deer and bison across the plains.

In the early 19th century fur traders moved into Wyoming, and settlers followed later along the Oregon Trail. Laramie and many of the state's other towns developed around old army forts built to protect wagon trains traveling through Wyoming. Today, fewer than 600,000 people live in all of Wyoming. The state's economy is based on agriculture—mainly grain and livestock production—and mining, especially energy resources. The state has some of the world's largest surface coal mines. In addition, the state is a source of petroleum, natural gas, industrial metals, and precious gems. The natural environment is also a major resource. People come to Wyoming for fishing and hunting, for rodeos, and for the state's majestic mountains and parks. Yellowstone, established in 1872, was the world's first national park.

WESTERN MEADOWLARK
INDIAN PAINTBRUSH

⊜ **WANT TO RACE?** Unique to the High Plains of the West, the pronghorn can sprint up to 60 miles an hour (97 km/h).

⊜ **DRAMATIC LANDSCAPE.** Rising more than 13,000 feet (3,900 m), the jagged peaks of the Tetons, one of the youngest western mountain ranges, tower over a barn on the valley floor.

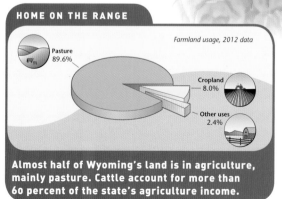

HOME ON THE RANGE

Farmland usage, 2012 data

Pasture 89.6%

Cropland 8.0%

Other uses 2.4%

Almost half of Wyoming's land is in agriculture, mainly pasture. Cattle account for more than 60 percent of the state's agriculture income.

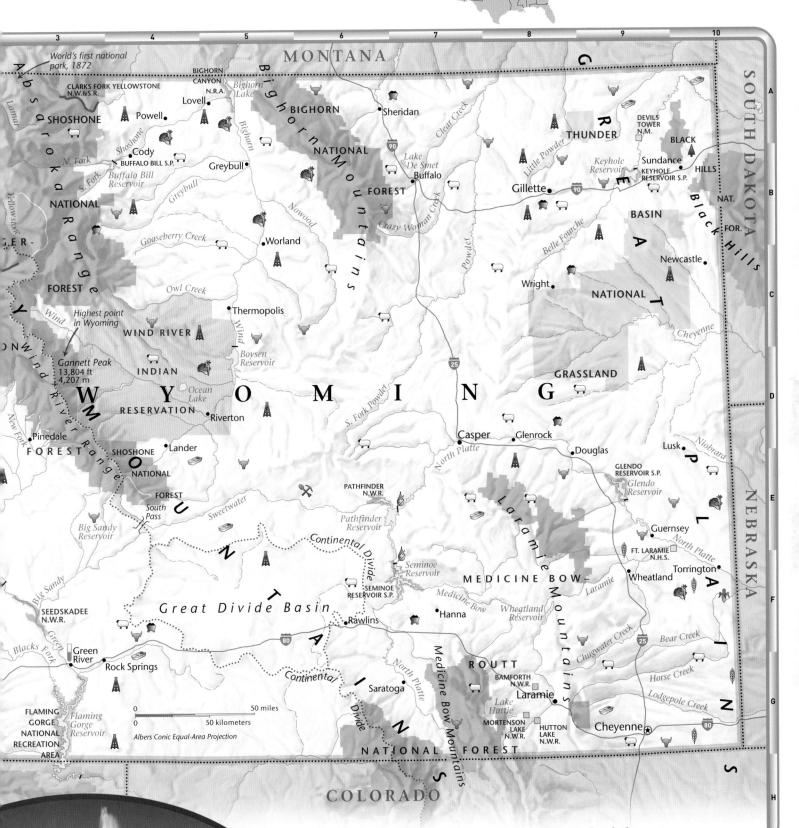

MONTANA

World's first national park, 1872

CLARKS FORK YELLOWSTONE
N.W.&S.R.

Absaroka

Lamar

Yellowstone

SHOSHONE

N. Fork

Powell

Lovell

BIGHORN
CANYON
N.R.A.

Bighorn Lake

Sheridan

BIGHORN

Cody

Shoshone

BUFFALO BILL S.P.

Greybull

Buffalo Bill Reservoir

Greybull

NATIONAL

Lake
De Smet

Buffalo

Clear Creek

THUNDER

DEVILS
TOWER
N.M.

BLACK

Keyhole
Reservoir

Sundance

KEYHOLE
RESERVOIR S.P.

HILLS

South Dakota

NATIONAL

Gooseberry Creek

Worland

Nowood

FOREST

Crazy Woman Creek

Gillette

Powder

Little Powder

Belle Fourche

BASIN

Black Hills

NAT.

FOR.

RANGE

Wind

Owl Creek

Highest point in Wyoming

WIND RIVER

Thermopolis

Wind

GER-

FOREST

Gannett Peak
13,804 ft
4,207 m

INDIAN

Boysen Reservoir

Wright

Newcastle

Cheyenne

GRASSLAND

W Y O M I N G

Ocean
Lake

Riverton

RESERVATION

S. Fork Powder

Casper

Glenrock

Lusk

Niobrara

New Fork

Pinedale

Wind River Range

FOREST

Lander

SHOSHONE

NATIONAL

Douglas

GLENDO
RESERVOIR S.P.

Glendo Reservoir

North Platte

Big Sandy
Reservoir

South Pass

Sweetwater

FOREST

MOUNTAINS

PATHFINDER
N.W.R.

Pathfinder Reservoir

Laramie Mountains

Guernsey

North Platte

FT. LARAMIE
N.H.S.

Torrington

SEEDSKADEE
N.W.R.

Big Sandy

Great Divide Basin

Seminoe
Reservoir

SEMINOE
RESERVOIR S.P.

MEDICINE BOW —

Laramie

Wheatland

Green
River

Blacks Fork

Green

Rock Springs

Continental Divide

Rawlins

Hanna

Medicine Bow

Wheatland
Reservoir

Chugwater Creek

Bear Creek

Horse Creek

North Platte

ROUTT

Medicine Bow Mountains

BAMFORTH
N.W.R.

Laramie

Lodgepole Creek

FLAMING
GORGE
NATIONAL
RECREATION
AREA

Flaming Gorge Reservoir

Saratoga

Lake
Hattie

MORTENSON
LAKE
N.W.R.

HUTTON
LAKE
N.W.R.

Cheyenne

NEBRASKA

P L A I N S

0   50 miles
0   50 kilometers
Albers Conic Equal-Area Projection

Continental

Divide

MEDICINE BOW MOUNTAINS

NATIONAL FOREST

COLORADO

⬤ POWERFUL PLUMBING.
Steam and water from
Old Faithful Geyser, in
Yellowstone National Park,
erupt more than 100 feet
(30 m) into the air.

Economy Symbols

🐑	Sheep	✕	Stone/gravel/cement
🐄	Dairy cows	🗆	Mining
🐂	Beef cattle	🪨	Coal
🥬	Vegetables	🛢	Oil/gas
🌾	Wheat	🍃	Hydro-electricity
🌽	Corn	🧪	Chemistry
🌲	Timber/forest products	📷	Tourism

The Territories

ACROSS TWO SEAS

Listed below are the five largest* of the fourteen U.S. territories, along with their flags and key information. Two of these are in the Caribbean Sea, and three are in the Pacific Ocean. Can you find the other nine U.S. territories on the map?

U.S. CARIBBEAN TERRITORIES

PUERTO RICO

Total area: 5,325 sq mi (13,791 sq km)
Land area: 3,424 sq mi (8,868 sq km)
Population: 3,598,357
Capital: San Juan
Languages: Spanish, English

U.S. VIRGIN ISLANDS

Total area: 733 sq mi (1,898 sq km)
Land area: 134 sq mi (348 sq km)
Population: 103,574
Capital: Charlotte Amalie
Languages: English, Spanish or Spanish Creole, French or French Creole

U.S. PACIFIC TERRITORIES

AMERICAN SAMOA

Total area: 581 sq mi (1,505 sq km)
Land area: 76 sq mi (198 sq km)
Population: 54,343
Capital: Pago Pago
Language: Samoan, English

NORTHERN MARIANA ISLANDS

Total area: 1,976 sq mi (5,117 sq km)
Land area: 182 sq mi (472 sq km)
Population: 52,344
Capital: Saipan (Capitol Hill)
Languages: Philippine languages, Chamorro, English

GUAM

Total area: 571 sq mi (1,478 sq km)
Land area: 210 sq mi (543 sq km)
Population: 161,785
Capital: Hagåtña (Agana)
Languages: English, Filipino, Chamorro

OTHER U.S. TERRITORIES

Baker Island, Howland Island, Jarvis Island, Johnston Atoll, Kingman Reef, Midway Islands, Navassa Island, Palmyra Atoll, Wake Island

*Close-up views of the five largest territories are highlighted in enlarged inset maps labeled with a letter. You can see where each territory is by looking for its corresponding letter on the main map.

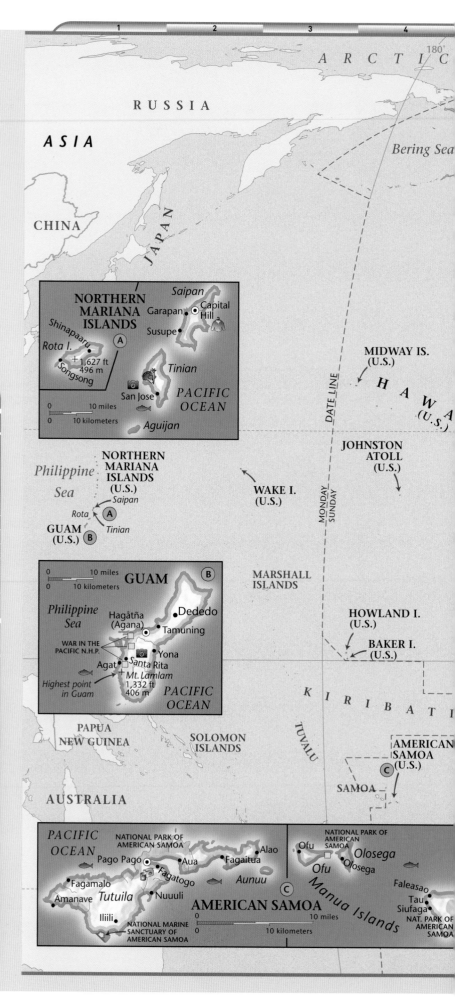

Economy Symbols

- Fishing
- Shellfish
- Fruits
- Vegetables
- Sugarcane
- Tobacco
- Coffee
- Chemistry
- Food processing
- Clothing/textiles
- Jewelry
- Electrical equipment
- Tourism

0   2,000 miles
0   2,000 kilometers

Eckert 4 Equal-Area Projection

OCEAN

ALASKA
(U.S.)

GREENLAND
(DENMARK)

CANADA

NORTH

AMERICA

UNITED STATES

ATLANTIC

OCEAN

TROPIC OF CANCER

MEXICO

Gulf of
Mexico

BAHAMAS

DOMINICAN
REPUBLIC

CUBA

HAITI

(E) PUERTO RICO (U.S.)

JAMAICA

U.S. VIRGIN IS.
(U.S.)

(D)

BELIZE

NAVASSA I.
(U.S.)

HONDURAS

Caribbean Sea

GUATEMALA

EL SALVADOR

NICARAGUA

COSTA RICA

GUYANA

VENEZUELA

SURINAME

PANAMA

KINGMAN REEF
(U.S.)

PACIFIC OCEAN

COLOMBIA

FRENCH
GUIANA
(FRANCE)

PALMYRA ATOLL
(U.S.)

EQUATOR

ECUADOR

SOUTH

JARVIS I.
(U.S.)

AMERICA

PERU

BRAZIL

BOLIVIA

FRENCH
POLYNESIA
(FRANCE)

ATLANTIC OCEAN

Crown
Mt.
1,556 ft
474 m

St. Thomas

Charlotte Amalie

Cruz Bay

St. John

BUCK ISLAND
N.W.R.

VIRGIN
ISLANDS
N.P.

(D) U.S. VIRGIN
ISLANDS

0   20 miles
0   20 kilometers

Caribbean Sea

GREEN CAY
N.W.R.

BUCK
ISLAND
REEF N.M.

SALT RIVER BAY N.H.P.
& ECOLOGICAL PRES.

CHRISTIANSTED
N.H.S.

Frederiksted

SANDY POINT
N.W.R.

St. Croix

Christiansted

PACIFIC
OCEAN

Tau

Maia

Leusoalii

Lata Mountain
3,170 ft
966 m

TROPIC OF CAPRICORN

(E)

Arecibo

Vega Baja

San Juan

SAN JUAN
N.H.S.

ATLANTIC
OCEAN

Aguadilla

Cataño

Carolina

Trujillo Alto

CULEBRA
N.W.R.

Mayagüez

PUERTO RICO

EL YUNQUE
N.F.

Fajardo

Culebra I.

LAGUNA
CARTAGENA
N.W.R.

Cordillera + *Central*

Highest point
in Puerto Rico

Cerro de Punta
4,390 ft 1,338 m

Caguas

Humacao

Cayey

VIEQUES
N.W.R.

Vieques I.

CABO ROJO
N.W.R.

Ponce

Guayama

0   20 miles
0   20 kilometers

Caribbean Sea

◗ **PRESERVING TRADITION.** Young dancers from American Samoa, dressed in costumes of feathers and pandanus leaves, prepare to perform in the Pacific Arts Festival, which is held once every four years to promote Pacific cultures.

The Territories
ISLANDS IN THE FAMILY

Fourteen territories and commonwealths scattered across the Pacific and Caribbean came under U.S. influence after wars or various international agreements. Although they are neither states nor independent countries, the U.S. government provides economic and military aid. Puerto Rico's more than 3.5 million residents give it a population greater than that of 23 U.S. states. Many tourists seeking sunny beaches visit the U.S. Virgin Islands, purchased from Denmark for $25 million in 1917. American Samoa, Guam, and the Northern Mariana Islands in the Pacific have sizable populations, but several tiny atolls have no civilian residents and are administered by U.S. military or government departments. In most cases, citizens of these territories are also eligible for American citizenship.

⬤ **RELIC OF THE PAST.** Sugar mill ruins on St. John, in the U.S. Virgin Islands, recall a way of life that dominated the Caribbean in the 18th and 19th centuries. Plantations used slave labor to grow cane and make it into sugar and molasses.

WHERE THE PICTURES ARE

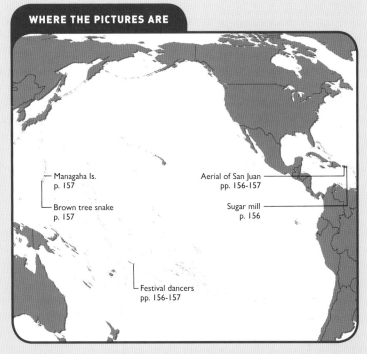

Managaha Is.
p. 157

Brown tree snake
p. 157

Aerial of San Juan
pp. 156-157

Sugar mill
p. 156

Festival dancers
pp. 156-157

◀ **PACIFIC JEWEL.** Managaha Island sits in the blue-green waters of a lagoon formed by a long reef along Saipan's western coast. Marine biologists fear that portions of the reef are dying due to pollution. The lagoon holds wrecks from battles fought in Northern Mariana waters during World War II.

◀ **ATLANTIC PLAYGROUND.** Modern hotels, catering to more than four million tourists annually, rise above sandy beaches in San Juan, Puerto Rico. Founded in 1521, the city has one of the best natural harbors in the Caribbean.

● **UNWELCOME STOWAWAY.** The brown tree snake probably arrived in Guam on cargo ships in the 1950s. The snake has greatly reduced the island's bird and small mammal populations and causes power outages when it climbs electric poles.

U.S. FACTS & FIGURES

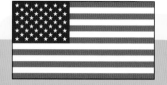

THE BASICS

Founding
1776

Total area (land and water)
3,796,742 sq mi (9,833,517 sq km)

Land area
3,531,905 sq mi (9,147,593 sq km)

Population
321,418,820

Capital
Washington, D.C.
Population 672,228

Largest city
New York
Population 8,550,405

Racial/ethnic groups
77.1% white; 13.3% African American;
5.6% Asian; 1.2% Native American;
17.6% Hispanic origin (any race)

Foreign born
13.5%

Urban population
80.7%

Population density
91.0 per sq mi (35.1 per sq km)

Language
No official national language;
language spoken at home: English
79.2%; Spanish 12.9%

Economy
Agriculture: 1.6%; Industry: 20.8 %;
Services: 77.6%

BALD EAGLE,
NATIONAL SYMBOL

Top States

Listed below are major producers of selected agricultural products, fish and seafood, and minerals.

Agricultural Products

Value of total U.S. agricultural production:
$421.5 billion (2014)

**Top 10 Agricultural Producing States
(based on cash receipts, 2014)**

1. California
2. Iowa
3. Texas
4. Nebraska
5. Illinois
6. Minnesota
7. Kansas
8. Indiana
9. North Carolina
10. Wisconsin

**Leading Agricultural Products and Top
Producers (based on cash receipts, 2014)**

Cattle and calves: Texas, Iowa, California, Nebraska, Kansas

Corn: Illinois, Iowa, Nebraska, Minnesota, Indiana

Milk/dairy products: California, Wisconsin, New York, Idaho, Pennsylvania

Soybeans: Illinois, Iowa, Indiana, Minnesota, Nebraska

Poultry and eggs: Georgia, North Carolina, Arkansas, Alabama, Mississippi

Hogs: Iowa, Minnesota, North Carolina, Illinois, Indiana

Fruit/tree nuts: California, Washington, Florida, Oregon, Michigan

Vegetables/melons: California, Florida, Washington, Idaho, Arizona

Potatoes: Idaho, Washington, Wisconsin, North Dakota, California

Fish and Seafood

Value of total U.S. seafood catch: $5.1 billion (2012)

Volume of wild catch: 9.5 billion lb (4.3 billion kg)

Volume of farmed catch: 662 million lb (300 million kg)

**Top 5 States in Fish and Seafood
(based on value of commercial
landings, 2012)**

1. Alaska
2. Massachusetts
3. Maine
4. Louisiana
5. Washington

**Leading Fish and Seafood Products
(based on U.S. consumption habits)**

1. Pollock
2. Salmon
3. Shrimp
4. Crab

Minerals

Leading Fossil Fuels and Top Producers

Petroleum: Texas, North Dakota, California, Alaska, Oklahoma (2013)

Natural gas: Texas, Louisiana, Wyoming, Oklahoma, Colorado (2011)

Coal: Wyoming, West Virginia, Kentucky, Pennsylvania, Illinois (2014)

Nonfuel Minerals

Value of total U.S. nonfuel mineral production: $78.3 billion (2015)

**Top 10 Nonfuel Mineral Producing
States (based on value, 2015)**

Nevada, Arizona, Texas, Minnesota, Wisconsin, California, Alaska, Utah, Florida, Michigan

**Important Nonfuel Minerals and Top
States in Terms of Production**

Copper: Arizona, Utah, New Mexico, Nevada, Montana

Crushed stone: Texas, Pennsylvania, Missouri, Ohio, Florida

Gold: Nevada, Alaska, Utah, Colorado, California (2011)

Iron ore: Michigan, Minnesota

Molybdenum: Colorado, Idaho, Arizona

Salt: Louisiana, Texas, New York, Kansas, Utah

Sand and Gravel: Texas, California, Minnesota, Washington, Michigan

Silver: Alaska, Nevada

Zinc: Alaska, Washington, Pennsylvania, North Carolina

Extremes

Strongest Surface Wind in U.S.

231 miles an hour (372 km/h), Mount Washington, New Hampshire, April 12, 1934

World's Tallest Living Tree

Hyperion; a coast redwood in Redwood National Park, California, 379.1 ft (115.55 m) high

World's Oldest Living Tree

Methuselah: a bristlecone pine, California; 4,789 years old

World's Largest Gorge

Grand Canyon, Arizona: 290 mi (466 km) long, 600 ft to 18 mi (183 m to 29 km) wide, 1 mile (1.6 km) deep

Highest Temperature in U.S.

134°F (56.6°C), Death Valley, California, July 10, 1913

Lowest Temperature in U.S.

Minus 80°F (-62.2°C), at Prospect Creek, Alaska, January 23, 1971

Highest Point in U.S.

Denali (Mount McKinley), Alaska: 20,320 ft (6,194 m)

Lowest Point in U.S.

Death Valley, California: 282 feet (86 m) below sea level

Longest River System in U.S.

Mississippi-Missouri: 3,710 mi (5,971 km) long

Rainiest Spot in U.S.

Wai'ale'ale (mountain), Hawai'i: average annual rainfall 460 in (1,168 cm)

**Metropolitan Areas With
More Than 5 Million People**

A metropolitan area is a city and its surrounding suburban areas.

1. New York, pop. 20,182,305
2. Los Angeles, pop. 13,340,068
3. Chicago, pop. 9,551,031
4. Dallas–Fort Worth, pop. 7,102,796
5. Houston, pop. 6,656,947
6. Washington, D.C., pop. 6,097,684
7. Philadelphia, pop. 6,069,875
8. Miami, pop. 6,012,331
9. Atlanta, pop. 5,710,795

GLOSSARY

aquaculture raising fish or shellfish in controlled ponds or waterways for commercial use

atoll a circular coral reef enclosing a tropical lagoon

arid climate type of dry climate in which annual precipitation is generally less than 10 inches (25 cm)

biomass total weight of all organisms found in a given area; organic matter used as fuel

bituminous coal a soft form of coal used in industries and power plants

bog a poorly drained area with wet, spongy ground

broadleaf forest trees with wide leaves that are shed during the winter season

canal an artificial waterway that is used by ships or to carry water for irrigation

center-pivot irrigation an irrigation system that rotates around a piped water source at its middle, often resulting in circular field patterns

city proper an incorporated urban place with boundaries and central government

continental climate temperature extremes with long cold winters and heavy snowfall

continental divide an elevated area that separates rivers flowing toward opposite sides of a continent

Creole a modified form of a language, such as French or Spanish, used for communication between two groups; spoken in some Caribbean islands

delta lowland formed by silt, sand, and gravel deposited by a river at its mouth

desert vegetation plants such as cactus and dry shrubs that have adapted to conditions of low, often irregular precipitation

fork in a river, the place where two streams join

Fortune 500 company top 500 U.S. companies ranked by revenue

fossil remains of or an impression left by the remains of plants or animals preserved in rock

geothermal energy a clean, renewable form of energy provided by heat from Earth's interior

grassland areas with medium to short grasses; found where precipitation is not sufficient to support tree growth

gross domestic product (GDP) the total value of goods and services produced in a country in a year

highland climate found in association with high mountains where elevation affects temperature and precipitation

hundredweight in the U.S., a commercial unit of measure equal to 100 pounds

ice age a very long period of cold climate when glaciers often cover large areas of land

intermittent river/lake a stream or lake that contains water only part of the time, usually after heavy rain or snowmelt

lava molten rock from Earth's interior that flows out on the surface during volcanic activity

levee an embankment, usually made of earth or concrete, built to prevent a river from overflowing

lignite low-grade coal used mainly to produce heat in thermal-electric generators

marine west coast climate type of mild climate found on the mid-latitude west coast of continents poleward of the Mediterranean climate

Mediterranean climate type of mild climate found on the mid-latitude west coast of continents

mesa a high, extensive, flat-topped hill; an eroded remnant of a plateau

metropolitan area a city and its surrounding suburbs or communities

mild climate moderate temperatures with distinct seasons and ample precipitation

nursery stock young plants, including fruits, vegetables, shrubs, and trees, raised in a greenhouse or nursery

pinnacle a tall pillar of rock standing alone or on a summit

plain a large area of relatively flat land that is often covered with grasses

plateau a relatively flat area, larger than a mesa, that rises above the surrounding landscape

population density the average number of people living on each square mile or square kilometer of a specific land area

precipitate process of depositing dissolved minerals as water evaporates, as in limestone caves

rangeland areas of grass prairie that are used for grazing livestock

reactor a device that uses controlled nuclear fission to divide an atomic nucleus to generate power

Richter scale ranking of the power of an earthquake; the higher the number, the stronger the quake

Rust Belt a region made up of northeastern and midwestern states that have experienced a decline in heavy industry and an out-migration of population

scale on a map, a means of explaining the relationship between distances on the map and actual distances on Earth's surface

stalactite column of limestone hanging from the ceiling of a cave that forms as underground water drips down and evaporates, leaving dissolved minerals behind

stalagmite column of limestone that forms on the floor of a cave when underground water drips down and evaporates, leaving dissolved minerals behind

staple main item in an economy; also, main food for domestic consumption

subtropical climate type of mild climate found in the southeastern areas of continents

Sunbelt a region made up of southern and western states that are experiencing major in-migration of population and rapid economic growth

temperate rain forest forests in the coastal Pacific Northwest region of the U.S. with heavy rainfall and mild temperatures

territory land that is under the jurisdiction of a country but that is not a state or a province

tropical zone the area bounded by the Tropic of Cancer and the Tropic of Capricorn, where it is usually warm year-round

tundra vegetation plants, often stunted in size, that have adapted to periods of extreme cold and a short growing season; found in polar regions and high elevations

urban area associated with a town or city in which most people are engaged in nonagricultural employment

volcanic pipe a vertical opening beneath a volcano through which molten rock has passed

wetland land that is either covered with or saturated by water; includes swamps, marshes, and bogs

POSTAL ABBREVIATIONS

AK- Alaska
AL- Alabama
AR- Arkansas
AS- American Samoa
AZ- Arizona
CA- California
CO- Colorado
CT- Connecticut
DC- District of Columbia

DE- Delaware
FL- Florida
GA- Georgia
GU- Guam
HI- Hawai'i
IA- Iowa
ID- Idaho
IL- Illinois
IN- Indiana
KS- Kansas

KY- Kentucky
LA- Louisiana
MA- Massachusetts
MD- Maryland
ME- Maine
MI- Michigan
MN- Minnesota
MO- Missouri
MP- Northern Mariana Islands

MS- Mississippi
MT- Montana
NC- North Carolina
ND- North Dakota
NE- Nebraska
NH- New Hampshire
NJ- New Jersey
NM- New Mexico
NV- Nevada
NY- New York

OH- Ohio
OK- Oklahoma
OR- Oregon
PA- Pennsylvania
PR- Puerto Rico
RI- Rhode Island
SC- South Carolina
SD- South Dakota
TN- Tennessee
TX- Texas

UT- Utah
VA- Virginia
VI- U.S. Virgin Islands
VT- Vermont
WA- Washington
WI- Wisconsin
WV- West Virginia
WY- Wyoming

MAP ABBREVIATIONS

°E .... degrees East	ME. .... Maine	OREG. .... Oregon
°N .... degrees North	mi .... miles	p., pp. .... page, pages
°S .... degrees South	MICH. .... Michigan	PA. .... Pennsylvania
°W .... degrees West	MINN. .... Minnesota	Pen. .... Peninsula
°C .... degrees Celsius	MISS. .... Mississippi	Pk. .... Peak
°F .... degrees Fahrenheit	MO. .... Missouri	Pres. .... Preserve
ALA. .... Alabama	MONT. .... Montana	Pt. .... Point
ARIZ. .... Arizona	Mt., Mts. .... Mount, Mountain, Mountains	R. .... River
ARK. .... Arkansas	N. .... North	Ra. .... Range
Br. .... Branch	Nat. .... National	Res. .... Reservoir
CALIF. .... California	NAT. MEM. .... National Memorial	RES. .... Reservation
COLO. .... Colorado	NAT. MON., N.M. .... National Monument	R.I. .... Rhode Island
CONN. .... Connecticut	NAT. RES. .... National Reserve	S. .... South
Cr. .... Creek	N.B. .... National Battlefield	S.C. .... South Carolina
D.C. .... District of Columbia	N.B.P. .... National Battlefield Park	S. DAK. .... South Dakota
DEL. .... Delaware	N.B.S. .... National Battlefield Site	S.H.P. .... State Historical Park
E. .... East	N.C. .... North Carolina	S.H.S. .... State Historical Site
Fk. .... Fork	N. DAK. .... North Dakota	S.P. .... State Park
FLA. .... Florida	NEBR. .... Nebraska	Sprs. .... Springs
ft .... feet	NEV. .... Nevada	sq km .... square kilometers
Ft. .... Fort	N.F. .... National Forest	sq mi .... square miles
GA. .... Georgia	N.G. .... National Grassland	St., Ste. .... Saint, Sainte
GDP .... Gross Domestic Product	N.H. .... New Hampshire	Str., Strs. .... Strait, Straits
I., Is. .... Island, Islands	N.H.A. .... National Historical Area	TENN. .... Tennessee
ILL. .... Illinois	N.H.P. .... National Historical Park	TVA .... Tennessee Valley Authority
IND. .... Indiana	N.H.S. .... National Historical Site	U.S. .... United States
INDIAN RES., I.R. .... Indian Reservation	N.J. .... New Jersey	VA. .... Virginia
KANS. .... Kansas	N. MEX. .... New Mexico	VT. .... Vermont
km .... kilometers	N.M.P. .... National Military Park	W. .... West
KY. .... Kentucky	N.P. .... National Park	WASH. .... Washington
L. .... Lake	N.R.A. .... National Recreation Area	WIS. .... Wisconsin
LA. .... Louisiana	N.W.R. .... National Wildlife Refuge	W. VA. .... West Virginia
m .... meters	N.W.&S.R. .... National Wild & Scenic River	WYO. .... Wyoming
MASS. .... Massachusetts	N.Y. .... New York	
MD. .... Maryland	OKLA. .... Oklahoma	

OUTSIDE WEBSITES

The following websites will provide additional valuable information about topics included in this atlas. Additional sites can be found by putting topics of interest into your favorite search engine.*

General information:
  States: www.state.al.us (This is for Alabama; for each state insert the two-letter state abbreviation where "al" is now.)
  Washington, D.C.: www.dc.gov
  Territories: www.cia.gov/library/publications/resources/the-world-factbook
  American Samoa: www.americansamoa.gov
  Guam: ns.gov.gu
  Northern Marianas: www.saipan.com/government.html
  Puerto Rico: welcome.topuertorico.org
  U.S. Virgin Islands: www.vi.gov

Natural Environment:
  Biomes: www.blueplanetbiomes.org
  Climate: www.eoearth.org
  Climate change: www3.epa.gov/climatechange

Climate:
  www.noaa.gov/climate
  www.world-climates.com
  www.cpc.ncep.noaa.gov

Natural Hazards:
  General: www.usgs.gov/hazards
  Droughts: droughtmonitor.unl.edu/
  Earthquakes: earthquake.usgs.gov
  Hurricanes: www.nhc.noaa.gov
  Tornadoes: www.tornadoproject.com
  Tsunamis: www.tsunami.noaa.gov
  Volcanoes: www.geo.mtu.edu/volcanoes/Volcanoes/Index.html
  Wildfires: www.nifc.gov and www.fs.fed.us/fire

Population:
  Population clock: www.census.gov
  States: quickfacts.census.gov/qfd/index.html
  Cities: www.city-data.com
  Population movement: census.gov/library/publications/2014/demo/p20-574.html
  Foreign-born population: census.gov/library/publications/2012/acs/acs-19.html

Energy:
  www.eia.gov/energyexplained/index.cfm
  www.nrdc.org/energy/renewables/
  profile.usgs.gov/myscience/upload_folder/ci2015Jun1012005755600Induced_EQs_Review.pdf

*Check with an adult before going on the Internet.

PLACE-NAME INDEX

Map references are in boldface (**59**) type. Letters and numbers following in lightface (G6) locate the place-names using the map grid. (Refer to page 7 for more details.)

Georgetown, SC — Holton

Koyukuk, North Fork N.W.&S.R. — Manti

N — Paint N.W.&S.R.

Painted Desert — Rainy Lake

Raisin — Seaman Range

Sunnyvale — Walnut Creek

Walnut Ridge — Zuni (river)

For more information, visit nationalgeographic.com, call
1-800-647-5463, or write to the following address:

National Geographic Partners
1145 17th Street N.W.
Washington, D.C. 20036-4688 U.S.A.

Visit us online at nationalgeographic.com/books

For librarians and teachers: ngchildrensbooks.org

More for kids from National Geographic:
kids.nationalgeographic.com

For information about special discounts for bulk
purchases, please contact National Geographic Books
Special Sales: specialsales@natgeo.com

For rights or permissions inquiries, please contact
National Geographic Books Subsidiary Rights:
bookrights@natgeo.com

Art directed by Kathryn Robbins
Designed by Nicole Lazarus

National Geographic supports K–12 educators
with ELA Common Core Resources.
Visit natgeoed.org/commoncore for more information.

Trade paperback ISBN: 978-1-4263-2831-2
Reinforced library binding ISBN: 978-1-4263-2832-9

Printed in Hong Kong
17/THK/1

The publisher would like to thank everyone
who worked to make this book come together:
Angela Modany, associate editor; Martha Sharma, writer/
researcher; Suzanne Fonda, project manager; Lori
Epstein, photo director; Mike McNey, map production;
Sean Philpotts, production director; Anne LeongSon,
design production assistant; Sally Abbey, managing
editor; Joan Gossett, editorial production manager; Molly
Reid, production editor; and Stuart Armstrong, illustrator.

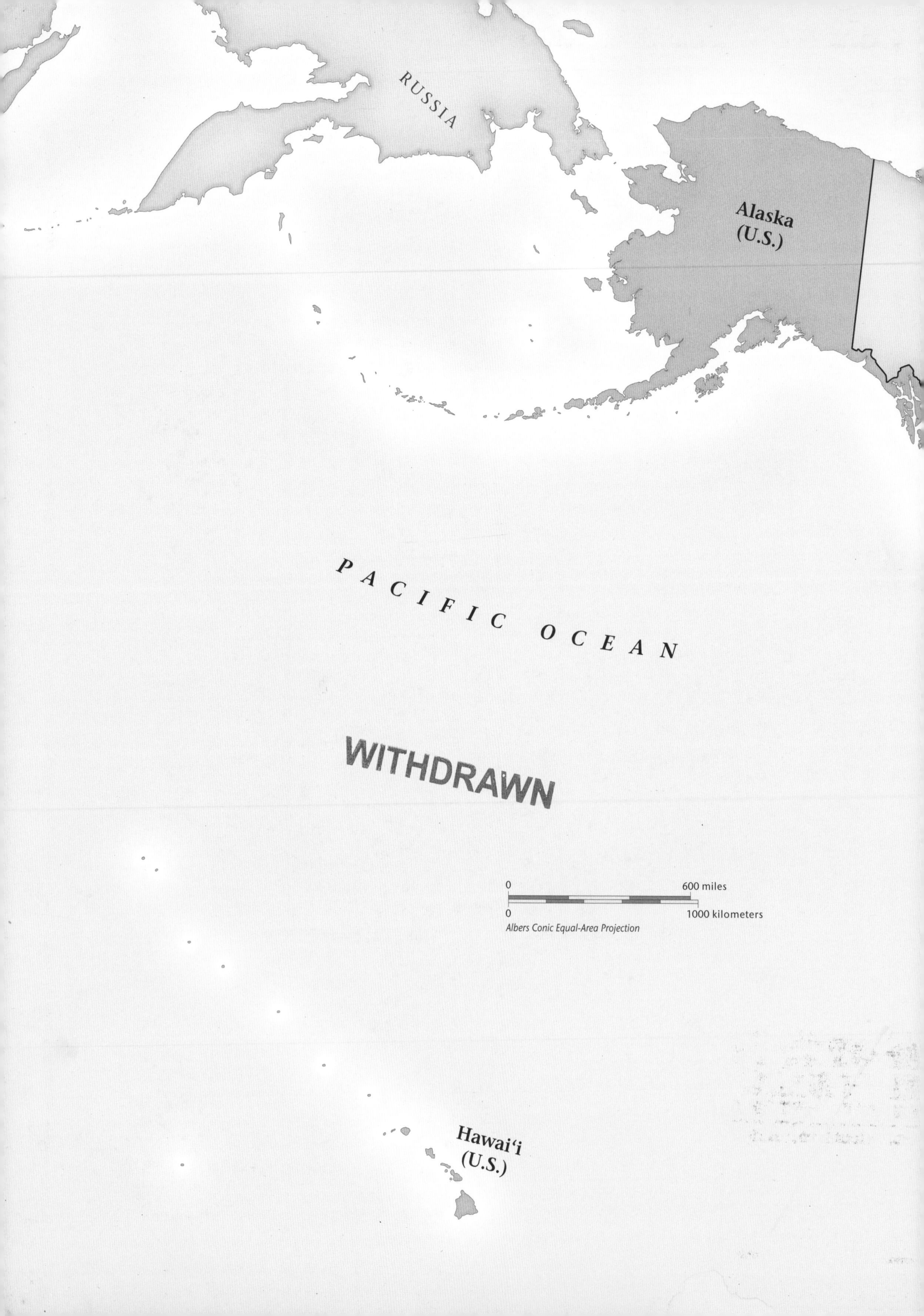

RUSSIA

Alaska
(U.S.)

P A C I F I C   O C E A N

WITHDRAWN

0 ———————————————— 600 miles
0 ———————————————— 1000 kilometers
Albers Conic Equal-Area Projection

Hawai'i
(U.S.)